Voluntary Assisted Dying

LAW? HEALTH? JUSTICE?

Voluntary Assisted Dying

LAW? HEALTH? JUSTICE?

EDITED BY DANIEL J FLEMING
AND DAVID J CARTER

Australian
National
University

ANU PRESS

Australian
National
University

ANU PRESS

Published by ANU Press
The Australian National University
Canberra ACT 2600, Australia
Email: anupress@anu.edu.au

Available to download for free at press.anu.edu.au

ISBN (print): 9781760465049
ISBN (online): 9781760465056

WorldCat (print): 1296178163
WorldCat (online): 1296100472

DOI: 10.22459/VAD.2022

Cover design and layout by ANU Press

Cover artwork: *Revive (after Canova)* by Elwyn Murray, © Elwyn Murray/Copyright
Agency, 2022

This book is published under the aegis of the Law Editorial Committee of the
ANU Press.

Contents

Synopsis

Since the introduction of plans for voluntary assisted dying and the passing of the *Voluntary Assisted Dying Act 2017* (Vic), a 'new moment' in the governance of life and death has opened up within the Australian context.

With the opening of this new moment, critical scholarship on topics related to or 'adjacent' to the questions that the voluntary assisted dying regime itself raises should be brought to bear on the regime and on this new era for law, healthcare and questions of justice.

This collection brings together critical perspectives on voluntary assisted dying itself, and on various practices 'adjacent' to it; including questions of state power, population ageing, the differential treatment of human and non-human animals at the time of death, the management of healthcare processes through silent 'workarounds', and the financialisation of death.

Acknowledging that voluntary assisted dying legislation is now part of most jurisdictions around Australia, this collection provides an overview of the Victorian regime in particular, and then introduces diverse critical views, broadening our engagement with euthanasia and voluntary assisted dying beyond the limited, but important, debates about its particular enactment in Australia.

Introduction

David J Carter and Daniel J Fleming

On 19 June 2019, the *Voluntary Assisted Dying Act 2017* (Vic) ('the Act')[1] came into effect in Victoria, Australia. Notwithstanding the Northern Territory's brief foray into legalised euthanasia in the mid-1990s, which was subsequently overturned by the federal government, this was the first time such a piece of legislation was brought into existence in an Australian jurisdiction.[2]

The Act opened up the possibility of two hitherto unavailable interventions in Victoria, known collectively as voluntary assisted dying ('VAD'). Terminally ill persons who meet the eligibility criteria and have been through the mandated process are now able to access a drug that when taken, will end their life. In some instances, when self-administration is impossible, a doctor is able to administer the substance to a person, again with a view to ending their life.

The enactment of VAD brought with it the mix of shock and praise in Victoria and around Australia that had been seen in other jurisdictions and during the debate. Lobby groups on both sides of the debate made grand claims, and the Victorian politicians responsible for implementing the regime constructed their role as one of statecraft becoming, with

---

1 Throughout this volume, 'voluntary assisted dying' is abbreviated to VAD, and the *Voluntary Assisted Dying Act 2017* (Vic) is referred to as the Act. For more of the Australian legal history on this topic see the work of Lindy Willmott et al '(Failed) Voluntary Euthanasia Law Reform in Australia: Two Decades of Trends, Models and Politics' (2016) 39(1) *University of New South Wales Law Journal* 1. The legal and other information contained in this collection was first presented in February 2019. The information contained is current as at June 2021 unless otherwise noted.
2 The Northern Territory had legalised euthanasia with its *Rights of the Terminally Ill Act 1995* (NT). This was almost immediately overturned by the Commonwealth. See *Euthanasia Laws Act 1997* (Cth).

the passing of the Act, 'the compassionate state'.[3] The enactment was productive too of a whole plethora of expert opinion and debate. Medical practitioners were asked to share their views on-air. Government and non-government health services were scrutinised. Legal academics provided commentary on the law itself, while the many safeguards built into the legislation became a matter of public commentary, a key feature of the Act and its operation.

In the midst of this debate, other voices became lost in the intensity of the rhetoric. This includes those for whom VAD and its legalisation speak to a broader set of concerns regarding the governance of death in Australia and elsewhere. Such critical reflection is best – and perhaps only – practised with the advantages of time and space from the moment of high-stakes debate and change. Wanting to ask both broader and more critical questions of the new regime, a group of scholars from a variety of disciplines and traditions gathered four months prior to the operationalisation of VAD to attempt to move beyond the public discussion to a more subtle and critical analysis of the Act, its assumptions and its impact on the governance of death. This volume is one result of that symposium, held in February 2019 at the University of Technology Sydney (UTS).

Scholarship from the disciplines of law, philosophy, ethics and theology was exchanged in a genuine attempt to reflect on the new era in the governance of death that the passage of the Act marked. Those gathered represented a diversity of views in terms of the morality of the interventions that the Act brought into law. In this context, they were challenged to use their expertise to study the Act and its implementation process from perspectives that had hitherto remained absent from discussion in public and in the academy. We, the organisers, were interested in what was not being seen because of the spectacle of the legislation: what assumptions underpin it? How does it relate to other legislation? What is new about it? What is familiar? What might we learn about VAD from aligned areas elsewhere?

This volume is the fruit of this gathering. And while the contributions were first developed prior to the Victorian Act coming into force, the authors have taken time between then and now to reflect on learnings

---

3   @JillHennessyMP (Twitter, 29 November 2017, 12:09pm AEST) <https://twitter.com/jill hennessymp/status/935676976064487424?lang=en>.

from the nearly three years of VAD in Victoria. In addition, most other Australian jurisdictions have now either passed or enacted similar legislation, making the enduring importance of the chapters that follow clear in the Australian context.

In the first chapter presented here, 'The Constitution of "Choice"', bioethicist Courtney Hempton engages with the logics of choice that undergird VAD. This is the first chapter of three that focus on the figure of choice, independence and relationships as they appear in the wake of VAD. From its ancestry in a Victorian Parliamentary Inquiry into End of Life Choices, to the ways in which the rhetoric of choice facilitates the state's governance of (voluntary assisted) dying, Hempton's target is the ways in which VAD first constitutes and then operationalises 'choice' in and through law, clinical practice and discourse for patients, their families and health practitioners. Hempton turns her gaze towards the conflict between a 'responsibilising' of patients for their own deaths through the mechanism of choice, and the cooption of health and medical practitioners in this process as 'assisted dying-gatekeepers'; whether they choose to participate or not. Hempton's contribution pushes us to see VAD within this broad rhetorical landscape, asking how the mobilisation of 'choice' in this regime is consistent or inconsistent with the state's governance of other medical care and decision-making practices.

This centrality of 'choice' as the rhetorical machinery that produces VAD and the state's continued governance of this (new) form of death is echoed in the jointly authored work of critical health geographer Hamish Robertson and health services researcher Joanne Travaglia. In the second chapter in this collection, Robertson and Travaglia think through ageing, aged care and the application of palliative care as a necropolitical technology. By posing a challenge to the construction of healthcare interventions, such as palliative care, as 'scientific' and 'evidence-based', their work demonstrates how the reality of variable levels of evidence and a corresponding raft of political and social choices, policies and practices that undergird them are occluded. For Robertson and Travaglia, ageing as *actually experienced* is not highly valued. Only where it is 'successful' is it valued, as measured by adherence to a model that values a certain form of independence and the exercise of particular forms of choice at all stages of life. With VAD now extending this structuring of ageing to include a 'successful' exercise of independence and 'choice' even as to death, this means an extension of the always-already vulnerability of older people. This opens up the potential for new pressure to engage in a variety of new interventions including advance directives, living wills and palliative care that can have life-or-death implications for the individual. And all of this in the name of the exercise of assertion of independence and choice.

These technologies of decision support are already being drawn upon in decision-making around health and other services like palliative and aged care. How VAD might place new pressures on these already complex decisions and technologies is a concern raised by Nola Ries and Elise Mansfield's contribution to this collection. They ask, in our third chapter, how might decision-making be 'done' in a manner that is responsive to the lived experience of individuals, and to the traditions of law that aim to protect the vulnerable in this new context. Ries and Mansfield's contribution makes an attempt at thinking through this challenge by way of 'supported decision-making'. Supported decision-making is grounded in the normative claim that adults have the right to make decisions for themselves and people with cognitive impairments should receive appropriate supports to maximise their decisional capacity. It is a deeply relational process, and in their empirical study those facing the question of supported decision-making highlight these very things. For participants, the formation and reliance on relationships of trust and support means a reduction in worry about being taken advantage of and a gain in confidence about decision-making; participants believe that this approach provides a context within which they would be able to more readily make their own decisions while giving expression to their own wishes. In short, the approach promises to achieve important outcomes for those facing decisions regarding end of life through a form of relational autonomy, recognising the reality that human beings exist always already in relation to one another.

Compassion is the topic of ethicist Daniel Fleming's contribution to this collection, and his contribution is the first of three that think through the economisation of death and the neoliberal tenor of the VAD regime. In his contribution, Fleming calls us to see how VAD is 'compassionate' only within a particular narrative: the narrative of neoliberalism with its ethical demand to create 'one's own story' and to 'provide for one's self'; the very opposite of the relational autonomy and care. Alasdair MacIntyre is a key dialogue partner in this undertaking, inspiring Fleming's interrogation of the incommensurability at the foundations of contemporary moral claims around VAD. For Fleming, we see this incommensurability most clearly in the fact that 'compassion' is able to be mobilised 'with equal public weight to describe VAD by those who are in favour of it, and to sharply critique it by those who are opposed to it'. Fleming demonstrates how the mobilisation of compassion in support of VAD can only make sense as an expression of a broader neoliberal frame. Those who mobilise compassion in this way do so by referencing and resonating with neoliberalism's hallmarks of autonomy without reference to the common good: the construction of a self-surveilling and self-regulating individual. The implications of such a frame are not merely theoretical. Mobilising compassion in its neoliberal form risks further compounding the signal features of a healthcare and economic system structured according to neoliberal norms: a tendency to serve those who have the means to act autonomously, and thus a privileging of those who hold economic power. His conclusion is that neoliberal 'compassion' can only distract us from other forms of justice and compassion, with its aversion to any form of economic or healthcare dependency, and a self-understanding of those who are unwell that prioritises self-governance and autonomy.

The figure of neoliberalism also motivates the contribution by legal academic Marc Trabsky, who in a rich contribution traces the neoliberal rationality of VAD as a legal technology. Trabsky describes VAD as a 'jurisdictional device'. Rather than VAD as only medical, as a jurisdictional device VAD is able to cultivate 'legal relations between … the living, the dying and the state'. Trabsky conceives of VAD as part of governmental practice that works by economising the relationship between the living, the dying and the state. This innovative analysis resonates with other contributions in the collection in its pointing to a 'thick' account of neoliberalism – beyond its thinner configuration as an economic doctrine – to a view of neoliberalism as it extends economisation into areas of life that were hitherto thought to be outside the economic. The analysis provided by Trabsky is put to work in showing that this movement of economisation has come to saturate VAD: by shaping legal relations between decision-makers, medical practitioners and the state, and by mobilising a model of 'human capital' as the model for government and governing the self. What is at stake here is the resulting exacerbation of socio-economic inequality and the further economisation of life through the regime of VAD – for both those who are able to access a (voluntary assisted) death, and those who cannot.

There are many significant shifts in the governance of death brought about by the entrance of VAD into law. While each contribution to this collection asks us to 'step back' and to critically assess what these shifts look like, the contribution of critical animal studies scholar Jessica Ison does so with a provocation: what about animals? Why are some animals not eligible to be euthanised? Why, instead, are they killed or slaughtered? Ison's intervention begins demonstrating the significant complexities that arise when we see that only some animals are considered worthy of euthanasia. For Ison, the pervasiveness of animal exploitation and our reliance on animal death in almost all facets of life further complicates why it is that these deaths are not rendered as 'deaths' at all. By tracing a history of animal euthanasia and its relation to animal anti-cruelty laws, Ison begins to draw our attention to the complex interplay of multiple interests within the domain of animal death: from entertainment, 'innovations' in worker control and exploitation, environmental pollution and other technologies of psychological conditioning and control made possible by the abattoir production line, to the rise of our contemporary form of domestic pet ownership. Ison ends her reflections by gesturing towards why it is time for animal death and VAD to be thought of together. For Ison, there is work to be done to render visible the figure of control and management within our ways of death dealing. Animal euthanasia is framed as offering comfort in death. Yet, even in this moment, we cannot escape that every facet of animal life is controlled, and their exploitation remains infinite and total: being 'put down' might be framed as care for animals, but it remains always a form of animal management and not an uncomplicated form of care. 'If nothing else', writes Ison, 'it shows us that we can construct elaborate layers of meaning that obfuscate cruelty and solidify a moral and ethical position that refuses to engage with the myriad inconvenient concerns'.

The potential for sanitising realities that are inconvenient is the warning issued by moral theologian Nigel Zimmermann's writing in this collection. Zimmermann begins with the promise that VAD offers a 'sanitising promise' to us and to those who suffer: 'your pain will be lessened and your autonomy increased'. But this promise of lightening the burden of death covers over what becomes in fact a far heavier burden placed on the shoulders of the dying person: responsibility for their own death. The thought of René Girard and Emmanuel Levinas stand as the two poles around which Zimmermann weaves his claims. Girard is mobilised primarily for his warning about the false promises of euthanasia, and Levinas for his ethics of alterity with its unsettling of views of human autonomy and the command not to kill. The conclusion Zimmermann draws highlights that what he terms the 'seductions of VAD' can in fact operate as a denial of the actual vulnerability and fragility of the Other – of us all – felt in especially heavy ways by those with fewer resources – spiritual, material, familial and social.

Those with few resources – particularly the aged – form the centre of criminal law and legal theory scholar Penny Crofts's chapter. In this contribution, Crofts takes the healthcare quality and safety failures at Gosport Hospital as an opportunity to interrogate law's inability to sustainably differentiate between unlawful and lawful homicide, particularly in the context of a health system that functions to veil such deaths – both consensual or not. Crofts mounts a discussion at the intersection of criminal theory of group culpability and systemic failure, of serial killer analysis and euthanasia. Her conclusions focus on the nature and productivity of vagueness in law and lexicon used to distinguish between various forms of unlawful homicides and euthanasia – presented by the central trope of 'foreshortening of life', used by *The Report of the Gosport Independent Panel* to describe the 456 deaths brought about by opioid prescribing practices that were used without appropriate clinical justification at Gosport Hospital.

Extending the discussion in this collection on VAD as 'law', health law scholar David Carter's contribution targets the place of the criminal law in relation to VAD. In his contribution, Carter notes how so much of the shift brought about with the introduction of VAD is as much about access to voluntary assisted dying as it is about a shift away from the criminal law's governance of this form of death. However true this transition is, Carter argues that it fails to fully capture the vital and ongoing role that the criminal law plays in the establishment and operation of VAD itself. In dialogue with Ben Golder's recent theorisation of biopolitics and the criminal law, this contribution first argues that the legal 'machinery' of VAD remains fundamentally criminal in nature. Building on that claim, Carter describes how criminal law is what then brings about the new biopolitical configuration of VAD, rendering visible the 'biopolitics of criminal law'; that is, how criminal law achieves a rationing of life by its organisation of a differential distribution of death within a population to be governed.

The VAD landscape is changing quickly across Australia. It is our hope that this volume provides some of the critical analysis of this area that has been largely missing as our community attempts to navigate this new terrain.[4]

4   The editors wish to acknowledge Jordan Roods and Katrina Mathieson for their research assistance, Beth Battrick for her copyediting, and the UTS Law Health | Justice | Research Centre for funding the initial symposium, which gave rise to this collection. David Carter is a National Health and Medical Research Council ('NHMRC') Early Career Fellow (Grant ID: 1156520). The contents are solely the responsibility of the individual authors and do not reflect the views of NHMRC.

1

The Constitution of 'Choice': Voluntary Assisted Dying in the Australian State of Victoria

Courtney Hempton[1]

The *Voluntary Assisted Dying Act* (2017) provides a safe legal framework for people who are suffering and dying to choose the manner and timing of their death.[2]

Introduction

On 19 June 2019 the *Voluntary Assisted Dying Act 2017* (Vic) came into effect, making Victoria the first state in Australia to establish a regime of physician-assisted death.[3] As summarised by the state's Department of Health and Human Services, the enacted model of 'voluntary assisted dying' 'provides a safe legal framework for people who are suffering and dying to

1   PhD Candidate, Monash Bioethics Centre, Monash University; courtney.hempton@monash. edu; orcid.org/0000-0001-9444-1170. This research was supported by an Australian Government Research Training Program (RTP) Scholarship. Information in this chapter is up to date as of November 2020.
2   Department of Health and Human Services, Government of Victoria, 'Voluntary Assisted Dying: Overview', *health.vic* (Web Page) <https://www.health.vic.gov.au/patient-care/overview>.
3   A brief note on terminology: I use the term 'voluntary assisted dying' to refer to the specific practice regulated in Victoria, though use the more generic term 'physician-assisted death' to refer more broadly to the practice of medical assistance to die, as variously conceived in different jurisdictions.

choose the manner and timing of their death'.[4] Such rhetoric of 'choice' is pivotal to the state's establishment and ongoing management of voluntary assisted dying. Notably, the historically significant law reform emerged from a state parliamentary Inquiry into End of Life Choices that focused broadly on 'the need for laws in Victoria to allow citizens to make informed decisions regarding their *own end of life choices*'[5] – specifically to 'assess the practices currently being utilised within the medical community to assist a person to exercise their preferences for the way they want *to manage their end of life*'.[6] Voluntary assisted dying thus emerges from a presupposition that 'end of life' may be medically managed through individual patient choice. As such, the emergence and formulation of voluntary assisted dying provokes consideration of the necessary and interrelated conditions permitting (and prohibiting) 'choice' in relation to voluntary assisted dying.

In this chapter, I critically examine the ways in which the state's distinct regulation of voluntary assisted dying constitutes and operationalises the concept of 'choice'. The state government's move to introduce voluntary assisted dying emerged from the recommendations of the aforementioned inter-party parliamentary Inquiry into End of Life Choices,[7] and an ensuing Ministerial Advisory Panel on Voluntary Assisted Dying;[8] the enacted *Voluntary Assisted Dying Act 2017* (Vic) is the cumulative product of these processes. A close reading of both the legislation and reports produced throughout the law reform process offer critical insight into the conception and operationalisation of voluntary assisted dying as a new 'end of life choice'. Despite the rhetoric of choice evident in the state's justification for establishing voluntary assisted dying, I contend there are pivotal ways in which the conditions created for 'choice' in relation to voluntary assisted dying are delimited, and markedly inconsistent with the

---

4   'Voluntary Assisted Dying: Overview' (n 2) (emphasis added).
5   Standing Committee on Legal and Social Issues, Parliament of Victoria Legislative Council, *Inquiry into End of Life Choices* (Final Report, June 2016) xiii (emphasis added).
6   Ibid xiii (emphasis added).
7   See generally Standing Committee on Legal and Social Issues, Parliament of Victoria Legislative Council, 'Community Views Sought on Choices for End of Life' (Media Release, 28 May 2015); Standing Committee on Legal and Social Issues, Parliament of Victoria Legislative Council, *Inquiry into End of Life Choices* (Interim Report, November 2015); *End of Life Choices* (Final Report) (n 5).
8   See generally Department of Health and Human Services, Government of Victoria, *Voluntary Assisted Dying Bill* (Discussion Paper, January 2017); Department of Health and Human Services, Government of Victoria, *Voluntary Assisted Dying Bill: Consultation Overview* (Interim Report, May 2017); Department of Health and Human Services, Government of Victoria, *Ministerial Advisory Panel on Voluntary Assisted Dying* (Final Report, July 2017); Margaret M O'Connor et al, 'Documenting the Process of Developing the Victorian Voluntary Assisted Dying Legislation' (2018) 42(6) *Australian Health Review* 621.

state's broader regulatory approach to medical care and decision-making. To demonstrate this claim, I will interrogate the state's constitution of 'choice' as evident in the Act, and briefly trace the emergence of consequential provisions through the law reform process, considered in terms of 'patient choices', and the interconnection with 'practitioner choices'. The aim of this chapter is not to analyse the state's rationale for establishing its particular regime of voluntary assisted dying,[9] nor to examine clinical implementation. Rather, I aim to demonstrate some of the distinct ways in which 'choice' in relation to voluntary assisted dying is produced – the state's institution of voluntary assisted dying in Victoria demarcates and deploys the concept of choice in unprecedented and anomalous ways. I will attend to the operationalisation of choice in voluntary assisted dying in the following sections, though first will overview the conceptualisation of voluntary assisted dying across stages of the law reform process, as conceived in relation to the notion of 'choice'.

'End of life choices': The conception of voluntary assisted dying

Victoria is the first state in Australia to develop and permit the practice of 'voluntary assisted dying'.[10] In essence, voluntary assisted dying refers to 'assistance to die provided in medical context'.[11] As specifically defined in the *Voluntary Assisted Dying Act 2017* (Vic) (hereafter 'the Act'), the term

---

9   For critical analysis of the state's rationale for voluntary assisted dying, see Marc Trabsky's chapter in this collection, 'The Neoliberal Rationality of Voluntary Assisted Dying'; see also John Keown, '"Voluntary Assisted Dying" in Australia: The Victorian Parliamentary Committee's Tenuous Case for Legalization' (2018) 33(1) *Issues in Law & Medicine* 55.

10   At the time of writing, other jurisdictions in Australia are actively considering the issue of 'end of life choices' including physician-assisted death. Most substantially in Western Australia, the *Voluntary Assisted Dying Act 2019* (WA) – legislation similar in nature to the Victorian legislation – passed on 10 December 2019, and will come into effect in mid-2021 after an approximate 18-month implementation period. The Western Australian legislation was introduced following a similar law reform process to Victoria; an initial inquiry into 'end of life choices', and consequent Ministerial Expert Panel on Voluntary Assisted Dying: see especially Joint Select Committee on End of Life Choices, Parliament of Western Australia, *My Life, My Choice: The Report of the Joint Select Committee On End Of Life Choices* (Report No 1, August 2018); Department of Health, Government of Western Australia, *Ministerial Expert Panel on Voluntary Assisted Dying* (Final Report, June 2019). Similar inquiries into 'end of life choices' are in progress in other states and territories (noting Australian territories are currently prohibited in effect by the federal *Euthanasia Laws Act 1997* (Cth) from permitting 'euthanasia'). For a history of law reform attempts across Australia see also Lindy Willmott, Ben White, Christopher Stackpoole et al, '(Failed) Voluntary Euthanasia Law Reform in Australia: Two Decades of Trends, Models and Politics' (2016) 39(1) *University of New South Wales Law Journal* 1.

11   *End of Life Choices* (Final Report) (n 5) 14.

voluntary assisted dying refers to 'the administration of a voluntary assisted dying substance',[12] 'for the purpose of causing a person's death'.[13] In effect, the state has established a particular regime of 'physician-assisted death' that provides primarily for the practice of patient 'self-administration' of a prescribed lethal substance;[14] in circumstances in which a patient is physically unable to self-administer, 'practitioner administration' is permitted, which allows a relevantly qualified and specifically trained medical practitioner to directly administer the substance to the patient.[15] The Act delineates the necessary conditions for access to voluntary assisted dying as an intentional life-ending option, and makes explicit the ways in which the practice will be governed as part of regulated medical care.

The broad framework of the state's voluntary assisted dying regime was outlined by the inter-party Victorian Legislative Council Legal and Social Issues Committee (Legislation and References) (hereafter the 'Committee'), which conducted the Inquiry into End of Life Choices (hereafter the 'Inquiry'), and later refined by the state-appointed Ministerial Advisory Panel on Voluntary Assisted Dying (hereafter the 'Panel'), which developed the Voluntary Assisted Dying Bill 2016 (Vic).[16] Alongside recommendations to improve aspects of palliative care and advance care planning,[17] the Committee's final recommendation – 'recommendation 49' – was that the state should introduce voluntary assisted dying;[18] specifically, that the state

> should introduce legislation to allow adults with decision making capacity, suffering from a serious and incurable condition who are at the end of life to be provided assistance to die in certain circumstances.[19]

The eventually adopted legislation emanates in essence from the 'assisted dying framework' proposed by the Committee,[20] though a number of consequential changes were introduced by the Panel, and amendments

---

12   *Voluntary Assisted Dying Act 2017* (Vic) s 3.1 (definition of 'voluntary assisted dying').
13   Ibid s 3.1 (definition of 'voluntary assisted dying substance').
14   Ibid s 47.
15   Ibid s 48.
16   Courtney Hempton and Catherine Mills, 'Constitution of "the Already Dying": The Emergence of Voluntary Assisted Dying in Victoria' (2021) 18(2) *Journal of Bioethical Inquiry* 265 doi.org/10.1007/s11673-021-10107-1.
17   *End of Life Choices* (Final Report) (n 5) xxix–xxxiv.
18   Ibid xxxiv.
19   Ibid 237.
20   Ibid 210–36.

further passed during parliamentary debate. While a complete history of the development of the state's model of voluntary assisted dying is beyond the scope of the current chapter, the rendering of 'choice' in the formulation of the voluntary assisted dying legislation is instrumental.

During the initial Inquiry stage of the law reform process, the Committee sought 'community views on the need for laws to allow people broader scope in their end of life choices'.[21] While the Inquiry addressed 'end of life' broadly, much attention was devoted to whether or not some form of lawful physician-assisted death ought to be introduced. The ensuing discourse predominantly followed familiar 'for' and 'against' arguments seen in the broader and ongoing debate[22] – arguments utilised by the those advocating for the introduction of physician-assisted death focused predominantly on the notion of patient choice.[23] Though in terms of the composition of 'choice' in relation to physician-assisted death, little definitional clarity was offered throughout the law reform process to distinguish between the meanings of various nebulous concepts and terms pertaining to patient choice; discourse concerning aspects of autonomy, control, decision-making, options and self-determination. For example, the Committee undertook a thematic analysis of arguments offered in public submissions[24] to the Inquiry arguing in support of (some form of) lawful voluntary assisted dying. The Committee's analysis provides an indication of community sentiment regarding the notion of choice in relation to voluntary assisted dying. Notably 'choice' is identified as the most dominant theme in arguments supporting voluntary assisted dying, and notions of choice also feature across a number of other themes identified by the Committee.[25] The primary analytic theme titled 'choice' is described by the Committee as:

---

21 'Community Views Sought on Choices for End of Life' (n 7).

22 *End of Life Choices* (Final Report) (n 5) 303–13. See generally Gerald Dworkin, RG Frey and Sissela Bok, *Euthanasia and Physician-Assisted Suicide: For and Against* (Cambridge University Press, 1998); Dieter Birnbacher and Edgar Dahl (eds), *Giving Death a Helping Hand—Physician-Assisted Suicide and Public Policy: An International Perspective* (Springer, 2008).

23 *End of Life Choices* (Final Report) (n 5) 296.

24 The Committee received a total 1,037 submissions throughout the course of the Inquiry, receiving 925 submissions from individuals and 112 from organisations. As advised by the Committee, only 1,023 submissions are included in its content analyses, as 14 were received too late for inclusion: Ibid 295.

25 Ibid 296–7.

> The manner of a person's death should be completely up to that person. *Each person should be able to choose how they die*, just as they choose how they live. As such, assisted dying should be legalised.[26]

The theme of 'control' is also relevant to voluntary assisted dying as an option or choice, described by the Committee as: 'Having the option of assisted dying would *give dying people a feeling of control over their death*, and remaining life'.[27] A further theme that explicitly mentions choice, though analytically separated from the principle theme of choice, is that the 'state should not prevent', described as:

> The state should not create laws that prevent people being able to choose when and how they die in the context of irremediable suffering. Doctors should be free from legal liability to provide assisted dying.[28]

Similarly, the theme 'others' morals should not prevent' reflects ideas of noninterference in personal choice and decision-making:

> The morals, religion, and ethics of other people should not affect a personal decision about ending your own life when experiencing irremediable suffering. The law on assisted dying should reflect this.[29]

Further, the theme 'legal options inhumane' reflects the idea of choice in relation to existing options, described as:

> The *current options for hastening death*, which include the patient refusing treatment, food and water, are inhumane. They subject patients to unnecessary pain and suffering that could be avoided by assisted dying.[30]

The Committee also offered a synopsis of the recurring arguments encountered throughout the Inquiry, drawing on written submissions received, oral testimony from witnesses and broader academic research. The Committee notes 'autonomy' is a common argument in favour of establishing lawful voluntary assisted dying. In describing the general

---

26 Ibid 297 (emphasis added).
27 Ibid 297 (emphasis added).
28 Ibid 297 (emphasis added).
29 Ibid 297 (emphasis added).
30 Ibid 297 (emphasis added).

content of autonomy-based arguments, the Committee notes 'submissions to the Inquiry that included the autonomy argument often used the word "choice", but sometimes also referred to "control"'.[31]

It is somewhat unclear how the Committee interpreted or weighted various arguments pertaining to the concept of 'choice' in moving to recommend the state establish lawful (voluntary) assisted dying as a new 'end of life' option, and more specifically to prescribe its particular 'assisted dying framework'. However, the Committee's general approach to 'end of life care' – in terms of which voluntary assisted dying is rendered – is most clearly articulated through the Committee's stated 'Core Values for End of Life Care' (hereafter 'Core Values'). The Core Values are described by the Committee as 'a set of shared core values for end of life care … [to] provide an understanding of the beliefs that underpin the Committee's approach to this subject';[32] the twelve 'beliefs' were developed by the Committee based on learnings throughout the Inquiry process.[33] A number of the Core Values and their descriptions reflect notions related to 'choice', including beliefs regarding promoting open discussion about mortality and planning for dying and death, self-determination, informed choices at the end-of-life, person-centred care and equitable access to end-of-life 'options', in terms of availability of high-quality care across geographic locations and preferred setting.[34] With regard to these Core Values, the Committee determined its model of lawful voluntary assisted dying reflected and aligned with 'the legal and medical values and culture that are essential to Victorians'.[35]

While the Committee's model of 'assisted dying' provided the foundation for the state's approach to voluntary assisted dying, the regime was then refined in accord with recommendations made by the Panel.[36] In regard to conceptualising voluntary assisted dying in terms of 'choice', the Panel highlighted 'clear and consistent themes [that] have emerged about what matters to Victorians for their care at the end-of-life',[37] including 'placing people at the centre of decision making about their own medical

31 Ibid 306.
32 Ibid 15.
33 Ibid 15.
34 Ibid 16.
35 Ibid 21.
36 See generally 'Voluntary Assisted Dying Bill' (Discussion Paper) (n 8); Voluntary Assisted Dying Bill: Consultation Overview (Interim Report) (n 8); Ministerial Advisory Panel on Voluntary Assisted Dying (Final Report) (n 8); O'Connor et al (n 8).
37 Ministerial Advisory Panel on Voluntary Assisted Dying (Final Report) (n 8) 34.

treatments', and 'genuine choice that responds to people's needs'.[38] Adapting the Committee's twelve 'Core Values', the Panel offered nine 'Guiding Principles' that underpin its recommendations.[39] In terms of choice, key 'Guiding Principles' include notions of 'respecting autonomy', 'informed decision-making' and 'genuine choice'. As demarcated by the Panel, 'respecting autonomy' means 'providing people with a degree of control over the timing and manner of death',[40] but 'does not mean allowing people to do whatever they want'.[41] 'Informed decision-making' entails being supported to make well-informed decisions; 'if a person is not properly informed, their decision will not necessarily reflect their will'[42] – 'it is critical that a person has all the necessary information available to them to identify the option that is the most consistent with their preferences and values'.[43] In terms of 'genuine choice', the Panel determined that voluntary assisted dying should only be an option for people 'who have a range of treatment options available to them … [it] cannot be an alternative to palliative care or being offered the best available treatment'.[44] As recommended by the Panel, its list of 'Guiding Principles' appear as 'Principles' in the Act, to guide interpretation of duties in relation to voluntary assisted dying.[45] Key Principles in relation to 'choice' featured in the Act include 'a person's autonomy should be respected',[46] 'a person has the right to be supported in making informed decisions about the person's medical treatment'[47] and 'individuals are entitled to genuine choices regarding their treatment and care'.[48] As summarised by Rosalind McDougall and Bridget Pratt, a number of the Principles listed in the Act contribute to fostering 'a normative environment that supports individual choice in relation to [voluntary assisted dying]'.[49]

38   Ibid 34.
39   Ibid 43–6.
40   Ibid 44.
41   Ibid 44.
42   Ibid 44.
43   Ibid 44.
44   Ibid 44.
45   *Voluntary Assisted Dying Act 2017* (Vic) s 5.
46   Ibid s 5(1)(b).
47   Ibid s 5(1)(c).
48   Ibid s 5(1)(h).
49   Rosalind McDougall and Bridget Pratt, 'Too Much Safety? Safeguards and Equal Access in the Context of Voluntary Assisted Dying Legislation' (2020) 21(1) *BMC Medical Ethics* 38, 8.

Voluntary assisted dying: Patient 'choices'

While a discourse of individual patient choice is drawn on to justify the state's institution of lawful voluntary assisted dying, the concept of choice is operationalised in distinct ways. Emerging from the state's law reform process, the Act in effect delineates the necessary conditions for access to voluntary assisted dying as an intentional life-ending medical option, and makes explicit a series of necessary and interrelated conditions permitting (and prohibiting) patient 'choice' in relation to voluntary assisted dying.

Foremost, the Act functions to distinguish between those deemed eligible (and ineligible) for voluntary assisted dying. Primarily, in formulating voluntary assisted dying exclusively for those medically prognosed to die 'within weeks or months',[50] elsewhere Catherine Mills and I contend the state constructs the bounds of a medico-legal category, which we term 'the already dying';[51] the category of the already dying is constituted through the interrelated (in)eligibility criteria specified in the Act. In effect, we contend this category of 'the already dying' functions to distinguish between lives the state deems terminable – those eligible for voluntary assisted dying, described by the state as 'those who are *already dying* from an incurable, advanced and progressive disease, illness or medical condition'[52] – and lives that are not.[53] I contend the most significant way in which the state constitutes choice in relation to voluntary assisted dying is rendered in terms of 'the already dying'. As summarised by the Committee, voluntary assisted dying 'should provide an option that can limit suffering at the very end of life, not a way to end life for those who are otherwise *not dying*'.[54] As such, the category of the already dying functions to frame choice in a particular way:

> The recommended eligibility criteria ensure voluntary assisted dying will allow a small number of people, at the end of their lives, to choose the timing and manner of their death. There is no intention to give people who are *not dying* access, and the legislation will *not* give these people an option to *choose between living and dying*.[55]

---

50 *Voluntary Assisted Dying Act 2017* (Vic) s 9(1)(d)(iii).
51 I provide a detailed argument regarding the constitution of 'the already dying' in Hempton and Mills (n 16).
52 'Voluntary Assisted Dying: Overview' (n 2) (emphasis added).
53 Hempton and Mills (n 16).
54 *End of Life Choices* (Final Report) (n 5) 224 (emphasis added).
55 *Ministerial Advisory Panel on Voluntary Assisted Dying* (Final Report) (n 8) 13 (emphasis added).

In this sense, the choice created by voluntary assisted dying is rendered as a choice that is not between 'living and dying' per se – not a choice between 'life' and 'death' – but rather an option for those *already dying* to 'choose the manner and timing of their death'. As recapitulated by the Panel, 'voluntary assisted dying would not give people the option *to choose to live or die*, as they must already be at the end of their life'.[56] In terms of choice then, the exclusive category of the already dying serves to *prohibit* choice for the corollary non-dying. The category of the already dying functions to 'safeguard' those 'people who are not dying' from being able to choose the manner and timing of death, while enabling '*only* those who are already dying'[57] to choose death.[58]

One of the other instrumental ways in which the concept of choice is constituted is through a distinct interpretation of medico-legal 'voluntariness'. Indeed, the original term adopted by the Committee – 'assisted dying' – was explicitly amended by the Panel to include the word *voluntary*; as determined by the Panel, the revised term 'voluntary assisted dying' 'puts the focus on the term "voluntary" as an emphatic statement that this is a decision initiated by a person who is suffering and *takes responsibility for the decision*'.[59] In this sense, voluntary assisted dying – by means of the necessary 'voluntariness' – is cast in relation to a decision, or choice, and in terms of 'responsibilisation'; the individual patient voluntarily making the decision is deemed solely responsible for the choice. Notably, the state's selected terminology, and 'emphatic' allocation of patient responsibility for voluntary assisted dying, obscures the necessary involvement of the medical discipline and professional responsibilities of individual medical practitioners involved in providing the patient with assistance to die. Not only does the term 'voluntary assisted dying' veil the medical aid or assistance inherent in voluntary assisted dying – the requisite action of physician-assisted death is indeed 'assistance' – the emphasis on patient responsibility further fails to account for the significant role of medical practitioners as gatekeepers to access voluntary assisted dying; a patient is not able to access or 'choose' voluntary assisted dying without the substantial involvement of medical practitioners.[60]

---

56   Ibid 44 (emphasis added).
57   'Voluntary Assisted Dying: Overview' (n 2) (emphasis added).
58   Hempton and Mills (n 16).
59   *Ministerial Advisory Panel on Voluntary Assisted Dying* (Final Report) (n 8) 8 (emphasis added).
60   *Voluntary Assisted Dying Act 2017* (Vic) s 6.

Relatedly, 'voluntariness' is demarcated in relation to 'decision-making capacity', such that to be eligible for voluntary assisted dying a 'person must have decision-making capacity in relation to voluntary assisted dying'.[61] Decision-making capacity is generally defined in the state's *Medical Treatment Planning and Decisions Act 2016* (Vic) in decision-relative terms,[62] such that:

> A person has decision-making capacity in relation to voluntary assisted dying if the person is able to—
>
> a. understand the information relevant to the decision relating to access to voluntary assisted dying and the effect of the decision; and
>
> b. retain that information to the extent necessary to make the decision; and
>
> c. use or weigh that information as part of the process of making the decision; and
>
> d. communicate the decision and the person's views and needs as to the decision in some way, including by speech, gestures or other means.[63]

In this sense, the concept of 'choice' – or the ability to *choose* – is medically assessed in terms of a patient's cognitive capacity in relation to deciding to 'manage their end of life' with voluntary assisted dying.[64] While a decision-relative account of decision-making capacity is in accord with the state's contemporary approach to legislatively regulating medical treatment decision-making,[65] the state's prohibition of requesting voluntary assisted dying through an advance care directive is inconsistent with other medical treatment and care decisions, including other 'end of life' (and in consequence life-ending) choices. In outlining the 'assisted dying framework' the Committee stated it 'does not support access to [voluntary] assisted dying through any kind of advance care directive'.[66]

---

61 Ibid s 9(1)(c).
62 See generally Courtney Hempton and Neera Bhatia, 'Deciding for When You Can't Decide: The *Medical Treatment Planning and Decisions Act 2016* (Vic)' (2020) 17(1) *Journal of Bioethical Inquiry* 109.
63 *Voluntary Assisted Dying Act 2017* (Vic) ss 4(1)(a)–4(1)(d).
64 I provide a more detailed overview of what we term the 'cognitive elements' of voluntary assisted dying (in)eligibility, including 'voluntariness' and decision-making capacity in Hempton and Mills (n 16); for a discussion regarding the clinical assessment of decision-making capacity in the context of voluntary assisted dying see Carmelle Peisah, Linda Sheahan and Ben White, 'The Biggest Decision of Them All—Death and Assisted Dying: Capacity Assessments and Undue Influence Screening' (2019) 49(6) *Internal Medicine Journal* 792.
65 Hempton and Bhatia (n 62).
66 *End of Life Choices* (Final Report) (n 5) 221.

The Committee's position was maintained by the Panel, which determined that 'requiring a person to have decision-making capacity *throughout* the voluntary assisted dying process represents an important safeguard to protect against abuse'.[67] The requirement to have decision-making capacity *throughout* the whole voluntary assisted dying process introduces a temporal condition for decision-making capacity in relation to voluntary assisted dying that is *not* necessitated for other medical decisions in Victoria, which are able to be effected in circumstances in which a patient does not have decision-making capacity, via an advance care directive or a proxy 'medical treatment decision-maker'.[68] In effect, the standard for decision-making capacity in relation to voluntary assisted dying is emphatically more demanding than that required for other medical treatment and care decisions in Victoria.

Even for an individual who prima facie meets all of the eligibility criteria, choosing voluntary assisted dying necessitates the navigation of a complex voluntary assisted dying apparatus; a patient's choice is absolutely contingent on the – largely obscured – choices of individual medical practitioners, health services and other care institutions, and ultimately the state. As outlined, 'choice' in voluntary assisted dying necessitates being diagnosed and prognosed as 'already dying', and further clinical assessment of one's 'voluntariness' and 'decision-making capacity' in relation to voluntary assisted dying,[69] in addition to a host of other (in)eligibility criteria as specified in the Act. Medical assessment of patient eligibility is then subject to approval by the state, requiring issuance of a 'voluntary assisted dying permit'[70] – literal permission from the state is required for a patient to choose voluntary assisted dying. Ultimately under the Victorian model of voluntary assisted dying, whether or not a particular patient is empowered to actually *choose* whether and when – or not – they may self-administer the voluntary assisted dying substance to cause their death (or have the substance administered by a practitioner if deemed medically necessary) is really available only once the relevant 'permit' is issued by the state, which then enables the patient to request access to

---

67   *Ministerial Advisory Panel on Voluntary Assisted Dying* (Final Report) (n 8) 8 (emphasis added).
68   For detailed discussion of the regulation of medical treatment decision-making in Victoria see Hempton and Bhatia (n 62); John Chesterman, 'Prioritising Patients' Preferences: Victoria's New Advance Planning and Medical Consent Legislation' (2017) 25(1) *Journal of Law and Medicine* 46.
69   For a discussion regarding the clinical assessment of decision-making capacity in the context of voluntary assisted dying, see Peisah, Sheahan and White (n 64).
70   *Voluntary Assisted Dying Act 2017* (Vic) ss 3(1) (definitions of 'voluntary assisted dying permit', 'self-administration permit', 'practitioner administration permit'), 45–53, 56.

the 'voluntary assisted dying substance', which will then be provided to the patient by the statewide pharmacy service. Rather than enabling a patient to 'choose the manner and timing of death' directly, the option that may be available to a patient is to merely make a request for voluntary assisted dying – or a request to be medically assessed for voluntary assisted dying. In terms of a patient actually being enabled to choose to die by means of voluntary assisted dying, such choice is wholly contingent on medical practitioner participation, which too is operationalised in distinct ways.

Voluntary assisted dying: Practitioner 'choices'

While the state's model of voluntary assisted dying deliberately emphasises the patient, the role of health practitioners in the management of voluntary assisted dying is inherent. In operationalising the concept of patient choice in its model of voluntary assisted dying, the state emphasises the extensive regulation of the eligibility and assessment and approval processes required for access to voluntary assisted dying, establishing medical practitioners as voluntary assisted dying gatekeepers, whether they choose to participate or not. However, the activities of health practitioners are further regulated by the state in ways peculiar to voluntary assisted dying, including the establishment of both new prohibitions and new rights for health practitioners.

A most extraordinary feature of the Victorian voluntary assisted dying legislation is its 'gag clause'[71] – the Act explicitly prohibits health practitioners from initiating a discussion about voluntary assisted dying with patients. As specified in the legislation, all registered health practitioners in the state are explicitly prohibited from initiating a discussion that is either in substance about voluntary assisted dying, or in substance suggests voluntary assisted dying to a patient in their care.[72] The inclusion of a gag clause was recommended by the Panel as a 'safeguard', with the stated policy intention '[t]o ensure a person is not coerced or unduly influenced into accessing voluntary assisted dying and to demonstrate the request for voluntary assisted dying is the person's

71 Bryanna Moore, Courtney Hempton and Evie Kendal, 'Victoria's Voluntary Assisted Dying Act: Navigating the Section 8 Gag Clause' (2020) 212(2) *Medical Journal of Australia* 1.
72 *Voluntary Assisted Dying Act 2017* (Vic) s 8.

own voluntary decision'.[73] To my knowledge at the time of writing, a gag-style clause is not a feature of any other physician-assisted death regime – Victoria is the *only* jurisdiction in the world to have a gag clause in effect in relation to physician-assisted death.[74] The gag clause has been critiqued on several grounds, foremost in relation to equitable access to voluntary assisted dying, and further in relation to potential issues regarding informed patient decision-making and consent.[75] Along with colleagues Bryanna Moore and Evie Kendal, I elsewhere critique the state's prohibition, outlining some of the ethically problematic implications for the provision of healthcare; we conclude 'section 8 is an unwarranted infringement on communication between health practitioners and their patients'.[76] In terms of 'choice', the gag clause

> places a burden of prior knowledge of voluntary assisted dying on patients … [c]ertain groups may end up missing vital information that could impact their end-of-life choices, particularly those with lower levels of health literacy.[77]

In this sense, the gag clause, while a prohibition regulating the activities of health practitioners, has the potential to impact patient choice, in terms of (lack of) awareness of available options. As noted by Carolyn Johnston and James Cameron, a patient

> will need to identify that voluntary assisted dying may be an option for them without the initial assistance of their health practitioner. This may limit access and prevent people who may be eligible for voluntary assisted dying from considering it as an option.[78]

---

73 *Ministerial Advisory Panel on Voluntary Assisted Dying* (Final Report) (n 8) 91.

74 The *Voluntary Assisted Dying Act 2019* (WA) will come into effect in mid-2021, and features a somewhat refined gag clause, relative to the Victorian legislation – in Western Australia medical practitioners and nurse practitioners will not be subject to a gag clause, but if initiating discussion about voluntary assisted dying must at the same time also inform the person of the treatment options and the palliative care options available, and the likely outcome of those options, while all other 'health care workers' in Western Australia (including all other registered health practitioners) will be prohibited from initiating discussion about voluntary assisted dying: *Voluntary Assisted Dying Act 2019* (WA) s 10.

75 See especially Moore, Hempton and Kendal (n 71); Carolyn Johnston and James Cameron, 'Discussing Voluntary Assisted Dying' (2018) 26(2) *Journal of Law and Medicine* 454; Lindy Willmott, Ben White, Danielle Ko et al, 'Restricting Conversations About Voluntary Assisted Dying: Implications for Clinical Practice' (2020) 10(1) *BMJ Supportive & Palliative Care* 105.

76 Moore, Hempton and Kendal (n 71) 1.

77 Ibid 2.

78 Johnston and Cameron (n 75) 458.

In this sense, voluntary assisted dying may be precluded from consideration as an end-of-life option, if perhaps patients are not aware the state now permits voluntary assisted dying, or are unaware of the state's protocol regarding patient-initiated requests for access – a patient cannot make a decision about voluntary assisted dying if they do not know voluntary assisted dying is an option available to them.

Relatedly, the gag clause highlights a further overt inconsistency between information provision regarding voluntary assisted dying, compared to other end-of-life choices, which may have implications for decision-making and 'informed consent'. In order to access voluntary assisted dying, as part of the clinical assessment protocol, each of the medical practitioners *must* inform the patient of 'the treatment options available to the person and the likely outcomes of that treatment; [and] the palliative care options available to the person and the likely outcomes of that care'.[79] This protocol appears to stem from the Principles of 'genuine choice' and 'informed decision-making' as described previously; voluntary assisted dying should only be an option in the context of alternatives, including the best available treatment and palliative care. However, in distinct contrast when making any other 'end of life' medical decisions, for example about treatment or palliative care, patients are *not* similarly required to be informed about voluntary assisted dying as an available option – indeed, not only is there no requirement to inform patients about voluntary assisted dying as an option, the 'section 8' gag clause expressly *prohibits* registered health practitioners from informing patients about voluntary assisted dying, unless the patient explicitly enquires. As summarised by Lindy Willmott and colleagues, 'the concern is that the section 8 restriction will prevent some patients approaching the [end of life] from making informed decisions'.[80] In practice then, patients considering choosing voluntary assisted dying are legally required have alternative treatment and palliative care options explained to them, while patients considering choosing treatment or palliative care options must *not* have voluntary assisted dying mentioned to them, except at their explicit request. In this regard, the principles of 'genuine choice' and 'informed decision-making' are operationalised differently in regard to considering choosing voluntary assisted dying, as compared to considering other end-of-life options.

---

79   *Voluntary Assisted Dying Act 2017* (Vic) ss 19(1)(b)–19(1)(c), 28(1)(b)–(c).
80   Willmott, White, Ko et al (n 75) 4.

Even if a patient is well-informed enough to request information about voluntary assisted dying, another way in which voluntary assisted dying is regulated differently to other medical options is through the practitioner 'conscientious objection' provision. As detailed in the Act, any registered health practitioner who has a 'conscientious objection to voluntary assisted dying has the *right* to refuse'[81] to support or participate in the practice of voluntary assisted dying in any way, including refusing to provide information about voluntary assisted dying, to participate in the assessment and permit-application process, to being involved in prescribing, dispensing, supplying or administering the voluntary assisted dying substance, and/or being present at the time of administration.[82] Unlike other legislated conscientious objection provisions in the state, this new right does not confer any obligations on health practitioners in order to support patients requesting information or access to voluntary assisted dying, for example requiring referral to another health practitioner.[83] In effect, the conscientious objection provision establishes more 'rights' for health practitioners than patients in regard to voluntary assisted dying – there are no new rights for patients established by the Act, while health practitioners have a new unfettered right to non-participation. In terms of 'choice', the potential impact of the conscientious objection provision, in the absence of a legislated obligation for health practitioners to provide minimal patient information or an appropriate referral, may impact the ability of patients to access information about voluntary assisted dying as a lawful option.

Further, briefly, I would be remiss not to note that the potential participation of individual health practitioners may be impacted by whether or not the health service within which they practice chooses to offer voluntary assisted dying. While the practice of voluntary assisted dying continues to evolve in Victoria, participation at an organisational level is discretionary, and there are health services and care providers that will not offer voluntary assisted dying services. For example, organisations without the necessary clinical staff or expertise may offer limited voluntary assisted dying services for logistical reasons, while faith-based institutions

---

81 *Voluntary Assisted Dying Act 2017* (Vic) s 7 (emphasis added).

82 Ibid ss 7(a)–7(f).

83 Cf the *Abortion Law Reform Act 2008* (Vic) features a 'conscientious objection' provision, which dictates 'obligations of registered health practitioner who has conscientious objection', including that a registered health practitioner, *must* 'refer the woman [sic] to another registered health practitioner in the same regulated health profession who the practitioner knows does not have a conscientious objection to abortion': *Abortion Law Reform Act 2008* (Vic) s 8.

may offer no voluntary assisted dying services for values-based reasons.[84] Overall, the specified medico-legal management of voluntary assisted dying makes evident what the administration of voluntary assisted dying actually produces in terms of 'choice'; the option or ability of a patient to *choose* voluntary assisted dying – to choose the manner and timing of their death – is absolutely contingent on the choices of others, including the necessary participation of health services and medical practitioners, and ultimately the state.

Conclusion

The establishment of voluntary assisted dying in Victoria is a historic transformation in the state's management of 'end of life choices'. As overviewed, the practice of voluntary assisted dying is operationalised through the *Voluntary Assisted Dying Act 2017* (Vic), as conceptualised through a state parliamentary Inquiry into End of Life Choices, subsequent Ministerial Advisory Panel on Voluntary Assisted Dying, and further parliamentary debate on the initially proposed Voluntary Assisted Dying Bill 2016 (Vic). Despite the rhetoric of patient choice evident in the state's justification for establishing voluntary assisted dying, in this chapter I have demonstrated some of the distinct ways in which 'choice' in relation to voluntary assisted dying is demarcated and deployed. While it is beyond the scope of this chapter to trace the state's rationale for establishing its particular regime of voluntary assisted dying, it is notable that a 'discourse of safety'[85] pervaded the development of voluntary assisted dying in Victoria – the model of voluntary assisted dying is claimed by the state to be the 'safest, and most conservative, in the world'.[86] As such, the distinct demarcation of 'choice' in relation to voluntary assisted dying as discussed may reflect a prioritisation of safety, including 'safeguards' to protect both patients and health practitioners.[87] However, as explicated

---

84 For a more detailed discussion of organisational-level participation in voluntary assisted dying, and the potential impact on (un)equal access in Victoria, see McDougall and Pratt (n 49).

85 McDougall and Pratt (n 49).

86 See, eg, Daniel Andrews, 'Debate of Historic Voluntary Assisted Dying Bill Starts' (Media Release, 17 October 2017) <https://www.premier.vic.gov.au/debate-historic-voluntary-assisted-dying-bill-starts>; 'Voluntary Assisted Dying: Overview' (n 2).

87 See generally *Ministerial Advisory Panel on Voluntary Assisted Dying* (Final Report) (n 8) 181–83, 216–28.

by Rosalind McDougall and Bridget Pratt, '[w]hile safety is of course an important value, safeguards have access consequences',[88] and the coherence and effects of voluntary assisted dying 'safeguards' warrant scrutiny.

The state's management of voluntary assisted dying is complex, and access to voluntary assisted dying entails navigating a new medico-legal voluntary assisted dying apparatus, which functions to delimit choice in relation to voluntary assisted dying in a number of ways that are pointedly inconsistent with the state's broader approach to regulating decision-making in a medical context. For patients, choice in regard to voluntary assisted dying is restricted to those who meet a number of necessary conditions that are not required in other medical decision-making circumstances, including holding prior knowledge of voluntary assisted dying as a potential option in order to make a sufficient request for voluntary assisted dying, in addition to maintaining decision-making capacity throughout the entire voluntary assisted dying request, assessment and administration process. Interrelatedly, the management of voluntary assisted dying necessitates the 'conscientious' participation of medical and potentially other health practitioners, though their involvement is constrained by the state with an unprecedented 'gag clause', and their necessary role as the essential administrators of voluntary assisted dying is obscured in a number of ways, given the state's emphasis on 'responsibilising' the patient. Ultimately, explicit approval from medical practitioners and authorisation from the state is required to permit an individual patient to 'choose' voluntary assisted dying – without permission, voluntary assisted dying is prohibited. In effect, the state's 'safeguarding' of choice in regard to voluntary assisted dying produces and deploys distinct meanings of choice that, while formulated in a values-discourse seemingly akin to broader medical care and decision-making in Victoria, delimits choice in the context of voluntary assisted dying in unprecedented and anomalous ways. In sum, the state's new option to 'choose the manner and timing of death' constitutes both patient and practitioner choice in new ways, such that voluntary assisted dying is not like other end-of-life choices.

---

88   McDougall and Pratt (n 49) 8.

Acknowledgements

A preliminary version of this chapter was discussed at an invitational symposium on 'Voluntary Assisted Dying: Law? Health? Justice?' at the University of Technology Sydney (7 February 2019), and I dearly thank hosts David Carter and Dan Fleming, and other attendees, for their thoughtful reflections, in particular Marc Trabsky for his continuing support. Parts of this chapter are drawn from my doctoral dissertation, and I extend my sincerest appreciation to my supervisors, Catherine Mills and Justin Oakley, for ongoing discussions that improved aspects of this broader work in progress. Much gratitude also to Ros McDougall and Bridget Pratt for generously sharing an advance copy of their manuscript under review, cited as published.

Bibliography

A Articles/books/reports

Birnbacher, Dieter and Edgar Dahl (eds), *Giving Death a Helping Hand: Physician-Assisted Suicide and Public Policy. An International Perspective* (Springer, 2008) doi.org/10.1007/978-1-4020-6496-8

Chesterman, John, 'Prioritising Patients' Preferences: Victoria's New Advance Planning and Medical Consent Legislation' (2017) 25(1) *Journal of Law and Medicine* 46

Department of Health, Government of Western Australia, *Ministerial Expert Panel on Voluntary Assisted Dying* (Final Report, June 2019)

Department of Health and Human Services, Government of Victoria, *Ministerial Advisory Panel on Voluntary Assisted Dying* (Final Report, 31 July 2017)

Department of Health and Human Services, Government of Victoria, *Voluntary Assisted Dying Bill: Consultation Overview* (Interim Report, May 2017)

Department of Health and Human Services, Government of Victoria, *Voluntary Assisted Dying Bill* (Discussion Paper, January 2017)

Dworkin, Gerald, RG Frey and Sissela Bok, *Euthanasia and Physician-Assisted Suicide: For and Against* (Cambridge University Press, 1998)

Hempton, Courtney and Catherine Mills, 'Constitution of "the Already Dying": The Emergence of Voluntary Assisted Dying in Victoria' (2021) 18(2) *Journal of Bioethical Inquiry* 265 doi.org/10.1007/s11673-021-10107-1

Hempton, Courtney and Neera Bhatia, 'Deciding for When You Can't Decide: The Medical Treatment Planning and Decisions Act 2016 (Vic)' (2020) 17(1) *Journal of Bioethical Inquiry* 109 doi.org/10.1007/s11673-020-09960-3

Johnston, Carolyn and James Cameron, 'Discussing Voluntary Assisted Dying' (2018) 26(2) *Journal of Law and Medicine* 454

Joint Select Committee on End of Life Choices, Parliament of Western Australia, *My Life, My Choice: The Report of the Joint Select Committee On End Of Life Choices* (Report No 1, August 2018)

Keown, John, '"Voluntary Assisted Dying" in Australia: The Victorian Parliamentary Committee's Tenuous Case for Legalization' (2018) 33(1) *Issues in Law & Medicine* 55

McDougall, Rosalind and Bridget Pratt, 'Too Much Safety? Safeguards and Equal Access in the Context of Voluntary Assisted Dying Legislation' (2020) 21(1) *BMC Medical Ethics* 38 doi.org/10.1186/s12910-020-00483-5

Moore, Bryanna, Courtney Hempton and Evie Kendal, 'Victoria's Voluntary Assisted Dying Act: Navigating the Section 8 Gag Clause' (2020) 212(2) *Medical Journal of Australia* 67 doi.org/10.5694/mja2.50437

O'Connor, Margaret M et al, 'Documenting the Process of Developing the Victorian Voluntary Assisted Dying Legislation' (2018) 42(6) *Australian Health Review* 621 doi.org/10.1071/AH18172

Peisah, Carmelle, Linda Sheahan and Ben P White, 'Biggest Decision of Them All – Death and Assisted Dying: Capacity Assessments and Undue Influence Screening' (2019) 49(6) *Internal Medicine Journal* 792 doi.org/10.1111/imj.14238

Standing Committee on Legal and Social Issues, Parliament of Victoria Legislative Council, *Inquiry into End of Life Choices* (Final Report, June 2016)

Standing Committee on Legal and Social Issues, Parliament of Victoria Legislative Council, *Inquiry into End of Life Choices* (Interim Report, November 2015)

Willmott, Lindy, Ben White, Christopher Stackpoole et al, '(Failed) Voluntary Euthanasia Law Reform in Australia: Two Decades of Trends, Models and Politics' (2016) 39(1) *University of New South Wales Law Journal* 1

Willmott, Lindy, Ben White, Danielle Ko et al, 'Restricting Conversations About Voluntary Assisted Dying: Implications for Clinical Practice' (2020) 10(1) *BMJ Supportive & Palliative Care* 105 doi.org/10.1136/bmjspcare-2019-001887

B Legislation

Abortion Law Reform Act 2008 (Vic)

Euthanasia Laws Act 1997 (Cth)

Voluntary Assisted Dying Act 2017 (Vic)

Voluntary Assisted Dying Act 2019 (WA)

C Other

Andrews, Daniel, 'Debate of Historic Voluntary Assisted Dying Bill Starts' (Media Release, 17 October 2017) <https://www.premier.vic.gov.au/debate-historic-voluntary-assisted-dying-bill-starts>

Department of Health and Human Services, Government of Victoria, 'Voluntary Assisted Dying: Overview', *health.vic* (Web Page) <https://www.health.vic.gov.au/patient-care/overview>

Standing Committee on Legal and Social Issues, Parliament of Victoria Legislative Council, 'Community Views Sought on Choices for End of Life' (Media Release, 28 May 2015)

2

Palliative Care as a Necropolitical Technology

Hamish Robertson and Joanne Travaglia

Introduction

We live in a century characterised by the phenomenon of population ageing . This is entirely new for humankind and it occurs at a time of many other significant societal changes; but also, we argue, some serious lags in political and economic ideologies. One of the consequences of this delay in the intellectual understanding of, and appreciation for, the success that population ageing represents is a wide-ranging, and often ageist, discourse in many public policy domains and areas of professional practice. Much of this discourse is underpinned by a medical paradigm that continues to focus on pathological interpretations of biological and physiological changes across the lifetime. Many social beliefs about ageing and old age are deeply culturally embedded, driven by capitalism's intersection with other aspects of national cultures. Thus, ageing is often represented as ugly and deforming, as in the common use of a disembodied, wrinkled hand image for ageing. Normal human dependency is considered undesirable because capitalism and its proponents see human needs and relationships as either monetiseable opportunities (the grey market etc) or individual failings (the result of bad 'lifestyle' choices). In other words, dependent ageing is framed within a wider deficit discourse and while this is not new, it has a variety of implications under contemporary health and social policy paradigms.

A correlate of these negative positionings, of both the ageing process and the status of old age, is a growing discourse about the 'quality of life', how this is measured, and how it can be used to inform medical treatment including what is provided, what is rationed and when and what forms of care may be withdrawn. This situation runs in parallel with a 'right to die' sub-discourse, which, not entirely unreasonably, positions issues such as chronic pain and terminal illness as experiences where any person might want to take some part in the 'decision-making' processes. The problematic issue is of course just how engaged the sick older person can be in such circumstances, and how they, and their carers, can be expected to negotiate complex scenarios when acutely medically unwell. While these issues are often framed around the issue of 'capacity', they can and should go well beyond the presence or absence of cognitive impairment. Clinicians will talk about 'letting your family member go', as increasingly aggressive treatments fail and human mortality looms despite the treatment regime, and regardless of the ideology of 'interventional successes at all cost' to the individual and their family. Our position is that advance directives may simplify this scenario but only because they are themselves an inherently neocritical technology in their own right, in which the patient may be asked to pre-empt their own response to critical health events. This rising tide of 'end-of-life' discourse, and the complexities it only partially acknowledges, raises the issue of one particular technological healthcare discourse, which is palliative care. In this piece, we explore palliative care in the context of population ageing and its broader sociopolitical implications.

In an ageing century, there is a need for critical scholarship on the ways in which age and ageing are represented in societies and how these representations are used by systems and professionals to justify specific interactions including when they choose not to act, or to withdraw care. Palliative care offers a highly illustrative case study for engaging with these issues as it is increasingly being represented as *the* caring and scientific option in end-of-life care policy and practice.[1] This includes the development of guidelines, agreements to implementation (eg advance directives) and a tranche of procedural and administrative practices that go alongside its implementation. While it is clear that the paradigm of palliative care is implemented in varying ways and to different degrees (ie not always in its 'ideal' form), this makes it all the more interesting as a case

---

1   Australian Government Department of Health, *National Palliative Care Strategy 2018* (2018).

study and exemplar of the issues considered here. We acknowledge that palliative care may be implemented well, just as it may be implemented badly. In this piece we seek to unpack and examine some of the persistent assumptions around ageing, illness and end-of-life care through the exemplar of palliative care.

Institutional power and individual vulnerability

One of the important considerations in this discussion is to take a closer look at the disproportionate power of institutions over individuals, and especially so over vulnerable individuals such as older people with various health conditions. This is not a passive relationship in which, for example, sick people enter hospital and come out well or die. Rather, what needs to be acknowledged is that the level of institutional and professional power is disproportionately in favour of the healthcare system, resulting in situations where the patient and their social supports may be dominated and encouraged to make decisions that are convenient for the institution rather than the patient. In this context, then, the institution (and its agents, the professionals) have the capacity to reinforce existing vulnerabilities, such as asking people to make pivotal treatment decisions in a time of crisis (often represented as another dimension of personal choice). The institution may also *generate* new vulnerabilities such as the types of incidents identified in patient safety research.[2] The field of iatrogenic harms illustrates this all too well. People die in hospitals not only because they are old and/or sick, but also because hospitals and health professions may fail to act appropriately in the patient's best interests or, more problematic still, they make the patient more vulnerable due to acts of omission (failing to act) or acts of commission (doing the wrong thing).[3] The complexities of this situation are likely to grow in scope and number as population ageing progresses, because ageing and death are intimately connected not only at a pragmatic level ('it happens') but also because there is a *necropolitics* associated with ageing and death,

---

2   Susannah Jane Long et al, 'What is Known about Adverse Events in Older Medical Hospital Inpatients? A Systematic Review of the Literature' (2013) 25(5) *International Journal for Quality in Health Care* 542; Eric J Thomas and Troyen A Brennan, 'Incidence and Types of Preventable Adverse Events in Elderly Patients: Population Based Review of Medical Records' (2000) 320(7237) *BMJ* 741.
3   Charles Vincent, *Patient Safety* (Wiley-Blackwell BMJ Books, 2nd ed, 2011).

in that there are individuals and institutions who '*exercise sovereignty* [by] *exercis*[ing] *control over mortality and ... defin*[ing] *life as the deployment and manifestation of power*'.[4]

The issue of who lives and who dies, and when, arises frequently in acute healthcare environments.[5] The people who make the most informed decisions in such circumstances are the medical practitioners, both because of their professional training and because rather than the one specific scenario a family might experience, they see many similar cases on a regular basis. In addition, this situation may be skewed by specialist services in which a narrow clinical focus is adopted in relation to a large client population, such as a cancer treatment facility. Here the vulnerability of the patient and their family/social supports may in fact be magnified.[6] The unequal power of the institution is itself magnified by the unequal knowledge base that the general public and patients usually have in comparison to the treating facility and its staff. This too can be seen as a source of vulnerability in that the treatment decisions a patient may be asked to make are rarely contextualised in this fashion, the clinicians know much more than the patient but the mythology of 'choice' in effect acts to reinforce institutional power rather than that of vulnerable patients.[7]

What we propose here is that this situation creates spaces of unequal knowledge and power. Healthcare can be understood as a territorial claim backed up by political and social authority. It may be mediated by factors such as money and experience, with few communities possessing the knowledge to negotiate directly with healthcare systems and the policies and practices they provide as 'choices'. Doctors' offices, nursing stations, wards, hospitals, pathology laboratories are all quite specific places with their own authority and systems of control. They are, at the aggregate level, a form of territory that only partially includes the people treated in them. As money is a factor in all healthcare treatment, this too creates a level of territorialisation and territorial separations (eg marketised versus public sector). This makes the concept of territory important in

---

4   Achille Mbembe, 'Necropolitics' (2003) 15(1) *Public Culture* 11, 11 (emphasis in original).

5   Albert R Jonsen, *Bioethics Beyond the Headlines: Who Lives? Who Dies? Who Decides?* (Rowman & Littlefield Publishers, 2005).

6   Miles Little et al, 'Liminality: A Major Category of the Experience of Cancer Illness' (1998) 47(10) *Social Science and Medicine* 1485.

7   Natalie Joseph-Williams, Glyn Elwyn and Adrian Edwards, 'Knowledge is Not Power for Patients: A Systematic Review and Thematic Synthesis of Patient-Reported Barriers and Facilitators to Shared Decision Making' (2014) 94(3) *Patient Education and Counseling* 291.

healthcare environments generally, and more particularly in technologies such as palliative care, where the care delivered may be provided in quite different environments and according to quite different principles.[8]

Healthcare as a territorial ambition

In following Agamben's use of Schmitt's notion of sovereignty, it can be suggested that any biopolitical agenda has specific *territorial* ambitions.[9] These ambitions may be geographical, ontological or epistemic in nature, without necessarily being exclusive to any one domain. So, for example, medicine can be seen as having territorial ambitions through its extensive use of political influence and a variety of epistemic strategies aimed at producing quite specific ontological effects. Medical practitioners have influenced the political system to make claims for control over and expertise in a variety of biopolitical domains including not solely 'illness' or 'disease', but 'life' itself. These territorial ambitions can be seen in the frequent objection to 'alternative' health paradigms and in their dominance over other types of health practitioner and their associated disciplines (pharmacy, nursing etc) as well as over 'alternative' treatments.[10] This is by its very nature a continually expanding territorial strategy. Medicine has also *affiliated* with various sciences (eg biochemistry, microbiology) but avoided deference to them, making claims for a unique interpretive perspective and an often imaginary 'partnership' between the doctor and the patient. The 'sacred' nature of the doctor–patient 'relationship' is itself a territorial claim in that it is frequently used to limit the agency of the patient and the role that other professionals might, potentially, play in the health of patients generally.

This kind of territorialisation is a necessarily incomplete agenda because medicine, and the health sciences more generally, keep extending their claims for expert management of various elements of human experience as healthcare knowledge and technologies grow. This frequently goes well beyond explicit disease states, an argument made forcefully by Illich

---

8   N Bradley, M Lloyd-Williams and C Dowrick, 'Effectiveness of Palliative Care Interventions Offering Social Support to People with Life-Limiting Illness—A Systematic Review' (2018) 27(3) *European Journal of Cancer Care* e12837:1–12.
9   Giorgio Agamben, *Homo Sacer: Sovereign Power and Bare Life* (Stanford University Press, 1998).
10   Mike Saks, *Orthodox and Alternative Medicine: Politics, Professionalization, and Health Care* (Sage, 2003).

in the mid-1970s and by a variety of medical sociologists since then.[11] This is acutely observable in ageing and end-of-life scenarios but can be seen to engage with almost any element of so-called 'lifestyle' factors in which individualised decisions are marked out from, and treated separately to, broader social, cultural and economic factors (eg obesity and diabetes) or what Michael Marmot calls 'the causes of the causes'.[12] This strategy permits the medicalisation of many factors arising from the intersectional nature of contemporary capitalist economics and associated political conditions.

Public health, once concerned directly with social conditions, can be seen to function in this manner in the richer economies, where infectious diseases are becoming less common and 'lifestyle' conditions (usually chronic diseases rising from environmental and social conditions) are framed in a discourse of 'choice'. This positioning suggests that no other societal factors need be considered in the 'choice' equation of health outcomes (pollution, housing, food access and quality, education etc). Marmot's 'causes of the causes', for example, would consider the higher number of fast food outlets in poorer socio-economic areas, rather than stopping with an analysis of the 'willingness' of individuals to adhere to a healthy eating regime.[13] Individualising health behaviour and its consequences allows both for an aggressive territorial claim (we know best) and an interventional paradigm that has very limited accountability (failure or success is located within the actions of the individual patient or client). This too is a form of territoriality since it sets the terms of state and state agent actions and accountabilities in relation to citizens.

This general epistemic strategy has profound ontological effects and can be analysed as the current iteration of a form of territorialisation of the body and society that has been developing for close to four centuries.[14] The first step was a deliberate acquisition of control over the human body, auspiced through claims to scientific reproducibility in medical diagnostic and treatment regimes. By the nineteenth century, medicine was well

---

11   Ivan Illich, *Medical Nemesis: The Expropriation of Health* (Pantheon Books, New York, 1977); Peter Conrad, *The Medicalization of Society: On the Transformation of Human Conditions into Treatable Disorders* (JHU Press, 2007).

12   Michael J Marmot, 'Inclusion Health: Addressing the Causes of the Causes' (2018) 391(10117) *Lancet* 186, 186.

13   Daniel D Reidpath et al, 'An Ecological Study of the Relationship Between Social and Environmental Determinants of Obesity' (2002) 8(2) *Health and Place* 141.

14   Nick J Fox, 'The Ill-Health Assemblage: Beyond the Body-with-Organs' (2011) 20(4) *Health Sociology Review* 359.

down the path of desacralising the human body through its dissection of cadavers drawn from prisons, slave plantations and workhouses, places where human life was already institutionally devalued.[15] This strategy was further developed using the umbrella term 'science' to produce a political right of medicine to use (and more recently to commodify) human bodies (gradually including parts of bodies, genetic material and even health data) for its own purposes, including the production of new medical knowledge, often with a variety of powerful social effects.[16] The authority of medicine to comment on and influence how human 'pathologies', social as well as clinical, were shaped and reproduced being a case in point. The idea that only women exhibit 'hysteria', for example, or that enslaved black bodies experience pain differently to and less than white ones are examples of medical knowledge and authority being used to produce social power over particular categories of person.[17]

To die in a hospital, as in prison, increasingly meant the loss of determination of how the individual's mortal remains were treated. Indeed, judicially directed dissection by medical practitioners was often included as a part of an individual's (post-mortem) punishment and, consequently, involuntary autopsy reduced the individual to a commodity, since individual identity and personhood could be harmed both in and beyond death.[18] This process of growing corporeal control was *territorially* extended by the mechanism of the autopsy. Even now, the right to dissect, remove and retain parts of the dead person's body remains a contested, and sometimes abused, part of this territorial ambition (for example as identified in the Alder Hey (Royal Liverpool) Inquiry 1988–1995,[19] and the case of Henrietta Lacks).[20] Traditional social and religious values are

15   See, eg, Michael Sappol, *A Traffic of Dead Bodies: Anatomy and Embodied Social Identity in Nineteenth-Century America* (Princeton University Press, 2002); Edward C Halperin, 'The Poor, the Black, and the Marginalized as the Source of Cadavers in United States Anatomical Education' (2007) 20(5) *Clinical Anatomy* 489.

16   Bryn Williams-Jones, 'Concepts of Personhood and the Commodification of the Body' (1999) 7(3) *Health Law Review* 11; Kara W Swanson, *Banking on the Body* (Harvard University Press, 2014).

17   Todd Lee Savitt, *Medicine and Slavery: The Diseases and Health Care of Blacks in Antebellum Virginia* (University of Illinois Press, 2002) Vol 82.

18   Kenneth C Nystrom, 'The Bioarchaeology of Structural Violence and Dissection in the 19th-Century United States' (2014) 116(4) *American Anthropologist* 765.

19   JL Burton and M Wells, 'The Alder Hey Affair: Implications for Pathology Practice' (2001) 54(11) *Journal of Clinical Pathology* 820; C Lawrence, 'Alder Hey: The Taken for Granted and Professional Practice' (2002) 56(1) *Journal of Epidemiology and Community Health* 4.

20   Rebecca Skloot, *The Immortal Life of Henrietta Lacks* (Crown Publishers, 2010); Sandra S-J Lee et al, '"I Don't Want to be Henrietta Lacks": Diverse Patient Perspectives on Donating Biospecimens for Precision Medicine Research' (2019) 21(1) *Genetic Medicine* 107.

rendered subordinate to medicine's authority, making the process of dying and the material fact of death part of an expansive *necropolitical* territory, often with the acquiescence of the law. Yet, these processes are deeply historical and themselves exhibit a necropolitics in relation to who was most at risk of punishment *by* death and punishment *in* death through the mutilation of the body for 'scientific' purposes.

The subjective body gradually became an objective site of medical inquiry and control. The socio-medical control over specific types or categories of bodies (criminals, the mentally ill, women, 'non-whites', people with disabilities, and people designated 'monsters') provided a premise for an authority over human bodies in a more general sense, living and dead. The ability to generalise from particular bodies to the concept of population(s) invests the medical perspective with sociopolitical authority. Yet much of this is achieved without any historical inquiry and the 'scientific' nature of the acquired right to dissect the dead is actively dehistoricised. This brings us to the situation of older people in this shifting sociopolitical regime.

Necropolitics and population ageing

As a consequence of the above points, it is possible to observe a rising necropolitics of ageing that exhibits some very familiar characteristics where medicine extends its control of situations in which it might usefully intervene and a contrarian position in which it maintains control over situations in which it feels unable or unwilling to intervene. In other words, medicine gets to choose when and if it intervenes while constituting patient 'choice' as the determining ethic. This scenario is especially notable in the context of population ageing, a scenario in which the numbers of older, frailer individuals (a majority of them female) will continue to grow in coming decades. Firstly there is the historical disinterest medicine has had in older people generally.[21] Secondly, when medicine has been interested in ageing, broadly conceived of as pathology in motion, it has often been deeply unhappy with older people and their illnesses because of their perceived social and clinical irrelevance. Even at its inception, the medical specialty of geriatrics was enmeshed in the social politics of

---

21   Desmond O'Neill, 'Do Geriatricians Truly Welcome Ageing?' (2016) 45(4) *Age and Ageing* 439.

ageing, gender and poverty because much of what we conceive of as the medical care of the elderly emerged in and through the institutional form of the workhouse infirmary.[22]

'Older people's medicine', now known as geriatric medicine, has remained a marginal player in the internal politics of medicine and, additionally, has been a nexus for both ageism and racism within medicine.[23] Geriatrics has now been a specialty on the medical margins for a century or so, and geriatricians in the UK National Health Service, for example, were frequently drawn from South Asian doctors who could not readily access the racially closed shop of British medicine.[24] In this context, geriatric medicine is not 'just' an uncontested clinical specialty addressing the medical needs of a specific population and category of person, it is a contested field of practice in which the patient is often secondary to the politics of medicine itself. This makes it a 'territory' that can be controlled and a technology through which that control can be acquired and maintained.

Consequently, this territorialisation intersects with the established necropolitics of medicine itself and produces a dynamic that invites serious consideration as population ageing progresses. One of the key reasons for doing so is that as new knowledge and 'technologies' emerge in the ageing space, they need to be accounted for against the historical backdrop of how medicine has developed, its influence on society and associated institutions (such as the law), and the implications for older people who find themselves framed in and through this expanding necropolitical environment. One of the means by which this interventional authority is exhibited is through the various technologies that healthcare gives rise to, including emergent clinical paradigms, policies and practices. A case in point is palliative care.

---

22   Alistair J Ritch, 'English Poor Law Institutional Care for Older People: Identifying the "Aged and Infirm" and the "Sick" in Birmingham Workhouse, 1852–1912' (2014) 27(1) *Social History of Medicine* 64.
23   Parvati Raghuram, Joanna Bornat and Leroi Henry, 'The Co-Marking of Aged Bodies and Migrant Bodies: Migrant Workers' Contribution to Geriatric Medicine in the UK' (2011) 33(2) *Sociology of Health and Illness* 321.
24   See, eg, Joanna Bornat, Leroi Henry and Parvati Raghuram, 'The Making of Careers, the Making of a Discipline: Luck and Chance in Migrant Careers in Geriatric Medicine' (2011) 78(3) *Journal of Vocational Behavior* 342.

Palliative care as a technology

Our interpretation here is that palliative care can be seen as a technology on multiple levels. As an area of medical subspecialisation and practice, it is an increasingly prominent component of the political technologies that healthcare as an industry seeks to control. It is also a territorial technology in the sense that a wide variety of spaces and places are explicitly (and many implicitly) connected to a 'systemic' focus on health and associated treatment modalities. For example, to die in hospital versus a hospice or other 'dedicated' dying space can engender very different types of experiences for a dying person and their family. This 'territorialism' is also an expansionist one in that, as Nikolas Rose has identified, the aim is control of 'life itself'.[25] It is also a necropolitical technology in that healthcare already sees itself as the quasi-secular custodian of the process of dying, of death itself and of the body after death. Not only can the autopsy be seen as part of this process but so too can the 'cause of death' determination that medical doctors make when a person dies in hospital. In this context, palliative care is an outgrowth of this growing medicalisation of life.[26]

As noted above, the assumptive control of the dead body and its component parts has been well entrenched in medicine for more than a century now. This was itself a political manoeuvre to gain access to corpses for anatomical and experimental purposes. Access to bodies was a significant problem in early modern medicine when the body was still seen as, mostly, sacred property.[27] However, the medical gaze and influence asserted itself through the acquisition of compliant bodies such as slaves, the workhouse dead, war casualties, occupants of mental asylums and so on.[28] The right to abuse the body under the rubric of 'science' persists in the present day. Even now, it is possible to see how the assumption of power over the dead offends those whose relatives (young or old) die in hospitals and whose

---

25   Nikolas Rose *The Politics of Life Itself: Biomedicine, Power, and Subjectivity in the Twenty-First Century* (Princeton University Press, 2007).

26   Denis Pereira Gray, Eleanor White and Ginny Russell, 'Medicalisation in the UK: Changing Dynamics, but Still Ongoing' (2016) 109(1) *Journal of the Royal Society of Medicine* 7.

27   See, eg, Piers D Mitchell et al, 'The Study of Anatomy in England from 1700 to the Early 20th Century' (2011) 219(2) *Journal of Anatomy* 91.

28   Stephen C Kenny, 'The Development of Medical Museums in the Antebellum American South: Slave Bodies in Networks of Anatomical Exchange' (2013) 87(1) *Bulletin of the History of Medicine* 32.

family members have had organs removed without familial consent.[29] This asks of us a closer inquiry on how the actual process of dying is framed, represented, communicated and clinically managed. This critical perspective becomes more important as population ageing progresses and societies respond to the growing numbers of very old, and often unwell, older people.

This scenario is extended into the politics of life itself through the technology of palliative care. While palliative care is often represented as a coherent and consistent application of medical care to the dying patient, in practice it can be a much more varied and variable form of intervention. At its most extreme, the use and abuse of opioids in treating older patients has led directly to situations such as the Gosport Inquiry in the United Kingdom in which older patients were being 'unlawfully killed' by a doctor, and affiliated health professionals, at the Gosport War Memorial Hospital.[30] This killing was frequently prefaced by the medical instruction 'please make comfortable',[31] as though differentiation of medical status and need in clinical environments is not a key aspect of treatment and care.[32] In other words, the elision of palliative actions can lead to the pre-emptive ending of lives even in cases where many older people might be (and were at Gosport) expected to recover and return to their homes.[33] This case, while an extreme one, is far from unique in the annals of aged care in the NHS or elsewhere. Older people are highly vulnerable in acute and subacute healthcare environments, as the Francis Inquiry into the Mid-Staffordshire Trust and the Harold Shipman affair

---

29 Edward A Glasper and Catherine Powell, 'Lessons of Alder Hey: Consent Must be Informed' (2001) 10(4) *British Journal of Nursing* 213.

30 Kieran Walshe, 'Gosport Deaths: Lethal Failures in Care Will Happen Again' (2018) 362 *BMJ* k2931; Simon Kenwright, 'Understanding Gosport' (2018) 362 *BMJ* k3422; Clare Dyer, 'Gosport Hospital: GP Prescribed Opioids that Shortened at Least 456 Lives' (2018) 361 *BMJ* k2706.

31 For a more in-depth discussion of the Gosport Inquiry, see Penny Crofts's contribution to this collection, 'Gosport Hospital, Euthanasia, and Serial Killing'.

32 Daniel Knights, Felicity Knights and Stephen Barclay, '"Please Make Comfortable": Prescribing Opioids in the Wake of Gosport' (2018) 68(675) *British Journal of General Practice* 462.

33 House of Commons, *Gosport War Memorial Hospital: The Report of the Gosport Independent Panel* (Report, June 2018).

showed.[34] Ideas about and attitudes towards palliation of the older patient may actually generate their own risks to those patients because older age is generally seen as inherently flawed and risky.

The technological nature of palliative care can also be observed in the more extreme examples through the ways in which regulatory authorities tend to support the authority of medicine and healthcare more broadly. This can be seen in the medical inquiry system, which is used in response to major abuses of, usually, highly vulnerable patients.[35] Patients, families and communities, and their concerns, often receive very limited and rarely any timely recognition (see the Gosport Inquiry, for example), a characteristic of many patient safety inquiries being the often considerable time it took for public concerns to be acknowledged and taken seriously. In both the Gosport and Mid-Staffordshire cases, patients and families had been voicing concerns for up to a *decade* before official inquiries into the activities of those services were launched. The result is that policies and practices in association with the established authority of medical and medically controlled or mediated systems generally prevail over the interests of vulnerable groups in these scenarios. By the time formal mechanisms such as inquiry processes are undertaken, the harms associated with these situations have generally multiplied significantly. This in turn raises the question of the current and potential impact of such technologies under conditions of population ageing and the enormous growth in older, frail and disproportionately female patients that this will produce.

Conclusion

This chapter draws together a number of concepts and ideas normally treated in isolation. More particularly, we put forward the concept of a *necropolitics of ageing* in which 'standard' medical strategies, palliative

---

34   Christopher Newdick and Christopher Danbury, 'Culture, Compassion and Clinical Neglect – Probity in the NHS after Mid Staffordshire' (2015) 41(12) *Journal of Medical Ethics* 946; DJ Roberts, 'The Francis Report on the Mid-Staffordshire NHS Foundation Trust: Putting Patients First' (2013) 23(2) *Transfusion Medicine* 73; Robert Francis, *Independent Inquiry into Care Provided by Mid Staffordshire NHS Foundation Trust January 2005 – March 2009* (The Stationery Office, 2010) Vol 1; Janet Smith, *The Shipman Inquiry* (Stationery Office, 2003); Richard Baker and Brian Hurwitz, 'Intentionally Harmful Violations and Patient Safety: The Example of Harold Shipman' (2009) 102(6) *Journal of the Royal Society of Medicine* 223.
35   See, eg, Kieran Walshe and Stephen M Shortell, 'When Things Go Wrong: How Health Care Organizations Deal with Major Failures' (2004) 23(3) *Health Affairs* 103.

care being a particular example, can be seen as territorial technologies of control in their own right. In this context, we suggest that medical responses to population ageing exist at a number of different levels but all of them are premised on medicine's right to determine and intervene in the politics of life itself. This right is a historically situated one, embedded in medicine's acquisition of political and social authority during the nineteenth century, long before clinical medicine became a safe option for patients seeking treatment for disease.[36] Furthermore, this authoritative positioning needs to be seen as a dynamic territorial strategy, one adaptive to changing situations and emerging themes, such as 'patient choice' and the 'right to die'. In this sense then, palliative care can be critiqued as a *territorial* technology just as many others identifiable within medicine and across healthcare policy and practices more broadly.

The right to govern and control the bodies of the vulnerable and powerless has been gradually expanded into an authority over many types of bodies – women, people with disabilities, the elderly and so forth – and hence to 'the body' more generally. The authority this right provided has extended from the bodies of the dead to those of the living and now increasingly encompasses transitional states such as still-birth, frailty, acute illness, people with delirium and those experiencing an imminent death. At every stage, then, medicine has extended its territorial authority as a social and political vehicle. Now, under conditions of growing numbers of older people and a deeply enmeshed politics of population ageing, we can observe palliative care as one more technology for maintaining and extending medical authority. The demographic reality of population ageing is often represented, rightly in our opinion, as a (partly) medical success story, with many more people living relatively healthy and longer lives than was the historical norm. Yet underneath this rhetoric of success lies a deep social history of contempt for the weak, the vulnerable, the dependent and the elderly. These attitudes are not exclusive to medicine but their interactions with an expanding medical territoriality represent a crisis in the making, one in which a necropolitics of ageing may be observed in many health and medical technologies of care. It is in this dynamic context that we have positioned palliative care as a component of a broader necropolitics of ageing.

---

36   Paul Starr, *The Social Transformation of American Medicine* (Basic Books, 1982).

Bibliography

A Articles/books/reports

Agamben, Giorgio, *Homo Sacer: Sovereign Power and Bare Life* (Stanford University Press, 1998) doi.org/10.1515/9780804764025

Australian Government Department of Health, *National Palliative Care Strategy 2018* (2018)

Baker, Richard and Brian Hurwitz, 'Intentionally Harmful Violations and Patient Safety: The Example of Harold Shipman' (2009) 102(6) *Journal of the Royal Society of Medicine* 223 doi.org/10.1258/jrsm.2009.09k028

Bornat, Joanna, Leroi Henry and Parvati Raghuram, 'The Making of Careers, the Making of a Discipline: Luck and Chance in Migrant Careers in Geriatric Medicine' (2011) 78(3) *Journal of Vocational Behavior* 342 doi.org/10.1016/j.jvb.2011.03.015

Bradley, N, M Lloyd-Williams and C Dowrick, 'Effectiveness of Palliative Care Interventions Offering Social Support to People with Life-Limiting Illness—A Systematic Review' (2018) 27(3) *European Journal of Cancer Care* e12837 doi.org/10.1111/ecc.12837

Burton, JL and M Wells, 'The Alder Hey Affair: Implications for Pathology Practice' (2001) 54(11) *Journal of Clinical Pathology* 820 doi.org/10.1136/adc.86.1.4

Conrad, Peter, *The Medicalization of Society: On the Transformation of Human Conditions into Treatable Disorders* (JHU Press, 2007)

Dyer, Clare, 'Gosport Hospital: GP Prescribed Opioids That Shortened at Least 456 Lives' (2018) 361 *BMJ* k2706 doi.org/10.1136/bmj.k2706

Fox, Nick J, 'The Ill-Health Assemblage: Beyond the Body-with-Organs' (2011) 20(4) *Health Sociology Review* 359 doi.org/10.5172/hesr.2011.20.4.359

Francis, Robert, *Independent Inquiry into Care Provided by Mid Staffordshire NHS Foundation Trust January 2005 – March 2009* (The Stationery Office, 2010), Vol 1

Glasper, Edward A and Catherine Powell, 'Lessons of Alder Hey: Consent Must Be Informed' (2001) 10(4) *British Journal of Nursing* 213 doi.org/10.12968/bjon.2001.10.4.12357

Halperin, Edward C, 'The Poor, the Black, and the Marginalized as the Source of Cadavers in United States Anatomical Education' (2007) 20(5) *Clinical Anatomy* 489 doi.org/10.1002/ca.20445

House of Commons, *Gosport War Memorial Hospital: The Report of the Gosport Independent Panel* (Report, June 2018)

Illich, Ivan, *Medical Nemesis: The Expropriation of Health* (Pantheon Books, New York, 1977)

Jonsen, Albert R, *Bioethics Beyond the Headlines: Who Lives? Who Dies? Who Decides?* (Rowman & Littlefield Publishers, 2005)

Joseph-Williams, Natalie, Glyn Elwyn and Adrian Edwards, 'Knowledge is Not Power for Patients: A Systematic Review and Thematic Synthesis of Patient-Reported Barriers and Facilitators to Shared Decision Making' (2014) 94(3) *Patient Education and Counseling* 291 doi.org/10.1016/j.pec.2013.10.031

Kenny, Stephen C, 'The Development of Medical Museums in the Antebellum American South: Slave Bodies in Networks of Anatomical Exchange' (2013) 87(1) *Bulletin of the History of Medicine* 32 doi.org/10.1353/bhm.2013.0016

Kenwright, Simon, 'Understanding Gosport' (2018) 362 *BMJ* k3422 doi.org/10.1136/bmj.k3422

Knights, Daniel, Felicity Knights and Stephen Barclay, '"Please Make Comfortable": Prescribing Opioids in the Wake of Gosport' (2018) 68(675) *British Journal of General Practice* 462 doi.org/10.3399/bjgp18X698705

Lawrence, C, 'Alder Hey: The Taken for Granted and Professional Practice' (2002) 56(1) *Journal of Epidemiology & Community Health* 4 doi.org/10.1136/jech.56.1.4

Lee, Sandra S-J et al, '"I Don't Want to Be Henrietta Lacks": Diverse Patient Perspectives on Donating Biospecimens for Precision Medicine Research' (2019) 21(1) *Genetics in Medicine* 107 doi.org/10.1038/s41436-018-0032-6

Little, Miles et al, 'Liminality: A Major Category of the Experience of Cancer Illness' (1998) 47(10) *Social Science & Medicine* 1485 doi.org/10.1016/S0277-9536(98)00248-2

Long, Susannah Jane et al, 'What is Known about Adverse Events in Older Medical Hospital Inpatients? A Systematic Review of the Literature' (2013) 25(5) *International Journal for Quality in Health Care* 542 doi.org/10.1093/intqhc/mzt056

Marmot, Michael, 'Inclusion Health: Addressing the Causes of the Causes' (2018) 391(10117) *The Lancet* 186 doi.org/10.1016/S0140-6736(17)32848-9

Mbembe, Achille, 'Necropolitics' (2003) 15(1) *Public Culture* 11 doi.org/10.1215/08992363-15-1-11

Mitchell, Piers D et al, 'The Study of Anatomy in England from 1700 to the Early 20th Century' (2011) 219(2) *Journal of Anatomy* 91 doi.org/10.1111/j.1469-7580.2011.01381.x

Newdick, Christopher and Christopher Danbury, 'Culture, Compassion and Clinical Neglect—Probity in the NHS after Mid Staffordshire' (2015) 41(12) *Journal of Medical Ethics* 946 doi.org/10.1136/medethics-2012-101048

Nystrom, Kenneth C, 'The Bioarchaeology of Structural Violence and Dissection in the 19th-Century United States' (2014) 116(4) *American Anthropologist* 765 doi.org/10.1111/aman.12151

O'Neill, Desmond, 'Do Geriatricians Truly Welcome Ageing?' (2016) 45(4) *Age and Ageing* 439 doi.org/10.1093/ageing/afw078

Pereira Gray, Denis, Eleanor White and Ginny Russell, 'Medicalisation in the UK: Changing Dynamics, but Still Ongoing' (2016) 109(1) *Journal of the Royal Society of Medicine* 7 doi.org/10.1177/0141076815600908

Raghuram, Parvati, Joanna Bornat and Leroi Henry, 'The Co-Marking of Aged Bodies and Migrant Bodies: Migrant Workers' Contribution to Geriatric Medicine in the UK' (2011) 33(2) *Sociology of Health & Illness* 321 doi.org/10.1111/j.1467-9566.2010.01290.x

Reidpath, Daniel D et al, 'An Ecological Study of the Relationship between Social and Environmental Determinants of Obesity' (2002) 8(2) *Health & Place* 141 doi.org/10.1016/S1353-8292(01)00028-4

Ritch, Alistair, 'English Poor Law Institutional Care for Older People: Identifying the "Aged and Infirm" and the "Sick" in Birmingham Workhouse, 1852–1912' (2014) 27(1) *Social History of Medicine* 64 doi.org/10.1093/shm/hkt071

Roberts, DJ, 'The Francis Report on the Mid-Staffordshire NHS Foundation Trust: Putting Patients First' (2013) 23(2) *Transfusion Medicine* 73 doi.org/10.1111/tme.12032

Rose, Nikolas, *The Politics of Life Itself: Biomedicine, Power, and Subjectivity in the Twenty-First Century* (Princeton University Press, 2007) doi.org/10.2307/j.ctt7rqmf

Saks, Mike, *Orthodox and Alternative Medicine: Politics, Professionalization, and Health Care* (Sage, 2003)

Sappol, Michael, *A Traffic of Dead Bodies: Anatomy and Embodied Social Identity in Nineteenth-Century America* (Princeton University Press, 2002) doi.org/10.2307/j.ctv36zrh7

Savitt, Todd Lee, *Medicine and Slavery: The Diseases and Health Care of Blacks in Antebellum Virginia* (University of Illinois Press, 2002)

Skloot, Rebecca, *The Immortal Life of Henrietta Lacks* (Crown Publishers, 2010)

Smith, Janet, *The Shipman Inquiry: Death Certification and the Investigation of Deaths by Coroners* (Third Report, June 2003)

Starr, Paul, *The Social Transformation of American Medicine* (Basic Books, 1982)

Swanson, Kara W, *Banking on the Body* (Harvard University Press, 2014)

Thomas, Eric J and Troyen A Brennan, 'Incidence and Types of Preventable Adverse Events in Elderly Patients: Population Based Review of Medical Records' (2000) 320(7237) *BMJ* 741 doi.org/10.1136/bmj.320.7237.741

Vincent, Charles, *Patient Safety* (John Wiley & Sons, 2nd ed, 2011)

Walshe, Kieran, 'Gosport Deaths: Lethal Failures in Care Will Happen Again' (2018) 362 *BMJ* k2931 doi.org/10.1136/bmj.k2931

Walshe, Kieran and Stephen M Shortell, 'When Things Go Wrong: How Health Care Organizations Deal With Major Failures' (2004) 23(3) *Health Affairs* 103 doi.org/10.1377/hlthaff.23.3.103

Williams-Jones, Bryn, 'Concepts of Personhood and the Commodification of the Body' (1999) 7(3) *Health Law Review* 11

3

Supported Decision-Making: A Good Idea in Principle but We Need to Consider Supporting Decisions about Voluntary Assisted Dying

Nola M Ries and Elise Mansfield[1]

Introduction

Australia has an ageing population and many older people will, at some point, experience an injury, such as a stroke, or develop a condition, like Alzheimer's disease, that results in impaired cognitive functioning. Alzheimer's disease is one of many dementia syndrome diseases characterised by impairments in memory, thinking, perception and language skills.[2] Dementia currently affects one out of ten adults over the age of 65 and three out of ten over age 85.[3] Each day in Australia, around

1   This research was funded by the National Health and Medical Research Council via a Dementia Research Team Grant (APP1095078). This research was also supported by infrastructure funding from the Hunter Medical Research Institute. The authors would like to thank Sandra Dowley, Max Katz-Barber and Lucy Boyd for assistance with data collection.
2   'Dementia', *Australian Institute of Health and Welfare* (Web Page) <http://www.aihw.gov.au/dementia/>.
3   Australia Bureau of Statistics, 'Dementia and Death in Australia', *Causes of Death, Australia, 2015* (Catalogue No 3303.0, 26 July 2017) <https://www.abs.gov.au/ausstats/abs@.nsf/Lookup/by%20Subject/3303.0~2015~Main%20Features~Dementia~10002>.

100 stroke events occur. Nearly 400,000 people across the country have had a stroke and over a third report disabling sequelae, including problems with thinking and communication.[4] People living with impaired cognition may experience difficulties in making decisions across a range of domains, including medical, financial and other personal domains.

Laws, such as 'guardianship' Acts, allow substitute decision-makers to be appointed and given the legal authority to make choices and manage the affairs for a person who is judged to lack decisional capacity. In principle, substitute decision-makers are expected to make decisions that reflect the will and preferences of the incompetent person (that is, to make the decision the person would make if they had capacity) or, if they are uncertain what the person would want, to act in the best interests of that person. In practice, a substitute decision-maker's knowledge of the person's preferences may be 'only slightly better than chance'[5] and many decision-makers report significant psychological burden in carrying out their role.

Laws based on guardianship and substitute decision-making models are increasingly criticised for perpetuating rigid notions of capacity as an 'all-or-nothing' concept and disempowering people who experience impaired capacity. Internationally and domestically, a major legal and policy shift is underway to adopt models of supported decision-making. This model is based on the premise that all people have the right to make decisions for themselves and people with cognitive impairments should receive appropriate supports to maximise their decisional capacity. These principles are articulated in the United Nations (UN) Convention on the Rights of Persons with Disabilities[6] and adopted by the Australian Law Reform Commission in its influential 2014 report, *Equality, Capacity and Disability in Commonwealth Laws.*[7]

---

4   Australian Institute of Health and Welfare, *Australia's Health 2016* (Australia's Health Series no 15, Catalogue no AUS 199, 2016) ch 3.6 ('Stroke') <https://www.aihw.gov.au/reports/australias-health/australias-health-2016/contents/summary>; Australia Bureau of Statistics, 'Stroke', *Profiles of Disability, Australia, 2009* (Catalogue No 4429.0, 27 June 2012) <http://www.abs.gov.au/ausstats/abs@.nsf/Lookup/4429.0main+features100262009>.

5   Lauren G Collins, Susan M Parks and Laraine Winter, 'The State of Advance Care Planning: One Decade After SUPPORT' (2006) 23(5) *American Journal of Hospice and Palliative Medicine* 378, 379; David I Shalowitz, Elizabeth Garrett-Mayer and David Wendler, 'The Accuracy of Surrogate Decision Makers: A Systematic Review' (2006) 166(5) *Archives of Internal Medicine* 493.

6   *Convention on the Rights of Persons with Disabilities*, opened for signature 13 December 2006, 2515 UNTS 3 (entered into force 3 May 2008).

7   Australian Law Reform Commission, *Equality, Capacity and Disability in Commonwealth Laws* (ALRC Report 124, 24 November 2014).

Governments across Australia are engaged in supported decision-making reform initiatives. Victoria amended its *Powers of Attorney Act 2014* and *Medical Treatment Planning and Decisions Act 2016* to recognise a 'supportive attorney' to assist with financial and personal decisions and a 'support person' for medical treatment decisions.[8] A person who anticipates a need for assistance with decision-making may appoint supporters whose role is to help the person understand their options and make and implement choices. In New South Wales, a 2018 Law Reform Commission review recommended replacing the state's decades-old *Guardianship Act 1987* with a new *Assisted Decision-Making Act* that would formally recognise supported decision-making.[9]

At the same time, voluntary assisted dying (VAD) is also an area of law reform activity. Victoria's *Voluntary Assisted Dying Act 2017* took effect in June 2019 and Western Australia's VAD legislation will come into force in mid-2021. Other states and territories have undertaken inquiries into legalisation of VAD and various bills have been introduced to seek legislative change.[10]

Laws for supported decision-making and VAD are both championed as promoting autonomy, dignity and rights to self-determination. Supported decision-making focuses on empowering people living with a disability to make or communicate decisions about their lives. VAD focuses on empowering people, typically those with advanced serious illness, to control the timing and manner of their death. Despite being grounded in shared principles and aims, there has been little attention to date on formal mechanisms of supported decision-making in the end-of-life context generally and VAD in particular.

Even aside from the contentious area of VAD, an Australian legal expert on disability rights and supported decision-making has criticised the 'minimal research to date on the practical implementation of supported

8   'Enduring Power of Attorney', *Office of the Public Advocate* (Web Page) <http://www.public advocate.vic.gov.au/power-of-attorney/supportive-attorney-appointments>.
9   NSW Law Reform Commission, *Review of the Guardianship Act 1987* (Report 145, 21 May 2018) ('*NSW Law Reform Commission Report*').
10   In March 2021, the Parliament of Tasmania passed the End of Life Choices (Voluntary Assisted Dying) Bill 2020, with implementation to follow: <https://www.parliament.tas.gov.au/Bills/Bills2020/30_of_2020.html>. In May 2021, the Voluntary Assisted Dying Bill 2021 was introduced in the Queensland Parliament: <https://www.health.qld.gov.au/system-governance/legislation/voluntary-assisted-dying-bill>. For an overview of legislative reform efforts in this area, see Ben White and Lindy Willmott, 'Future of Assisted Dying Reform in Australia' (2018) 42 *Australian Health Review* 616.

decision-making', emphasising that '[t]he issues at stake for people with cognitive and psychosocial disabilities and the public interest are too significant and potentially grave to be decided … [without] careful' study.[11] Similarly, Douglas and Bigby observe that there is 'little evidence about the practice of support or [its] essential ingredients'[12] to ensure the will and preferences of persons with disability are at the centre of decisions that affect them. Where projects have been undertaken, they have mostly focused on younger people with intellectual disability and strategies to help them gain more confidence in areas such as money management and living independently.[13] In such contexts, the aim of supported decision-making is to enhance participation and integration into the community and enhance life satisfaction.[14] Supporting decision-making to access medical assistance to die is somewhat outside these typical objectives and raises new issues for consideration.

With further law reforms on supported decision-making and VAD anticipated in Australia, it is timely to advance the empirical research base on formal supporter arrangements and to consider how people with serious illness and decision-making impairments can be supported in the context of decisions about accessing VAD. These are the key topics this chapter addresses. First, the chapter reports on a New South Wales survey that investigated the views of community members in a health service setting on supported decision-making. The survey was undertaken during the NSW Law Reform Commission's review of the *Guardianship Act 1987*, which provided an opportunity to elicit community opinions on a formal system of supported decision-making recognised by law. Second, the chapter considers supported decision-making in the context of VAD, drawing on the survey findings and literature to consider the needs of people seeking assistance with decision-making, formal (and informal)

---

11   Terry Carney and Fleur Beaupert, 'Public and Private Bricolage – Challenges Balancing Law, Services and Civil Society in Advancing *CRPD* Supported Decision-Making' (2013) 36(1) *University of New South Wales Law Journal* 175, 199.

12   Jacinta Douglas and Christine Bigby, 'Development of an Evidence-Based Practice Framework to Guide Decision Making Support for People with Cognitive Impairment due to Acquired Brain Injury or Intellectual Disability' (2018) 42(3) *Disability and Rehabilitation* 434.

13   See eg, projects summarised in Anna Arstein-Kerslake et al, 'Future Directions in Supported Decision-Making' (2017) 37(1) *Disability Studies Quarterly* 1.

14   These aims are reflected in outcome measures recommended for supported decision-making programs: Karrie A Shogren and Michael L Wehmeyer, 'A Framework for Research and Intervention Design in Supported Decision-making' (2015) 3(1) *Inclusion* 17.

supporters and clinicians. As the intersection of supported decision-making and VAD is a novel and fraught area, the paper proposes areas for future research.

The survey study

Participant eligibility and recruitment

A survey study was designed to seek the views of community members on the impacts of chronic illness on people's lives. The questions on supported decision-making, discussed in detail below, were a module within this chronic illness survey.[15] The study involved people attending outpatient clinics at a major tertiary referral hospital in regional New South Wales, Australia.[16] Eligible participants for the survey were aged 18 years and older, either a patient attending the clinic for a medical appointment or a person accompanying the patient, English-speaking, able to provide informed consent, and mentally and physically well enough to complete a touchscreen survey.

An information statement about the study was displayed at the clinic reception. A trained research assistant approached people in the waiting area to check their eligibility and interest in doing the survey. Consent was confirmed by undertaking the survey. The survey was completed on an iPad and took approximately 10 minutes to complete. The research assistant recorded the gender and age group of individuals who declined to participate in the survey. Data were collected in September and October 2017.

Survey questions on supported decision-making

The survey module on supported decision-making provided the following background information:

---

15   Other modules in the survey investigated knowledge and attitudes about chronic diseases. It is important to note that the survey respondents were not prompted to consider supported decision-making in the context of end-of-life decisions generally or VAD in particular.
16   Ethics approval for the study was obtained from the Hunter New England Health Human Research Ethics Committee (17/03/15/4.06) and the University of Newcastle Human Research Ethics Committee (H-2017-0146).

> Some conditions may affect peoples' ability to make important decisions on their own. A law may be passed to allow people to legally appoint a formal supporter to help them make decisions. For example, the formal supporter might attend appointments with the person, or help them understand their options.

With this context in mind, respondents were asked to answer questions by indicating their level of agreement with given response options on a four-point Likert scale (strongly agree, agree, disagree, strongly disagree). Some questions included 'unsure' or 'not applicable' response options, as noted in Tables 1 and 2.

Survey respondents were first asked to indicate their level of agreement with the statement that allowing people to legally appoint a formal supporter is a good idea. They were then asked to indicate their level of agreement with specified benefits and downsides of supported decision-making.

> Having a formal supporter would allow me to: (1) Still make my own decisions; (2) Be more confident that I was making the right decisions; (3) Have my wishes respected; and (4) Worry less about being taken advantage of.

> I would be worried that a formal supporter may: (1) Not be trustworthy; (2) Not have the time to help me; (3) Cost me money; (4) Try to get me to make the decisions they want; (5) Have disagreements with me; (6) Not know when I need them to help me.

Last, respondents were asked to indicate their level of agreement as to whom they would appoint as their formal supporter, with the following options presented: my wife/husband/partner; my adult child/children; another family member; a friend; a community volunteer; a care worker/disability services worker; a lawyer.

Survey results

A total of 408 people were approached. Of these, 17 were ineligible. A further 21 were called into their appointment before they were asked for consent. Of the remaining 370 eligible individuals, 250 consented to participate (consent rate of 68 per cent). There was no significant difference in gender between people who consented and did not consent to participate ($p = 0.18$). However, people aged 65–74 years were significantly less likely to consent compared to other age groups (p = 0.045). Sixty-five people who consented to participate were removed from the dataset as they did not provide complete data for at least one item, leaving 185 participants available for analysis.[17] Participants' average age was 56 years (SD = 17 years), and there were approximately equal numbers of each gender (48 per cent male, n = 89).

Is a formal system of supported decision-making a good idea?

There was nearly universal agreement among survey respondents that allowing people to legally appoint a formal supporter is a good idea: of the 185 respondents who answered this question, 95 per cent (n = 176) of respondents either agreed (66 per cent, n = 122) or strongly agreed (29 per cent, n = 54). Just 3 per cent of respondents (n = 5) expressed disagreement and 2 per cent (n = 4) were unsure.

Perceived benefits and downsides of having a formal supporter

As reported in Table 1, a substantial majority of respondents (87–96 per cent) agreed that having a formally appointed supporter would enable them to continue to exercise decision-making autonomy and self-determination.

Table 1. Perceived benefits of a formally appointed supporter (n = 180)

A formal supporter would allow me to:	Agreement (n)
Have my wishes respected	96% (172)
Be more confident that I was making the right decisions	90% (162)
Worry less about being taken advantage of	90% (162)
Still make my own decisions	87% (156)

Source: Authors' summary of survey results.

Table 2. Perceived downsides of a formally appointed supporter (n = 173)

I would be worried that a formal supporter may:	Agreement (n)
Have disagreements with me	73% (125)
Not know when I need them to help me	66% (115)
Try to get me to make the decisions they want	58% (101)

---

17 Frequencies and proportions are calculated based on the number of responses available for each question. These may total less than 185 due to missing data (eg where participants skipped questions).

I would be worried that a formal supporter may:	Agreement (n)
Not have the time to help me	56% (97)
Cost me money	54% (93)
Not be trustworthy	53% (92)

Source: Authors' summary of survey results.

There was less unanimity in respondents' perceptions of the downsides of having a formally appointed supporter, as reported in Table 2. Respondents had divided views on potential areas of concern, such as the trustworthiness of a supporter and their availability to perform their role. However, nearly three-quarters of respondents (73 per cent, $n = 125$) would worry about disagreements with their supporter and around two-thirds (67 per cent, $n = 115$) were concerned the supporter might not know when they should help. Over half of respondents (58 per cent, $n = 101$) were worried about coercion from their supporter.

Preferred person to appoint as a supporter

When asked who they would appoint as their formal supporter, a majority of respondents agreed or strongly agreed they would choose their spouse/partner (84 per cent, $n = 144$), their adult child (81 per cent, $n = 138$) or another family member (64 per cent, $n = 110$). Around half would choose a lawyer (56 per cent, $n = 96$), a care or disability services worker (50 per cent, $n = 85$) or a friend (49 per cent, $n = 84$). A community volunteer was the least popular option, with only 30 per cent ($n = 52$) of respondents expressing agreement with this option. Around 10 per cent of respondents selected 'not applicable' for the spouse/partner and adult child response options (12 per cent, $n = 21$, and 9 per cent, $n = 16$, respectively), indicating they may not have such people in their lives.

Discussion

Supported decision-making: A good idea in principle and considerations for VAD

An important finding from this survey is that nearly all respondents thought legal recognition of supported decision-making is a good idea. Law reforms to allow formal supporter appointments therefore appear to accord with community views. Moreover, there was substantial agreement (87–96 per cent) with the benefits of supported decision-making in enabling people to make and have confidence in their own decisions, have their choices respected and worry less about others taking advantage of them. The areas the survey identified as being of concern – having disagreements and not knowing when the person with a disability might need support – highlight that supported decision-making is a relational process that needs its own supports. People who choose to enter formal supporter agreements need guidance on identifying their needs, communicating effectively and resolving disputes. Supporters must understand and act in their role as a *supporter*, not as someone who takes over and substitutes their values and preferences for that of the person living with cognitive impairment.

These findings provide a foundation for identifying and discussing specific considerations in relation to supported decision-making and VAD. Effective support for decision-making is an area for attention in high-quality end-of-life care, including support for VAD decisions, where this option is among the legally available choices. For people with advanced serious illness, maintaining control, dignity and self-respect are identified as factors that improve their dying and death experience.[18] Moreover, in the end-of-life context, being free from coercion is vital to a voluntary choice to access medical assistance to die.

Capacity and the level of support required

Issues of decision-making capacity are central to both supported decision-making and VAD. A person who wishes to appoint a formal supporter must have the capacity to do so;[19] for instance, they must be able to understand the nature and effect of making such an appointment. Since formal support arrangements are targeted for people with cognitive disability, ascertaining decision-making capacity will typically be an important part of the process. Once a supporter appointment is in place, the individual in the role is responsible for enhancing the decision-making capacity of the person with a disability. They may do so by gathering and explaining information relevant to a decision, accompanying the person to appointments with service providers to help ask questions and weigh up options.

---

18   Lois Downey et al, 'The Quality of Dying and Death Questionnaire (QODD): Empirical Domains and Theoretical Perspectives' (2009) 39(1) *Journal of Pain and Symptom Management* 9.
19   See eg, Victoria's *Medical Treatment Planning and Decisions Act 2016* s 31(1).

Restricting access to VAD for adults with capacity to make their own choice on the matter is an important legislative safeguard.[20] This raises the question of whether a person who requires decision-making support is an eligible person to access VAD. Victoria's *Voluntary Assisted Dying Act 2017* makes it clear that 'a person has decision-making capacity to make a decision if it is possible for the person to make a decision with practicable and appropriate support'.[21] A 2018 Western Australian parliamentary inquiry into end-of-life choices stated:

> Consistent with the United Nations Convention on the Rights of Persons with Disabilities (to which Australia is a signatory) individuals with a disability must be afforded the same legal rights as the rest of the community.[22]

The inquiry cited submissions from People with Disabilities WA and the Australian Federation of Disability Organisations advocating that everyone has 'the right to be supported in making properly informed decisions about their medical treatment'.[23] Western Australia's *Voluntary Assisted Dying Act 2019* adopts this language, stating:

> a person has the right to be supported in making informed decisions about the person's medical treatment, and should be given, in a manner the person understands, information about medical treatment options including comfort and palliative care and treatment.[24]

Further, the legislation encourages people to 'openly discuss death and dying'[25] and states that 'a person should be supported in conversations with the person's health practitioners, family and carers and community about treatment and care preferences'.[26]

---

20 For discussion, see eg, Carmelle Peisah, Linda Sheahan and Ben White, 'Biggest Decision of Them All – Death and Assisted Dying: Capacity Assessments and Undue Influence Screening' (2019) 49(6) *Internal Medicine Journal* 792.

21 *Voluntary Assisted Dying Act 2017* (Vic) s 4(4)(d).

22 Joint Select Committee on End of Life Choices, Parliament of Western Australia, *My Life, My Choice: The Report of the Joint Select Committee on End of Life Choices* (Report 1, August 2018) 221, <http://www.parliament.wa.gov.au/parliament/commit.nsf/(Report+Lookup+by+Com+ID)/71C9AFECD0FAEE6E482582F200037B37/$file/Joint+Select+Committe+on+the+End+of+Life+Choices+-+Report+for+Website.pdf>.

23 Ibid 222.

24 *Voluntary Assisted Dying Act 2019* (WA) s 4(1)(c).

25 Ibid s 4(1)(f).

26 Ibid s 4(1)(g).

Recent inquiries into VAD in other Australian jurisdictions also recognise that people with disabilities must not be discriminated against, implying that, with appropriate supports, individuals with cognitive disability can be enabled to make choices about VAD. For example, the Australian Psychological Society takes the view that supported decision-making can be appropriate in the context of VAD choices:

> People with a disability should be provided with appropriate support to make decisions, and having a disability does not negate their right to assisted dying or any other service that is legal for non-disabled persons.[27]

In its 2018 review of guardianship legislation, the NSW Law Reform Commission recommended that a new *Assisted Decision-Making Act* should provide that 'if a person ... has decision-making ability in relation to a healthcare decision only when assisted by the supporter, the person has decision-making ability for the purposes of [the law]'.[28]

The ways in which capacity is understood and applied in the VAD context may, however, undermine the principle of non-discrimination. An analysis of submissions to a UK commission on assisted dying found:

> [a] tendency towards a conceptual and clinical shift toward a presumption of *incapacity*. This appeared to be based on the belief that assisted suicide should only be open to those with a high degree of mental capacity to make the decision.[29]

In contrast, early commentary on supported decision-making argued:

> The starting point is not a test of capacity, but the presumption that every human being is communicating all the time and that this communication will include preferences. Preferences can be built up into expressions of choice and these into formal decisions.

---

27 Australian Psychological Society, *Submission to the Inquiry into End of Life Choices in the ACT* (March 2018) <https://psychology.org.au/getmedia/bc8fd1fb-d944-4d2e-8f64-d70445e8de5c/APS-Submission-ACT-Inquiry-into-end-of-life-choices.pdf>.
28 *NSW Law Reform Commission Report* (n 9) 157.
29 Annabel Price et al, 'Concepts of Mental Capacity for Patients Requesting Assisted Suicide: A Qualitative Analysis of Expert Evidence Presented to the Commission on Assisted Dying' (2014) 15(32) *BMC Medical Ethics* 1 (emphasis added).

> From this perspective, where someone lands on a continuum of capacity is not half as important as the amount and type of support they get to build preferences into choices.[30]

An Irish study of psychologists' views and experiences of supported decision-making also revealed that the legal presumption of capacity is undermined by a 'culture of incapacity' that is embedded in attitudes and practices.[31] European bioethics experts echoed concern that 'the bar [for decision-making capacity] is sometimes set too high' for people seeking access to VAD.[32] They contend:

> Any doctor who attempts to prevent a patient who is mentally competent from accessing assisted suicide is adopting an over-paternalistic stance that is contrary to the more general emphasis on autonomy in biomedical ethics. One might never choose assisted suicide for oneself or might think that the practice itself is deeply unethical, but to impose those values on one's patients is deeply unethical and unprofessional.[33]

Decision-making domains: Complex or 'high-risk' decisions

There has been some discussion as to whether certain domains of decision-making, such as significant financial decisions, should be excluded from the scope of formal supported decision-making arrangements. In the NSW review of the *Guardianship Act 1987*, several stakeholders suggested that people with cognitive disability are at heightened vulnerability to financial exploitation and that appointed supporters should not assist with major financial decisions.[34] The Law Reform Commission rejected such a restriction, arguing instead that if supported decision-making laws exclude support for particular kinds of decisions then support for such

---

30 Stephanie Beamer and Mark Brookes, *Making Decisions: Best Practice and New Ideas for Supporting People with High Support Needs to Make Decisions* (Values into Action, 2001) 4, cited in Arstein-Kerslake et al (n 13).

31 E Rogers et al, 'Psychologists' Perspectives on Supported Decision Making in Ireland' (2020) 64(3) *Journal of Intellectual Disability Research* 234.

32 David Shaw, Manuel Trachsel and Bernice Elger, 'Assessment of Decision-Making Capacity in Patients Requesting Assisted Suicide' (2018) 213(1) *British Journal of Psychiatry* 393, 394.

33 Ibid.

34 *NSW Law Reform Commission Report* (n 9) 82, citing submissions: NSW Disability Network Forum, Submission GA39 (25 January 2017) 11; Royal Australian and New Zealand College of Psychiatrists NSW Branch, Submission GA53 (31 January 2017) 2–3; Seniors Rights Service, Submission GA61 (31 January 2017) 14.

decisions would occur on an informal basis, outside the safeguards in the law.[35] Moreover, the commission felt that complex areas of decision-making are precisely the areas where support should be available.

By analogy, formal support for understanding VAD and making end-of-life care decisions may also be desirable and would ensure that safeguards both in VAD laws and supported decision-making rules are available. Ultimately, it is contended that supported decision-making recognises that adults, including those in formal supporter arrangements, 'have the right to make decisions, including the right to make risky or "bad" decisions'.[36] At the same time, it is not a straightforward process to support decision-making 'in difficult situations where the decision may pose some harm to the individual'.[37] Supporters report being more risk-averse in such circumstances and prioritising protection from harm over promotion of autonomy.[38] The issue of supporting VAD decision-making will run up against persistent debates about the harms of hastening death and whether choosing assistance to die is in a person's best interests.[39]

Eligibility to be a supporter

In Australia, law reform discussions on supported decision-making have generally favoured wide latitude in who is eligible to be a formally appointed supporter to assist with health-related decisions.[40] In its recommendations for a new *Assisted Decision-Making Act,* the NSW Law Reform Commission stated: 'we want to provide people looking for support with as many options as possible to suit their circumstances'.[41]

---

35   A person making a support agreement can, however, choose to exclude certain matters from their arrangement with an appointed supporter.

36   *NSW Law Reform Commission Report* (n 9) 19.

37   Arstein-Kerslake et al (n 13).

38   See Rogers et al (n 31); Christine Bigby, Mary Whiteside and Jacinta Douglas, 'Providing Support for Decision Making to Adults with Intellectual Disability: Perspectives of Family Members and Workers in Disability Support Services' (2019) 44(4) *Journal of Intellectual & Developmental Disability* 396.

39   See eg, James Downar, 'Is Physician-Assisted Death in Anyone's Best Interest? Yes.' (2015) 61(4) *Canadian Family Physician* 314; and Edward T St Godard, 'Is Physician-Assisted Death in Anyone's Best Interest? No.' (2015) 61(4) *Canadian Family Physician* 316.

40   Other requirements may apply for supporters who assist with financial decisions. Under Victoria's *Powers of Attorney Act 2014* and the NSW recommendations, if an appointee is to support financial decision-making, they must not have prior bankruptcy or conviction for a dishonesty offence unless this has been acknowledged in the support agreement.

41   *NSW Law Reform Commission Report* (n 9) 74 [7.29].

Under Victoria's *Medical Treatment Planning and Decisions Act 2016* and the NSW recommendations, a person under age 18 may be appointed as a supporter provided they understand the role and its responsibilities.[42]

Our survey respondents identified people within their family network as their preferred supporters, while community volunteers were their least preferred option. However, investing resources in volunteer programs may be vital to provide access to supported decision-making for people who are socially isolated or otherwise do not have relatives or friends able to assist them in a supporter arrangement.[43] To this end, a Victorian pilot project matched people with mild intellectual disability with a trained volunteer to assist them with decision-making. It was found that success depended on 'skilled volunteers who were committed to spending many months developing a relationship with participants and persevering through many barriers when supporting them to make and act on their own decisions'.[44]

This finding highlights that a community volunteer model may be poorly suited to VAD decision-making if legislation (or practice) restricts access to terminally ill people with a limited life expectancy. A short time period of only months of life may be insufficient for a volunteer to establish a relationship with the person to support them in decision-making about VAD. Moreover, just as medical practitioners may conscientiously object to being involved in VAD,[45] some prospective supporters, such as community volunteers, may not wish to offer support for decision-making about assisted dying.

---

42   *Medical Treatment Planning and Decisions Act 2016* (Vic) ss 31 and 34. The NSW Law Reform Commission recommends a minimum age of 16 years for a formally appointed supporter.

43   Arstein-Kerslake et al (n 13). Social isolation is increasingly recognised as a serious issue among older people: Nicholas R Nicholson, 'A Review of Social Isolation: An Important but Underassessed Condition in Older Adults' (2012) 33(2–3) *Journal of Primary Prevention* 137; Thomas KM Cudjoe et al, 'The Epidemiology of Social Isolation: National Health and Aging Trends Study' (2020) 75(1) *The Journals of Gerontology: Series B* 107 (reporting US survey data that approximately one quarter of older adults experience social isolation, accounting for 7.7 million Americans). As family sizes shrink and more people have few or no children, a growing number of people may reach older age without traditional family support systems: C Deindl and M Brandt, 'Support Networks of Childless Older People: Informal and Formal Support in Europe' (2017) 37(8) *Ageing and Society* 1543.

44   Brenda Burgen, 'Reflections on the Victorian Office of the Public Advocate Supported Decision-Making Pilot Project' (2016) 3(2) *Research and Practice in Intellectual and Developmental Disabilities* 165, 177.

45   See eg, Australian Medical Association, *Conscientious Objection – 2019* (Position Statement, 27 March 2019) <https://ama.com.au/position-statement/conscientious-objection-2019>.

Attitudes and approaches to supporting the decision-making of another person may vary depending on whether the supporter is a family member or a third party, such as a disability support worker or a health or legal professional. Family members feel a stronger entitlement to be involved in decision-making and may be more paternalistic and protective.[46] Supporters who are paid carers or professional advisors feel their role is to be neutral, however they report tensions between promoting individual autonomy and meeting their legal duty of care, especially for higher-risk decisions.[47] Accordingly, they identify resources they need, including opportunities to talk through ethical dilemmas with colleagues or supervisors and guidelines on supported decision-making from their organisations or professional associations.

The end-of-life context

Even where support for VAD decision-making is possible in principle, barriers may exist in practice.

Legal or practical barriers to accessing support for end-of-life decision-making, including VAD, could have negative impacts such as denying the seriously ill person with cognitive disability access to a service available to others and also reinforcing stigma about dying and death. The notion of a disenfranchised death has been used to describe end-of-life circumstances where a person with a cognitive or intellectual disability 'is socially excluded from the process of dying and deliberately excluded from the decision-making process surrounding the terminal illness'.[48]

A recent UK interview study of people with intellectual disabilities, supporters and social care professionals found

---

46   Bigby, Whiteside and Douglas, (n 38).
47   Ibid; Craig Sinclair et al, 'Professionals' Views and Experiences in Supporting Decision-Making Involvement for People Living with Dementia' (2021) 20(1) *Dementia* 84.
48   S Read, 'Communication in the Dying Context', in S Read, ed, *Palliative Care for People with Learning Disabilities* (Quay Books, 2006) 93, 96, cited in Sue Read and Heather Morris, *Living and Dying with Dignity: The Best Practice Guide to End-of-Life Care for People with a Learning Disability* (Report, Mencap, 7 November 2008) <http://supporteddecisionmaking.com/sites/default/files/end-of%20life-care-best-practice-guide.pdf>.

> limited availability of support for more complex decisions, by which we mean decisions which may require the decision-maker to understand and process greater quantities of, or more difficult, information, or wider and/or more abstract potential effects.[49]

Examples included decisions about end-of-life planning and refusals of medical treatments. Moreover, '[t]he amount of support available to disabled people from frontline care professionals appeared to reduce in an inverse relationship to the complexities of the decision they needed to make'.[50]

Similarly, Australian stakeholders have expressed concern about people being excluded from supported decision-making arrangements when their support needs are perceived as more complex. For example, Arstein-Kerslake cites comments from a participant at a University of Melbourne symposium on supported decision-making:

> As is the case for supported decision-making, to date, these movements have been dominated by people with mild, as opposed to more severe cognitive disability. As articulated by one of the symposium participants 'I think we are once again leaving a whole group of people out. We've been there before. Like with [healthcare] planning. For these people it's different, and it's not easy. I don't know, perhaps they will always be in the too hard basket'.[51]

However, as the need for decision-making support increases, the line between supported and substituted decision-making can become blurred. A case study project in Victoria examined supported decision-making for five people with profound intellectual disability.[52] One participant in the study, who 'did not use or appear to understand formal communication', developed aspiration pneumonia. His (informal) supporters, including his parents and care workers from his group home, 'were faced with assisting him with a life and death related decision', that is whether to undergo

---

49   Rosie Harding and Ezgi Taşcıoğlu, 'Supported Decision-Making from Theory to Practice: Implementing the Right to Enjoy Legal Capacity' (2018) 8(2) *Societies* 25. Fifteen disabled people, six supporters and 25 social care professionals from across England and Wales participated in the study.
50   Harding and Taşcıoğlu (n 49).
51   Arstein-Kerslake et al (n 13).
52   Joanne Watson, Erin Wilson and Nick Hagiliassis, 'Supporting End of Life Decision Making: Case Studies of Relational Closeness in Supported Decision Making for People with Severe or Profound Intellectual Disability' (2017) 30(6) *Journal of Applied Research in Intellectual Disabilities* 1022.

a live-saving tracheotomy procedure. While labelled supported decision-making, the process described reveals a substitute decision-making process guided by knowledge of the person's will and preferences:

> The group spoke with Neil's medical team about his options, and spent time collaboratively weighing these up. They drew heavily from their relationships with Neil as well as his past life experiences, specifically his past experiences of tracheotomy. … Guided by the preferences Neil had communicated [through means such as body language and vocalisations during] his past experiences … the group collectively made the difficult decision that a tracheotomy would not be carried out.[53]

Changing the issue in this situation to one of accessing VAD instead of refusing a tracheotomy, the process described above would not count as a voluntary, supported decision; the supporters appear to *make* the decision, not assist Neil to understand his options and help him express his wishes to the doctors. This example underscores the importance of clarity about the formal and informal roles of family members, friends, care workers and others involved in the life – and death – of a person with disability.

The needs of supporters

Healthcare professionals recognise family members and others close to the patient as important supporters – either informally or potentially in a formal supporter role. At the same time, these supporters may be seen as 'second patients who could be traumatized by a patient's situation and needed special attention, care and time investment'.[54] Studies have investigated the impacts of being a *substitute* decision-maker for a loved one in the end-of-life context and this research can identify possible stressors that formally appointed supporters may encounter. For many people, the substitute decision-making role is emotionally stressful and can generate conflicts with clinicians, as well as relatives and friends of the seriously ill person. Substitute decision-makers are troubled by uncertainty about the person's preferences and by guilt when they perceive that following the person's wishes is at odds with best interests as perceived by others. Effective communication with the person prior to loss of capacity and

---

53   Ibid 1031.
54   Katsiaryna Laryionava et al, 'The Second Patient? Family Members of Cancer Patients and their Role in End-of-Life Decision Making' (2018) 17(29) *BMC Palliative Care* 1.

clinicians helps to improve substitute decision-makers' confidence in the choices they make but may not assuage guilt or reduce family conflicts.[55] The negative psychosocial sequelae of substitute decision-making can be long-lasting.[56]

The needs of clinicians

Australian studies have revealed gaps in clinicians' knowledge of end-of-life law, including lack of knowledge of who is the lawful decision-maker for a person who lacks decisional capacity.[57] With law reforms to recognise formal supporter roles, there will be a need to ensure that clinicians understand the role and responsibilities of a supporter and have the skills needed to work effectively with patients and their formal supporters. Effective practices for supported decision-making may, in fact, demand more from clinicians, a point acknowledged by the Royal Australian and New Zealand College of Psychiatrists:

> The intent of SDM [supported decision-making] is not to merely shift risk and responsibility for decision-making and treatment outcomes from mental health clinicians and onto consumers, their families and carers. Instead, it places increased responsibility on clinicians to improve their way of practising in order to strengthen consumers' capacity to make decisions, whilst reducing practices viewed as coercive or manipulative.[58]

Areas for future research

As law reforms continue, it is important to ensure that supported decision-making is 'constructed, led, and continually guided by those using the support'.[59] To the extent that supported decision-making is implemented

---

55   Alyssa Majesko et al, 'Identifying Family Members who May Struggle in the Role of Surrogate Decision Maker' (2012) 40(8) *Critical Care Medicine* 2281.

56   David Wendler, 'The Theory and Practice of Surrogate Decision-Making' (2017) 47(1) *Hastings Center Report,* 29.

57   See Ben White et al, 'Doctors' Knowledge of the Law on Withholding and Withdrawing Life-Sustaining Medical Treatment' (2014) 18(201) *Medical Journal of Australia* 229; Ben White et al, 'Knowledge of the Law about Withholding or Withdrawing Life-Sustaining Treatment by Intensivists and Other Specialists' (2016) 18(2) *Critical Care and Resuscitation: Journal of the Australasian Academy of Critical Care Medicine,* 109.

58   Royal Australian and New Zealand College of Psychiatrists, Victorian Branch, *Enabling Supported Decision-Making* (Position Paper, May 2018) <https://www.ranzcp.org/files/branches/victoria/enabling-supported-decision-making-vic-branch-posi.aspx>.

59   Anna Arstein-Kerslake et al (n 13).

in relation to end-of-life choices, it will be vital to understand the perspectives and experiences of those who seek support for VAD decisions, as well as the supporters.

Where VAD is legal, routine data collection should be expanded to include information on the use of supported decision-making, including the types of support used and the reasons for needing support; for example, does the person requiring support have a communication disorder or a neurocognitive illness with fluctuating or reduced capacity. A recent review of 20 years of experience of Oregon's *Death with Dignity Act* does not elaborate on issues related to decision-making capacity and whether those who access assisted dying have had support in their decision-making.[60]

The circumstances of people with specific neurocognitive disorders, such as dementia, warrant investigation. To date, the literature on access to assisted dying by people with dementia does not yet appear to address supported decision-making; for instance, on the issue of decisional capacity, a 2017 literature review concludes:

> Assisted dying in dementia raises numerous questions that remain to be answered empirically. It is of major interest to determine how long the capacity to decide about one's own death is retained during the course of dementia, which factors influence this capacity and how this capacity can reliably be assessed.[61]

A factor that influences decisional capacity is the availability of appropriate supports and future research should investigate this topic. A recent multidisciplinary project on supported decision-making for people with dementia has started to fill the gaps in resources with a consumer guidebook and a policy development document for aged care providers.[62] These materials discuss health-related decisions and advance care planning, however, VAD decision-making is a specific topic where future evidence-based guidance will be needed.

---

60 Katrina Hedberg and Craig New, 'Oregon's Death with Dignity Act: 20 Years of Experience to Inform the Debate' (2017) 167(8) *Annals of Internal Medicine* 579.
61 J Diehl-Schmid et al, 'Suicide and Assisted Dying in Dementia: What We Know and What We Need to Know. A Narrative Literature Review' (2017) 29(8) *International Psychogeriatrics* 1247.
62 Cognitive Decline Partnership Centre, 'Supported Decision-Making', *The University of Sydney* (Web Page) <http://sydney.edu.au/medicine/cdpc/resources/supported-decision-making.php>.

Conclusion

In Australia, law reform is underway in the separate but potentially intersecting areas of supported decision-making and VAD. To meet their obligations under the UN Convention on the Rights of Persons with Disabilities, Australia and other signatory nations must 'ensure all citizens are considered when developing legislation, policy and practice guidelines around supported decision-making. This includes those who historically have not been invited to the self-determination "party"'.[63] An analogous comment can be made about VAD, another area where self-determination is a driving principle. An important area of intersection is to consider how support for decision-making can be provided for people facing end-of-life choices, particularly older people with neurocognitive disorders such as dementia, a group that has been on the sidelines of the self-determination 'parties' both of supported decision-making and VAD.

Bibliography

A Articles/books/reports

Arstein-Kerslake, Anna et al, 'Future Directions in Supported Decision-Making' (2017) 37(1) *Disability Studies Quarterly* 1 doi.org/10.18061/dsq.v37i1.5070

Australian Institute of Health and Welfare, *Australia's Health 2016* (Australia's Health Series No 15, Catalogue no AUS 199, 2016)

Australian Law Reform Commission, *Equality, Capacity and Disability in Commonwealth Laws: Final Report* (ALRC Report 124, 24 November 2014)

Australian Psychological Society, *Submission to the Inquiry into End of Life Choices in the ACT* (March 2018) <https://psychology.org.au/getmedia/bc8fd1fb-d944-4d2e-8f64-d70445e8de5c/APS-Submission-ACT-Inquiry-into-end-of-life-choices.pdf>

Beamer, Stephanie and Mark Brookes, *Making Decisions: Best Practice and New Ideas for Supporting People with High Support Needs to Make Decisions* (Values into Action, 2001)

---

63   Arstein-Kerslake et al (n 13).

Bigby, Christine, Mary Whiteside and Jacinta Douglas, 'Providing Support for Decision Making to Adults with Intellectual Disability: Perspectives of Family Members and Workers in Disability Support Services' (2019) 44(4) *Journal of Intellectual & Developmental Disability* 396 doi.org/10.3109/1366 8250.2017.1378873

Burgen, Brenda, 'Reflections on the Victorian Office of the Public Advocate Supported Decision-Making Pilot Project' (2016) 3(2) *Research and Practice in Intellectual and Developmental Disabilities* 165 doi.org/10.1080/23297018. 2016.1199969

Carney, Terry and Fleur Beaupert, 'Public and Private Bricolage – Challenges Balancing Law, Services and Civil Society in Advancing CRPD Supported Decision-Making' (2013) 36(1) *University of New South Wales Law Journal* 175

Collins, Lauren G, Susan M Parks and Laraine Winter, 'The State of Advance Care Planning: One Decade After SUPPORT' (2006) 23(5) *American Journal of Hospice and Palliative Medicine* 378 doi.org/10.1177/1049909106292171

Cudjoe, Thomas KM et al, 'The Epidemiology of Social Isolation: National Health and Aging Trends Study' (2020) 75(1) *The Journals of Gerontology: Series B* 107 doi.org/10.1093/geronb/gby037

Deindl, C and M Brandt, 'Support Networks of Childless Older People: Informal and Formal Support in Europe' (2017) 37(8) *Ageing and Society* 1543 doi.org/ 10.1017/S0144686X16000416

Diehl-Schmid, J et al, 'Suicide and Assisted Dying in Dementia: What We Know and What We Need to Know. A Narrative Literature Review' (2017) 29(8) *International Psychogeriatrics* 1247 doi.org/10.1017/s1041610217000679

Douglas, Jacinta and Christine Bigby, 'Development of an Evidence-Based Practice Framework to Guide Decision Making Support for People with Cognitive Impairment Due to Acquired Brain Injury or Intellectual Disability' (2018) 42(3) *Disability and Rehabilitation* 434 doi.org/10.1080/09638288. 2018.1498546

Downar, James, 'Is Physician-Assisted Death in Anyone's Best Interest?: Yes' (2015) 61(4) *Canadian Family Physician* 314

Downey, Lois et al, 'The Quality of Dying and Death Questionnaire (QODD): Empirical Domains and Theoretical Perspectives' (2010) 39(1) *Journal of Pain and Symptom Management* 9 doi.org/10.1016/j.jpainsymman.2009.05.012

Harding, Rosie and Ezgi Taşcıoğlu, 'Supported Decision-Making from Theory to Practice: Implementing the Right to Enjoy Legal Capacity' (2018) 8(2) *Societies* 25 doi.org/10.3390/soc8020025

Hedberg, Katrina and Craig New, 'Oregon's Death With Dignity Act: 20 Years of Experience to Inform the Debate' (2017) 167(8) *Annals of Internal Medicine* 579 doi.org/10.7326/M17-2300

Joint Select Committee on End of Life Choices, Parliament of Western Australia, *My Life, My Choice: The Report of the Joint Select Committee on End of Life Choices* (Report No 1, August 2018)

Joint Select Committee on End of Life Choices, Submission to Parliament of Western Australia, *Inquiry into the Need for Laws in Western Australia to Allow Citizens to Make Informed Decisions Regarding Their Own End of Life Choices* (23 August 2018)

Laryionava, Katsiaryna et al, 'The Second Patient? Family Members of Cancer Patients and Their Role in End-of-Life Decision Making' (2018) 17(29) *BMC Palliative Care* 1 doi.org/10.1186/s12904-018-0288-2

Majesko, Alyssa et al, 'Identifying Family Members Who May Struggle in the Role of Surrogate Decision Maker' (2012) 40(8) *Critical Care Medicine* 2281 doi.org/10.1097/CCM.0b013e3182533317

Nicholson, Nicholas R, 'A Review of Social Isolation: An Important but Underassessed Condition in Older Adults' (2012) 33(2–3) *Journal of Primary Prevention* 137 doi.org/10.1007/s10935-012-0271-2

NSW Law Reform Commission, *Review of the Guardianship Act 1987* (Report No 145, 21 May 2018)

Peisah, Carmelle, Linda Sheahan and Ben P White, 'Biggest Decision of Them All – Death and Assisted Dying: Capacity Assessments and Undue Influence Screening' (2019) 49(6) *Internal Medicine Journal* 792 doi.org/10.1111/imj.14238

Price, Annabel et al, 'Concepts of Mental Capacity for Patients Requesting Assisted Suicide: A Qualitative Analysis of Expert Evidence Presented to the Commission on Assisted Dying' (2014) 15(32) *BMC Medical Ethics* 1 doi.org/10.1186/1472-6939-15-32

Read, S, 'Communication in the Dying Context' in S Read, (ed), *Palliative Care for People with Learning Disabilities* (Quay Books, 2006) 93

Read, Sue and Heather Morris, *Living and Dying with Dignity: The Best Practice Guide to End-of-Life Care for People with a Learning Disability* (Report, Mencap, 7 November 2008) <http://supporteddecisionmaking.com/sites/default/files/end-of%20life-care-best-practice-guide.pdf>

Rogers, E et al, 'Psychologists' Perspectives on Supported Decision Making in Ireland' (2020) 64(3) *Journal of Intellectual Disability Research* 234 doi.org/10.1111/jir.12712

Royal Australian and New Zealand College of Psychiatrists, Victorian Branch Committee, *Enabling Supported Decision-Making* (Position Paper, May 2018)

Shalowitz, David I, Elizabeth Garrett-Mayer and David Wendler, 'The Accuracy of Surrogate Decision Makers: A Systematic Review' (2006) 166(5) *Archives of Internal Medicine* 493 doi.org/10.1001/archinte.166.5.493

Shaw, David, Manuel Trachsel and Bernice Elger, 'Assessment of Decision-Making Capacity in Patients Requesting Assisted Suicide' (2018) 213(1) *The British Journal of Psychiatry* 393 doi.org/10.1192/bjp.2018.81

Shogren, Karrie A and Michael L Wehmeyer, 'A Framework for Research and Intervention Design in Supported Decision-Making' (2015) 3(1) *Inclusion* 17 doi.org/10.1352/2326-6988-3.1.17

Sinclair, Craig et al, 'Professionals' Views and Experiences in Supporting Decision-Making Involvement for People Living with Dementia' (2021) 20(1) *Dementia* 84 doi.org/10.1177/1471301219864849

St Godard, Edward (Ted), 'Is Physician-Assisted Death in Anyone's Best Interest?: No' (2015) 61(4) *Canadian Family Physician* 316

Watson, Joanne, Erin Wilson and Nick Hagiliassis, 'Supporting End of Life Decision Making: Case Studies of Relational Closeness in Supported Decision Making for People with Severe or Profound Intellectual Disability' (2017) 30(6) *Journal of Applied Research in Intellectual Disabilities* 1022 doi.org/10.1111/jar.12393

Wendler, David, 'The Theory and Practice of Surrogate Decision-Making' (2017) 47(1) *Hastings Center Report* 29 doi.org/10.1002/hast.671

White, Ben and Lindy Willmott, 'Future of Assisted Dying Reform in Australia' (2018) 42(6) *Australian Health Review* 616 doi.org/10.1071/AH18199

White, Ben et al, 'Doctors' Knowledge of the Law on Withholding and Withdrawing Life-Sustaining Medical Treatment' (2014) 201(4) *Medical Journal of Australia* 229 doi.org/10.5694/mja13.00217

White, Ben et al, 'Knowledge of the Law about Withholding or Withdrawing Life-Sustaining Treatment by Intensivists and Other Specialists' (2016) 18(2) *Critical Care and Resuscitation: Journal of the Australasian Academy of Critical Care Medicine* 109

B Legislation

End of Life Choices (Voluntary Assisted Dying) Bill 2020 (Tas)
Medical Treatment Planning and Decisions Act 2016 (Vic)
Powers of Attorney Act 2014 (Vic)
Voluntary Assisted Dying Act 2017 (Vic)
Voluntary Assisted Dying Act 2019 (WA)

C Treaties

Convention on the Rights of Persons with Disabilities, opened for signature 13 December 2006, 2515 UNTS 3 (entered into force 3 May 2008)

D Other

Australia Bureau of Statistics, 'Dementia and Death in Australia', *Causes of Death, Australia, 2015* (Catalogue No 3303.0, 26 July 2017) <https://www.abs.gov.au/ausstats/abs@.nsf/Lookup/by%20Subject/3303.0~2015~Main%20Features~Dementia~10002>

Australia Bureau of Statistics, 'Stroke', *Profiles of Disability, Australia, 2009* (Catalogue No 4429.0, 27 June 2012) <https://www.abs.gov.au/ausstats/abs@.nsf/Lookup/4429.0main+features100262009>

Australian Medical Association, *Conscientious Objection – 2019* (Position Statement, 27 March 2019) <https://ama.com.au/position-statement/conscientious-objection-2019>

Cognitive Decline Partnership Centre, 'Supported Decision-Making', *The University of Sydney* (Web Page) <https://cdpc.sydney.edu.au/research/planning-decision-making-and-risk/supported-decision-making/>

'Dementia', *Australian Institute of Health and Welfare* (Web Page) <https://www.aihw.gov.au/reports-data/health-conditions-disability-deaths/dementia/overview>

'Enduring Power of Attorney', *Office of the Public Advocate* (Web Page) <http://www.publicadvocate.vic.gov.au/power-of-attorney/supportive-attorney-appointments>

NSW Disability Network Forum, Submission GA39 to NSW Law Reform Commission, *Review of the Guardianship Act 1987* (25 January 2017)

Royal Australian and New Zealand College of Psychiatrists NSW Branch, Submission GA53 to NSW Law Reform Commission, *Review of the Guardianship Act 1987* (31 January 2017)

Seniors Rights Service, Submission GA61 to NSW Law Reform Commission, *Review of the Guardianship Act 1987* (31 January 2017)

4

The Compassionate State? 'Voluntary Assisted Dying', Neoliberalism, and a Virtue Without an Anchor[1]

Daniel J Fleming

On 28 November, 2017, the Victorian Minister for Health and Ambulance Services, Jill Hennessy, published a Twitter post that read 'Victoria … the compassionate state. ✓ #VAD #assisteddying #springst'.[2] The Tweet remained pinned to Hennessy's account (meaning that it was the first post seen there) until October 2018. It followed the marathon debate in the Victorian parliament – lasting more than 100 hours – which culminated in the passing of the *Voluntary Assisted Dying Act 2017*. This Act makes it legal in Victoria for individuals who meet certain criteria and have followed a set process to end their own lives by consuming a lethal substance or, in certain cases, have that substance administered to them by a doctor.[3] It came into effect 19 June 2019.

1   An earlier version of this article is published in ABC Religion and Ethics Online, see Daniel Fleming, 'The Compassionate State? Voluntary Assisted Dying, Neoliberalism and the Problem of Virtue Without an Anchor', *ABC Religion and Ethics* (Opinion, 25 March 2019) <https://www.abc.net.au/religion/compassionate-state-voluntary-assisted-dying-neoliberalism-and/10937504>.
2   @JillHennessyMP (Twitter, 29 November 2017, 12:09pm AEST) <https://twitter.com/jillhennessymp/status/935676976064487424?lang=en>.
3   *Voluntary Assisted Dying Act 2017* (Vic) pt 4, div 1.

This article does not focus on the ethical issues surrounding the newly legal interventions that the Act legalises, referred to by the *Cambridge Textbook of Bioethics* as 'physician assisted suicide' and 'euthanasia'.[4] Commentaries that analyse the ethics of these acts already abound. Nor does the article in substance seek to grapple with the tragedy of those who die in pain or without adequate care: that indeed is a crucial moral question, globally, which equally tragically is circumvented when the fact of inadequate care is used as a bait-and-switch argument to propose only one solution to it. Instead, it presents an analysis of the use of the term 'compassion' in Hennessy's tweet, which itself is reflective of the language and thrust of political and public sentiment following the voluntary assisted dying (hereafter referred to as VAD) debate. The claim here is that the state that legislates for VAD is the 'compassionate state'. In the words of the Premier of Victoria, Daniel Andrews, in the media conference following the Act's passing:

> This is a day of reform, a day of compassion, a day of giving control to those who are terminally ill … I'm proud today that we have put compassion right at the centre of our parliamentary and our political process.[5]

Compassion is a virtue – a stable, consistent and morally praiseworthy character disposition.[6] This article considers the following question: according to what narrative is 'VAD' an expression of the virtue of compassion?

These questions build on the seminal work of Alasdair MacIntyre in his 1981 book *After Virtue*, which observed that contemporary moral discourse is so dysfunctional because it has lapsed into an emotivism in which ethical terminology is used in an incongruent manner, because it (1) is separated from its anchors in the bodies of thought that make it meaningful, (2) rests on different and often incommensurable assumptions or narratives, and yet (3) is communicated in public as if it has a universal foundation and meaning.[7]

---

4   *Voluntary Assisted Dying Act 2017* (Vic) pt 4 div 1; Bernard M Dickens, Joseph M Boyle Jr and Linda Ganzini, 'Euthanasia and Assisted Suicide' in Peter A Singer and AM Viens (eds), *The Cambridge Textbook of Bioethics* (Cambridge University Press, 2008) 72.

5   Cited in Jean Edwards, 'Euthanasia: Victoria Becomes the First Australian State to Legalise Voluntary Assisted Dying', *ABC News* (online, 29 November 2017) <https://www.abc.net.au/news/2017-11-29/euthanasia-passes-parliament-in-victoria/9205472>.

6   James Rachels and Stuart Rachels, *The Elements of Moral Philosophy* (McGraw-Hill, 2007) 176.

7   Alasdair C MacIntyre, *After Virtue: A Study in Moral Theory* (Bloomsbury USA Academic, 3rd ed, 2013) 10–12.

In such a context, moral discourse is unintelligible because there is no shared system of meaning that can be used to reconcile or adjudicate over moral differences – hence 'compassion' can be used with equal public weight to describe VAD by those who are in favour of it, and to sharply critique it by those who are opposed to it. In seeking to understand the narrative according to which VAD is seen as an expression of compassion, I therefore aim to provide a more robust framework for assessing the legitimacy of this claim. As I will show in the article, legislation for VAD makes sense as an expression of compassion only within the narrative of neoliberalism, especially in its manifestations in healthcare.

The article's analysis proceeds in three parts. First, it uses two tangential examples and two virtues other than compassion to illustrate how the claim to virtue rests on particular narratives: the case of a solider on a battlefield contrasted with a pacifist protester inasmuch as this refers to the virtue of courage, and the case of a Qantas flight that was delayed on account of missing pyjamas inasmuch as this refers to the virtue of justice. This allows for a deeper appreciation of the three aspects of MacIntyre's critique noted above, and their implications.

Second, it develops an understanding of neoliberalism, including with an analysis of several ideas related to health and healthcare that are common within the neoliberal narrative. These can be summarised in an aversion to any form of economic or healthcare dependency, and a self-understanding of those who are unwell that prioritises self-governance and autonomy. In this way, I am using a 'thick' description of neoliberalism, which takes it beyond its thinner configuration as an economic doctrine and links this to a broader sociopolitical framework, which is also experienced by individuals on the level of self-understanding. It then considers what the virtues of courage and justice look like in this framework, before introducing the virtue of compassion and considering how VAD might be an expression of compassion according to a neoliberal narrative. The article then considers data from Oregon, which sheds further light on this point.

Third, the article considers how positioning 'VAD' as compassion according to the neoliberal narrative distracts from other visions of justice and compassion, and provides a number of final observations about the consequences of this.

Current thinking in virtue ethics: The battlefield and the pyjamas that delayed QF94

To begin our illustrations of how virtue is used today, we begin with a consideration of the virtue of courage. Consider the claim that a soldier on the battlefield in war is exercising the virtue of courage in contrast to the claim that a pacifist protesting against the same war is exercising the virtue of courage.[8] Notwithstanding a retreat into some form of relativism or subjectivism, it is impossible to adjudicate on which of these is defensibly courage unless we appeal to a more comprehensive narrative, which will necessarily make claims about what the good life is, what justice is and in this particular case whether or not war is justified. On these foundations the worldview will provide a framework for determining what kind of acts are truly virtuous.[9] On this basis, we can note that a strongly pacifist world view would not see the soldier's fighting on the battlefield as courageous (perhaps as foolhardiness), and a world view that sees the given war as entirely justifiable would not see the protester's pacifism as courageous (again, perhaps as foolhardiness or even cowardice). As the Notre Dame scholar Jean Porter argues, it is even possible to imagine such a contrast in the same person: a soldier who has a radical change of world view – perhaps on the basis of an experience of war – and becomes a pacifist.[10]

What is at stake here is not simply a case of the same virtue being exercised in a different context, but rather two different understandings of what constitutes virtue in the first place, founded on different narratives, and the different interests that these seek after and ultimately serve. The extreme pacifist narrative would see the good life as bound up with a commitment to nonviolence, and on that basis judge that fighting on the battlefield is not an expression of virtue. Instead, it would see the stable and consistent opposition of war as courageous. The pro-war position might see a soldier on the battlefield as the paradigmatic case of

---

8   Jean Porter, *Nature as Reason: A Thomistic Theory of the Natural Law* (William B. Eerdmans Publishing Company, 2005) 227–8.

9   Here my use of the word 'world view' is a replacement for MacIntyre's use of the words 'narrative' and 'story'. See for example MacIntyre (n 7) 250–2.

10   Porter (n 8) 227–8. Of course, it is possible to imagine a case in which someone says 'I admire the soldier's courage, but I do not agree with the soldier's cause'. However, most coherent theories of virtue claim that the virtues are held together as a comprehensive whole. Hence courage is only defensibly courage when it is set in the context of justice, and so on.

the virtue of courage, founding itself on a narrative that sees conflict as inevitable, holds up the capacity to fight as part and parcel of the good life, and judges the moral merits of individuals on this basis. This helps to demonstrate a key aspect of MacIntyre's critique of contemporary moral discourse: that often our moral claims rest on incommensurable visions of what constitutes the good life, and without a capacity to deal with the truth or falsity of these narratives we are doomed to an ultimately hopeless form of moral debate.[11]

In a peculiar way, this leads us to QF94 and the virtue of justice. In August, 2012, the *Herald Sun* reported on an incident at Los Angeles airport that delayed a Qantas A380 bound for Melbourne.[12] Passengers in first and business class on Qantas long-haul flights are provided with pyjamas as part of the airline's premium package. In this case, the aircraft did not have XL-sized first-class pyjamas available for two of its first-class passengers. Declining the offer of the business-class alternative, the passengers demanded to be let off the plane. According to the *Sun*'s article, one of the passengers demanded of the crew 'Make sure you tell everyone why we're so late: they didn't have pyjamas for us'. The Captain obliged, announcing to the rest of the plane's passengers, 'Just to inform you all, the reason we've had the delay is because two of our first-class passengers refused to fly on this plane as there was no extra large pyjamas on board for them'. As the story was told, the cabin erupted into laughter, though as one passenger observed it was clear that the pyjama-less pair expected common outrage.

Though a strange case, we can note a similar feature here to that which we saw in the context of the virtue of courage above, this time in relation to the virtue of justice. It is the Code of Justinian (sixth century CE) that gives us the most common definition of justice, that 'each person be given what is due to them'.[13] In the case of the first-class pyjamas, that which was considered 'due' to each person was different when read through the lens of different classes. What was seen as a matter of just deserts in first class was an object of laughter across the rest of the plane. We can assume that for others what was considered 'due' was a safe, comfortable and timely trip to

---

11   See MacIntyre (n 7) 2–3.

12   Lachlan Hastings and Huda Hayek, 'Qantas Flight Delayed After Passengers Go Bananas for Pyjamas', *Herald Sun* (online, 10 August 2012) <https://www.heraldsun.com.au/news/national/qantas-passengers-refuse-to-fly-from-la-to-melbourne-because-there-were-no-xl-sized-first-class-pyjamas/news-story/d68291bcd9eac75d1d560bf620c6cdeb>.

13   Refer to Caesar Flavius Justinian, *The Institutes of Justinian*, tr JB Moyle (Project Gutenberg, 2009) <https://www.gutenberg.org/files/5983/5983-h/5983-h.htm> Book I of Persons, no I.1.

Melbourne, with or without branded pyjamas. The incommensurability of the concepts of justice at play here rests not only at a theoretical level, but also importantly at the social and practical level too: responding to the world view of the first-class passengers – or at least admitting defeat in the face of it – led to the delay of the flight for everyone else. This is no mere game of concepts: whichever vision of justice is given the trump card in a particular context will have implications for those who do not subscribe to it, and may also – at the level of action – overcome or interrupt what they consider as 'due' to them.[14]

There is a further consideration here that warrants attention. Referring back to MacIntyre's analysis above, we can note the way in which each concept of justice is universalised by those who hold it, despite the incommensurable assumptions that sit underneath. In their request for the rest of the plane to be informed of the incident with the pyjamas, the first-class passengers revealed an expectation that others on the flight would be similarly outraged that they did not receive what they considered as their due. In the response of collective laughter, the rest of the plane demonstrated that they were operating out of a different understanding altogether. Both consider their standpoint as correct, despite the unacknowledged assumptions that rest behind them. For the first-class passengers, these assumptions included the idea that what they considered their 'due' was more important than the on-time departure of the flight. Many would argue that the rest of the plane was correct in its critique of this response, but that position itself rests on assumptions about which and whose priorities take precedence over others, and when.

These two examples lead us to a point at which we can now ask more nuanced and enlightening questions about the claim that the legislation of VAD is an act of the compassionate state. First, they invite a deeper consideration of the world view out of which specific moral claims arise, and hence the question we began with: according to what world view is 'VAD' an expression of the virtue of compassion? Second, they challenge us to critique the universalising use of moral concepts in the service of particular ends through the observation that such language can obscure the fact that those ends themselves serve the interests of particular groups and in so doing might interrupt or overcome the just deserts of others, as was the case on QF94.

---

14   It is hard to imagine the airline acquiescing to the delay on account of economy passengers complaining that an in-flight amenity kit was not available, for example.

Courage, justice and compassion according to neoliberalism

In answer to the first question, I argue that the world view out of which legislation for VAD can be considered compassionate is neoliberalism. Loïc Wacquant proposes that, among other features, neoliberalism includes 'the reassertion of the prerogatives of capital and the promotion of the market-place' as well as holding up the cultural trope of individual responsibility as the centre of personhood.[15] Together, these aspects form the dominant narrative of individuals in neoliberal societies, who have internalised a framework that prioritises the construction of the individual self, largely in entrepreneurial terms and set aside from connections to tradition, history and community. Such a narrative casts suspicion on any form of dependency on others.[16]

Following this, the dominant ethical demand of neoliberalism is to create one's own story and to 'provide for one's self', which has both economic and health implications.[17] As Peacock et al note, the neoliberal narrative coheres

> around a valuing of the self-regulating, self-surveillant and autonomous self, where those who are not equal to this task face both strain and fears that others will judge them as insufficiently responsible.[18]

The 'neo' in neoliberalism takes what is laudable from liberalism (an emphasis on individual rights and autonomy for all people, balanced against the needs of the common good), and totalises the emphasis on autonomy without clear reference to the common good. In so doing, it tends to serve those who have the means to act autonomously, and so privileges those who have a certain degree of economic power, normally associated with higher socio-economic status. In so doing, it aligns neatly with various forms of free market capitalism.

---

15 Loïc Wacquant, 'Crafting the Neoliberal State: Workfare, Prisonfare, and Social Insecurity' (2010) 25(2) *Sociological Forum* 197, 213–14.
16 Wacquant (n 15) 213.
17 Marian Peacock, Paul Bissell and Jenny Owen, 'Dependency Denied: Health Inequalities in the Neo-Liberal Era' (2014) 118 *Social Science & Medicine* 173.
18 Peacock, Bissell and Owen (n 17) 175.

Such a narrative is reflected in the context of neoliberal policy frameworks and the way in which they address social problems. Deirdre Howard-Wagner analyses this point in regard to Australian federal policy on Indigenous disadvantage, in which neoliberal solutions address 'disadvantage through an individualistic framework of individual rights – the rights to a job, an education and housing' with the ultimate target as 'individual agency'.[19] In its crudest form, this position is reflected in then prime minister Tony Abbott's recommendations for addressing Indigenous disadvantage as 'getting an education' and 'getting a job'.[20]

This framework also leads to certain assumptions in the context of health, wherein the health of those operating out of a neoliberal narrative is predominantly seen as an individual (rather than communal) responsibility. In their fascinating study on attitudes to health among disadvantaged people in neoliberal societies, Peacock et al uncovered a common set of assumptions and beliefs, which they refer to as 'no legitimate dependency'. Collectively, they describe these as:

> multi-stranded narratives in which almost everything about participants' lives were deemed to be the responsibility of the individual, who alone should be able to manage whatever was happening to them and where turning to others, or even acknowledging the need for help, was seen as weak and unacceptable. Participants described being alone with this responsibility (although in some circumstances it might be acceptable to turn to partners, but with a fear that they might not deliver and that ultimately, you would still be on your own).[21]

Furthermore:

> attempts to make sense of this experience of responsibility using anything other than an individualistic frame of reference was cited as evidence of a wish to shirk one's responsibilities and duties. In other words, taking a socially contextualised perspective was interpreted as a self-serving attempt to rationalise or justify either failure or personal inadequacy.[22]

---

19   Deidre Howard-Wagner, 'Governance of Indigenous Policy in the Neo-Liberal Age: Indigenous Disadvantage and the Intersecting of Paternalism and Neo-Liberalism as a Racial Project' (2018) 41(7) *Ethnic and Racial Studies* 1332, 1340.

20   Howard-Wagner (n 19) 1340.

21   Peacock, Bissell and Owen (n 17) 176.

22   Peacock, Bissell and Owen (n 17) 176.

4. THE COMPASSIONATE STATE?

With these aspects of the neoliberal narrative in mind, we can consider how they relate to expressions of virtue along the lines that we explored above. First, courage, according to a neoliberal narrative, is predominantly concerned with the courage to undertake the human project as an individual. The paradigm of neoliberal courage is the person who 'goes it alone', creates their own self-identity against the expectations of others and is their own person. This is illustrated in contradistinction through the quotes above, which show what the lack of courage – cowardice – looks like according to a neoliberal framework. Moral heroes, on the neoliberal view, are those who exemplify self-mastery and self-sufficiency, able to craft their own path without undue reliance on those around them. 'Be yourself' is the relevant, popular, trope. The condition of possibility for realising this is often aligned with the opportunities afforded by one's socio-economic status. It is much more straightforward for Bill Gates to be considered a neoliberal hero than it is for someone living in poverty.

As it relates to the virtue of justice, what is due in the context of neoliberalism is predominantly what can extend on the interests of the self-regulated, self-surveillant and autonomous self, held closely alongside a concept of just deserts that is indistinguishable from what is earned or bought. The first-class passengers on QF94 are an example of a neoliberal concept of justice *par excellence*. What is considered an offence against justice in this framework is therefore anything that might moderate autonomy or self-regulation, or which limits access to what can be bought. What is due to me is my self-mastery, autonomy and that which I have earned. Incidentally, it is also in this context that it makes sense to refer to those receiving care in the health or aged care systems as 'consumers', implying an economic mobility to be able to choose what health services one will purchase, and when. The inevitable correlate of this is that doctors, nurses and hospitals function like supermarkets – there to deliver what the consumer wants, when they want it. The relevant trope here is something along the lines of 'I earned my place here: no-one has a right to tell me what to do with my life'.

As Aquinas noted, following Aristotle and Cicero, the virtues are inherently connected, and so now is an appropriate time to extend on this analysis and introduce the virtue of compassion.[23] This virtue takes its name from

---

23   Thomas Aquinas provides a synthesis of this tradition of thinking, see *The Summa Theologiae of St. Thomas Aquinas*, tr Fathers of the English Dominican Province (New Advent, 2nd rev ed, 2008) Part I-II, Question 65.

two Latin words, meaning to 'suffer with'. In its traditional form, it has been a cornerstone of the Jewish and Christian ethical traditions, which have held it up as the highest virtue: to enter into suffering with others and respond to them is an ultimate expression of what it means to be human. The paradigmatic case of compassion in the Christian tradition is found in the story of the Good Samaritan, whose stomach turns at the sight of another person beaten and left for dead, and at personal cost and with an enduring commitment seeks to respond to him.[24]

As we have seen, moral terms are used now in a manner absent from their original foundations, and hence it is important to note that – just as with courage and justice – compassion has a different 'face' in a neoliberal context. That face refers it to the dominant concerns of neoliberalism, which, as noted above, extend on the interests of the self-regulated, self-surveillant and autonomous self, held closely alongside a concept of just deserts that align with what can be earned and bought. Suffering in this context reflects the concerns of neoliberalism, which means that suffering predominantly relates to the loss of capacity in regards to self-regulation, self-surveillance and autonomy, and the capacity to be a productive citizen and thereby to earn and buy what is due. To be compassionate in this context is to suffer with the suffering that neoliberalism prescribes, and to offer solutions to that suffering that equally align with neoliberal concerns.[25] Abbott's proposals to Australia's Indigenous people make sense as an expression of 'compassion' in this context, and so too do the words often heard in today's palliative care wards 'grandma can no longer feed or go to the toilet herself – she has lost her dignity'. Both are perfectly configured, neoliberal positions.

VAD: Compassion according to a neoliberal framework

It is here that we can see how VAD makes sense as an act of compassion within a neoliberal framework. Importantly, this has little to do with a major feature of the public and political advocacy related to VAD, namely that it is necessary because of grave physical suffering. While

---

24   See Luke 10:25–37.
25   Cf Abbott's response to Indigenous disadvantage above, which could be claimed as 'compassionate' on the neoliberal narrative precisely because it seeks to deliver what neoliberalism prescribes.

cases of such suffering do exist, they are relatively rare and most experts agree that the majority can be responded to with existing (not to mention future) techniques in the discipline of palliative care. However, such techniques cannot necessarily restore what is central to the neoliberal narrative. According to this view, physical suffering is less a concern than the suffering incurred by the dependency that fragility and illness entails, and its consequent loss of autonomy, self-regulation and self-surveillance. To be compassionate according to the neoliberal narrative is to suffer with these particular concerns. The commitment following such suffering with is to open up hitherto unavailable options for the exercise of autonomy in order to reinstate what has been lost, even to the extent of that ultimate expression of individual choice: to end one's life.

This position is not mere speculation. In jurisdictions in which VAD or its equivalents have been legislated, by far the dominant reasons for it being sought have to do with loss of autonomy, loss of dignity (which is left undefined in the data, though would be understood according to the dominant narrative), loss of capacity to engage in activities considered worthwhile, and becoming a burden on others. In Oregon, which has had such legislation for 20 years and has seen 1,275 individuals die through the regime, 'inadequate pain control *or* concern about it' is sixth on the list of end-of-life concerns cited by individuals who accessed VAD, with 25.8 per cent noting this as a concern in comparison to 90.9 per cent noting 'losing autonomy'.[26] These same trends have been reflected in Victoria, including in the recent release of the state's third Voluntary Assisted Dying Review Board report, which, while not providing statistical data, noted the same dominant reasons as Oregon for accessing VAD (loss of autonomy, loss of capacity to engage in activities considered worthwhile, and loss of dignity). Grave physical suffering as a reason for accessing VAD is not mentioned in the report.[27]

This same narrative is reflected in an article written by members of the Ministerial Advisory Panel, which was established to consult on, and ultimately produce the framework for, the Victorian VAD legislation. The article has the express purpose of assisting other jurisdictions

26 These categories are not mutually exclusive. See Oregon Health Authority Public Health Division, *Oregon Death with Dignity Act 2017 Data Summary* (Report, 9 February 2018) <https://www.oregon.gov/oha/PH/PROVIDERPARTNERRESOURCES/EVALUATIONRESEARCH/DEATHWITHDIGNITYACT/Documents/year20.pdf>.
27 Voluntary Assisted Dying Review Board, Safer Care Victoria, *Report of Operations January–June 2020* (Report No 3, 31 August 2020).

who are 'considering similar legislative changes'.[28] That the neoliberal
framework rests behind their considerations is borne out with great clarity
throughout the document. The authors begin by noting the significance
for the VAD movement of 'the rise of the value of individualism and
personal autonomy'.[29] This is consistent throughout: in an article of less
than four thousand words, derivatives of 'autonomy', 'individual' and
'choice' appear nearly 40 times, and the word 'pain' does not appear once.
Consistent with the analysis above, the neoliberal framework is assumed
here rather than stated, and so deeper questions about the common
good and whose interests are served by the legislation, not to mention its
neoliberal underpinning, are avoided.

Those questions are helped by further consideration of the data set from
Oregon noted earlier. This is updated yearly, and is readily available on
the Oregon Health Authority's website. Here I note particularly racial
and socio-economic factors (the latter is indicated in this data set through
educational achievement, which can be mapped to socio-economic status
in Oregon). These factors relate to a further question within the article:
namely, if neoliberalism is the framework according to which the virtue
of compassion is being claimed, which group in society's interests does it
serve? This takes us beyond that simplistic notion introduced earlier that
the claim of a virtue indicates an automatic universality, and invites us
into a much deeper analysis.

First, racial demographics in Oregon. Of the 1,275 people who have
'died from ingesting a lethal medication as of January 19, 2018' since the
legislation was enacted, 1,223 were white. That's 95.92 per cent. Across
the 20 years, of other races who sought and out VAD and died as a result
of it, one was African American (0.08 per cent), two were American
Indians (0.16 per cent), 19 were Asian (1.49 per cent), one was a Pacific
Islander (0.08 per cent), 15 were Hispanic (1.18 per cent), and those
classed as two or more races, other or unknown make up the remaining
14 (1.1 per cent).

---

28 Margaret M O'Connor et al, 'Documenting the Process of Developing the Victorian Voluntary
Assisted Dying Legislation' (2018) 42(6) *Australian Health Review* 621.
29 Ibid.

While these statistics alone suggest that the legislation is primarily used by those who are white, it is important to consider them against demographic data from Oregon itself (if the trends match the demographic differences in the population, then the disparity is not significant but instead is representative of the population). One comparison suffices for this analysis – in Oregon, whites account for 87.1 per cent of the population and African Americans account for 2.2 per cent of the population. Measured against the trends in accessing physician-assisted suicide, this means that on balance white people are 30.9 times more likely to access this option at the end of their lives compared to the African American population.

Next, education demographics. Of the 1,275 people who have 'died from ingesting a lethal medication as of January 19, 2018', 46.5 per cent had a bachelor's degree or higher, 26 per cent had some college education, 22 per cent were high school graduates and 5.5 per cent had less than high school education. In comparison with the population of Oregon, 31.4 per cent have a bachelor's degree or higher, meaning that those at the top tier of educational achievements are 2.7 times more likely to access VAD than those with less than a high school education. As noted above, such educational demographics map clearly to socio-economic status in Oregon.

Similar trends in the area of race exist in Washington State[30] and California,[31] in which VAD is legal and reports are publicly available. With some subtle differences, they also show similar trends in the area of class, and in gender, which sees that in all states bar California men are slightly more likely to access the legislation than women. Montana and Vermont do not publish their data, and the remaining jurisdictions, in which similar legislation exists – Colorado, the District of Columbia and Hawaii – are too recent for data to be available. Thus far, the reports provided by the Victorian VAD Review Board do not include sufficient data to undertake a similar analysis of demographic details of those accessing the regime.

---

30   Washington State Department of Health, *Washington State Death With Dignity Act Report* (Report, March 2018) <https://www.doh.wa.gov/Portals/1/Documents/Pubs/422-109-DeathWith DignityAct2017.pdf>.
31   California Department of Public Health, *California End of Life Option Act 2016 Data Report* (Annual Report, June 2017) <https://www.cdph.ca.gov/Programs/CHSI/CDPH%20Document%20 Library/CDPH%20End%20of%20Life%20Option%20Act%20Report.pdf>.

First class or economy? Whose interests are being served through the VAD legislation? And what might a contrast between them teach us?

I have already noted that the virtues are necessarily connected to one another. In any Aristotelian or Thomistic account of the virtues, all of the virtues are considered in relation to the virtue of justice. Hence, each claim to virtue must be considered against the framework that requires that each be given their due. A critical question of any claim to virtue is therefore whether it is being expressed in such a way that serves the good of all (as a vision of justice should) or only the interests of some (which we can expect of a virtue claimed on behalf of a highly specific narrative, such as neoliberalism). Autonomy is a laudable goal, but as we have seen under neoliberalism it is the autonomy of those higher on the socio-economic ladder that is served. This contradicts the virtue of justice when it is concerned with the good of all. To make a link back to our earlier example of the virtue of justice, we can now consider whether the link between VAD and compassion is more like the claims of the first-class passengers on QF94 or the claims of those spread throughout the rest of the plane. It seems clear, based on this analysis, that it is more like the former. This is a 'first-class' vision of compassion, though it is curious – and perhaps the result of the pervasiveness of neoliberal ideology in our context – that the claim to compassion gathered such wide-reaching public support in Victoria, including among groups that are normally suspicious of neoliberal agendas, and that it was led by a Labor government. That fact requires another paper for another time.

We saw in the case of QF94 that placing different visions of virtue alongside one another helped to illustrate some of the deeper concerns at play in that situation, including whose interests were being served as a priority. Here I would like to briefly place the neoliberal narrative alongside the longstanding ethic of medicine, held together across that which is broadly considered the 'Hippocratic' tradition of medicine and also the Judeo-Christian conception of healthcare and its expressions through compassion. As they pertain to end-of-life care, both of these traditions express care in the following commitments: to always comfort and accompany, to never abandon, to offer fully sufficient pain relief, even if that has the effect of hastening the end of a person's life, and to honour requests to withdraw or withhold treatments that a person wishes to withdraw or withhold, or which have become overly burdensome. In this way, both of these traditions have developed an ethic of respecting autonomy but hold this alongside a commitment to several norms that are at the heart of healthcare practice: that one should never intentionally kill, nor assist a person to kill themselves. As examples, this is the current position of the World Health Organization, and the same is held by the official teaching of the Catholic Church. Importantly, both traditions of healthcare see access to this kind of care as a right, which aligns with the current teaching of the United Nations. On both of these views, what is due to every person – and what the 'compassionate state' looks like – is the state that provides such care for all of its citizens.

We saw in the context of QF94 that the privileging of the first-class vision of justice led to a small, but significant, inconvenience to the passengers who had different considerations of justice. There are more serious implications for the privileging of one narrative in the case of VAD. Before the marathon debate regarding VAD in 2017, Palliative Care Victoria noted that of the 40,000 Victorians who die every year a full 10,000 do not have access to the universally agreed upon methods of compassionate care. They estimated that it would cost a minimum of $65 million a year to address this gap.[32]

In the lead-up to that same debate, the Andrews Government announced an extra $62 million investment in such care spread across five years, so less than 20 per cent of what was needed.[33] In the election campaign in 2018 an additional one-off $23.4 million was added to this amount, which still falls short at only 27 per cent of what was needed. In contrast to this amount, $6.35 million was announced for the implementation of VAD, which the government believes would be accessed by around 150 people a year (a number that was premised on Oregon's data).[34]. The recurring costs of VAD are unknown, and most who have been close to the implementation agree that it has – to date – cost the government far more than what was committed. This of course does not include the

---

32   'New Victorian Palliative Care Funding Announcements are Disappointing and Inadequate', *Palliative Care Victoria* (Blog Post, 15 November 2017) <https://www.pallcarevic.asn.au/new-victorian-palliative-care-funding-announcements-disappointing-inadequate/>.

33   Daniel Andrews, 'Palliative Care Boost to Support Terminally Ill Victorians', *Premier of Victoria, The Hon Daniel Andrews* (Media Release, 16 November 2017) <https://www.premier.vic.gov.au/palliative-care-boost-to-support-terminally-ill-victorians>.

34   Stephanie Anderson, 'Euthanasia in Victoria: How the State's Assisted Dying Laws will Work', *ABC News* (online, 22 November 2017) <https://www.abc.net.au/news/2017-11-22/euthanasia-in-victoria-how-assisted-dying-laws-will-work/9115210>.

incidental costs to healthcare organisations who are attempting to respond to the regime, whether or not they are participating. And then there are the significant establishment costs and resources that were committed to the passing of the legislation, which are highlighted as a matter of pride in the Ministerial Advisory Panel's article cited earlier.[35] This casts in clear light whose interests are being served, and what 'compassion' according to the neoliberal narrative costs. Many palliative care physicians yearn for the moment in history wherein their service is given this much attention and resourcing.

Aside from the obvious contrast with the Hippocratic and Judeo-Christian traditions of care, it is also relevant to consider how a different political narrative sees this issue, so to avoid any accusation that I am simply falling into 'right' vs 'left' or 'religious' vs 'secular' politics. To close, therefore, I refer to the telling case of Portugal in May 2018, at which time their parliament voted against the legalisation of euthanasia. This caught some by surprise, given the general direction of cultural change in Portugal, which has seen a succession of left-leaning governments and the waning influence of the Catholic Church.[36] In a BBC report in the lead-up to the vote, the euthanasia debate was framed as pitting 'left-leaning parties in parliament against the Catholic Church and traditional social order'. The record of the vote is far more interesting: the vote against was carried by the Portuguese Communist Party (PCP), a work of the left that explicitly founds itself in Marxist theory, and so a tradition that is diametrically distinct from neoliberalism.[37] António Filipe of the PCP put to the Assembly of the Republic that:

> Faced with the problems of human suffering, illness, disability or incapacity, the solution is not to remove responsibility from society by promoting the early death of people in these circumstances, but to promote social progress in order to ensure conditions for a decent life.[38]

---

35   O'Connor et al (n 28).

36   Associated Press, 'Portugal Considers Allowing Euthanasia and Assisted Suicide', *Los Angeles Times* (online, 28 May 2018) <http://www.latimes.com/world/la-fg-portugal-assisted-suicide-20180528-story.html>.

37   'A Dignidade Da Vida Não Se Assegura Com a Consagração Legal Do Direito à Antecipação Da Morte [The Dignity of Life Is Not Guaranteed by the Legal Consecration of the Right to Anticipate Death]', *Partido Comunista Português* (Web Page, 29 May 2018) <https://www.pcp.pt/dignidade-da-vida-nao-se-assegura-com-consagracao-legal-do-direito-antecipacao-da-morte>; On the PCP's statutes, see: 'Estatutos Do PCP [PCP Statutes]', *Partido Comunista Português* (Web Page) <https://www.pcp.pt/estatutos-do-pcp>.

38   'A Dignidade Da Vida' (n 37).

Conclusion

In this article, I have undertaken an analysis of the claim that the state that legalises 'voluntary assisted dying' is the compassionate state. I have drawn on Alasdair MacIntyre's observations regarding the separation of moral language from the narratives that make sense of it in order to uncover the narrative framework according to which it makes sense to refer to VAD as an expression of compassion. I have argued that this makes most sense in the context of neoliberalism, and have illustrated the implications for this in terms of whose preferences are served through the VAD legislation. That neoliberalism predominantly serves the preferences of the socially privileged is borne out in discussions of its impact in healthcare, and is also reflected in the data related to who accesses VAD in Oregon. Placing this framework in contrast to different narratives, including the Hippocratic and Judeo-Christian ethics of compassion, reveals the stark contrast here, and the substantial concerns that arise when neoliberalism is used to claim that VAD is compassionate. As many laughed with the economy passengers in the story of QF94, these observations should cause any of us who object to the neoliberal narrative and its competency in matters of healthcare to pause and think before accepting the claim that Victoria is now 'the compassionate state'.

Bibliography

A Articles/books/reports

Aquinas, Thomas, *The Summa Theologiae of St. Thomas Aquinas*, tr Fathers of the English Dominican Province (New Advent, 2nd rev ed, 2008)

California Department of Public Health, *California End of Life Option Act 2016 Data Report* (Annual Report, June 2017) <https://www.cdph.ca.gov/Programs/CHSI/CDPH%20Document%20Library/CDPH%20End%20of%20Life%20Option%20Act%20Report.pdf>

Dickens, Bernard M, Joseph M Boyle and Linda Ganzini, 'Euthanasia and Assisted Suicide' in Peter A Singer and AM Viens (eds), *The Cambridge Textbook of Bioethics* (Cambridge University Press, 2008) 72 doi.org/10.1017/CBO9780511545566.013

Howard-Wagner, Deirdre, 'Governance of Indigenous Policy in the Neo-Liberal Age: Indigenous Disadvantage and the Intersecting of Paternalism and Neo-Liberalism as a Racial Project' (2018) 41(7) *Ethnic and Racial Studies* 1332 doi.org/10.1080/01419870.2017.1287415

Justinian, Caesar Flavius, *The Institutes of Justinian*, tr JB Moyle (Project Gutenberg, 2009) <https://www.gutenberg.org/files/5983/5983-h/5983-h.htm>

MacIntyre, Alasdair C, *After Virtue: A Study in Moral Theory* (Bloomsbury USA Academic, 3rd ed, 2013)

O'Connor, Margaret M et al, 'Documenting the Process of Developing the Victorian Voluntary Assisted Dying Legislation' (2018) 42(6) *Australian Health Review* 621 doi.org/10.1071/AH18172

Oregon Health Authority Public Health Division, *Oregon Death with Dignity Act 2017 Data Summary* (Report, 9 February 2018) <https://www.oregon.gov/oha/PH/PROVIDERPARTNERRESOURCES/EVALUATIONRESEARCH/DEATHWITHDIGNITYACT/Documents/year20.pdf>

Peacock, Marian, Paul Bissell and Jenny Owen, 'Dependency Denied: Health Inequalities in the Neo-Liberal Era' (2014) 118 *Social Science & Medicine* 173 doi.org/10.1016/j.socscimed.2014.08.006

Porter, Jean, *Nature as Reason: A Thomistic Theory of the Natural Law* (William B. Eerdmans Publishing Company, 2005)

Rachels, James and Stuart Rachels, *The Elements of Moral Philosophy* (McGraw-Hill, 5th ed, 2006)

Voluntary Assisted Dying Review Board, Safer Care Victoria, *Report of Operations January–June 2020* (Report No 3, 31 August 2020)

Wacquant, Loïc, 'Crafting the Neoliberal State: Workfare, Prisonfare, and Social Insecurity' (2010) 25(2) *Sociological Forum* 197 doi.org/10.1111/j.1573-7861.2010.01173.x

Washington State Department of Health, *Washington State Death With Dignity Act Report* (Report, March 2018) <https://www.doh.wa.gov/Portals/1/Documents/Pubs/422-109-DeathWithDignityAct2017.pdf>

B Legislation

Voluntary Assisted Dying Act 2017 (Vic)

C Other

'A Dignidade Da Vida Não Se Assegura Com a Consagração Legal Do Direito à Antecipação Da Morte [The Dignity of Life Is Not Guaranteed by the Legal Consecration of the Right to Anticipate Death]', *Partido Comunista Português* (Web Page, 29 May 2018) <https://www.pcp.pt/dignidade-da-vida-nao-se-assegura-com-consagracao-legal-do-direito-antecipacao-da-morte>

Anderson, Stephanie, 'Euthanasia in Victoria: How the State's Assisted Dying Laws Will Work', *ABC News* (online, 22 November 2017) <https://www.abc.net.au/news/2017-11-22/euthanasia-in-victoria-how-assisted-dying-laws-will-work/9115210>

Andrews, Daniel, 'Palliative Care Boost To Support Terminally Ill Victorians', *Premier of Victoria, The Hon Daniel Andrews* (Media Release, 16 November 2017) <https://www.premier.vic.gov.au/palliative-care-boost-support-terminally-ill-victorians>

Edwards, Jean, 'Euthanasia: Victoria Becomes the First Australian State to Legalise Voluntary Assisted Dying', *ABC News* (online, 29 November 2017) <https://www.abc.net.au/news/2017-11-29/euthanasia-passes-parliament-in-victoria/9205472>

'Estatutos Do PCP [PCP Statutes]', *Partido Comunista Português* (Web Page) <https://www.pcp.pt/estatutos-do-pcp>

Fleming, Daniel, 'The Compassionate State? Voluntary Assisted Dying, Neoliberalism and the Problem of Virtue without an Anchor', *ABC Religion & Ethics* (Opinion, 25 March 2019) <https://www.abc.net.au/religion/compassionate-state-voluntary-assisted-dying-neoliberalism-and/10937504>

Hastings, Lachlan and Huda Hayek, 'Qantas Flight Delayed after Passengers Go Bananas over Pyjamas', *Herald Sun* (online, 10 August 2012) <https://www.heraldsun.com.au/news/national/qantas-passengers-refuse-to-fly-from-la-to-melbourne-because-there-were-no-xl-sized-first-class-pyjamas/news-story/d68291bcd9eac75d1d560bf620c6cdeb>

@JillHennessyMP (Twitter, 29 November 2017, 12:09PM AEST) <https://twitter.com/jillhennessymp/status/935676976064487424?lang=en>

'New Victorian Palliative Care Funding Announcements Are Disappointing and Inadequate', *Palliative Care Victoria* (Web Page, 15 November 2017) <https://www.pallcarevic.asn.au/new-victorian-palliative-care-funding-announcements-disappointing-inadequate/>

'Portugal Considers Allowing Euthanasia and Assisted Suicide', *Los Angeles Times* (online, 28 May 2018) <https://www.latimes.com/world/la-fg-portugal-assisted-suicide-20180528-story.html>

5

The Neoliberal Rationality of Voluntary Assisted Dying

Marc Trabsky

In the first volume of *The History of Sexuality*, Michel Foucault traces a shift in the eighteenth century from the sovereign's 'right to decide life and death' towards a 'power of life and death'.[1] The latter was more concerned with techniques for managing life, maximising its efficacy and exploiting its vitality, evinced by a governmental preoccupation with monitoring fluctuations in birth and death rates. Foucault calls this new relation of power–knowledge 'biopower', which consisted of an *anatomo-politics* of the body and a *bio-politics* of the population.[2] The regulation of death, including its control by the state and a range of medical, legal and financial institutions, also gave rise to a new arrangement of *thanato-politics*, or the government of death.[3] For Foucault, government does not simply refer to an institution, but to a historical practice that had as its ultimate aim the care of a population. In the nineteenth century, the art of governing developed a range of techniques for managing populations of the dying.[4]

---

1   Michel Foucault, *The History of Sexuality, Volume 1: The Will to Knowledge*, tr Robert Hurley (Penguin Books, 1998) 136.
2   Ibid 139.
3   Michel Foucault, 'The Political Technology of Individuals' in Luther H Martin, Huck Gutman and Patrick H Hutton (eds), *Technologies of the Self: A Seminar with Michel Foucault* (University of Massachusetts Press, 1st ed, 1988) 160.
4   See further, Marc Trabsky, *Law and the Dead: Technology, Relations and Institutions* (Routledge, 2019), which writes an institutional history of the dead that pays attention to questions of technology, jurisdiction and office. The book emphasises the importance of conceptualising law as a network of institutions, relations and technologies when examining how coroners encountered the dead in the nineteenth and twentieth centuries.

The *Voluntary Assisted Dying Act 2017* (Vic) provides an opportunity to reflect upon the transformations of the government of death in the twenty-first century. In 'The Political Technology of Individuals', Foucault recounts how 'caring' for individual life emerged as 'a duty for the state' in the eighteenth century.[5] In the nineteenth century, the medicalisation of the deathbed framed 'care for the dying' as an object of state governance. 'The medical hastening of death', Shai Lavi writes, 'became a last resort to the problem of dying, a limited hope of mastery in the face of a hopeless condition.'[6] This chapter conceives of 'voluntary assisted dying' as a legal technology, that is, not simply a *political* or *medical* technology, but a jurisdictional device that cultivates legal relations between, and holds together, the living, the dying and the state. It describes the legislative framework that authorises voluntary assisted dying as part of a repertoire of governmental practices that tether the dying to law in the twenty-first century. The chapter thus invites readers to approach law in terms of the materiality of its institutions, the technologies that congeal around institutional practices and the performances of different roles that sustain the vitality of legal institutions.

When examining the institutional practices of caring for the dying, the concept of technology should not be limited to lethal medication or life-supporting machinery that sustain life or hasten death. The term finds its etymological roots in the Ancient Greek word for technique (*technê*), which denotes a skill, art or craft. *Technê* was conceptualised by Aristotle as 'craft-knowledge', or rather '"productive knowledge", [which] bears upon the domain of what is mutable, in the process of becoming, and comes to be'.[7] If technology is a tool or instrument that is capable of constructing meaning, then in managing populations of the dying, it includes the provision of legal advice and the application of statutory interpretation, operational manuals and guidance notes, record-keeping and form-filling, and an array of bureaucratic procedures for determining whether an individual can lawfully self-administer or access medical assistance for hastening their death. The 'Easy Booklet' released by the Victorian Department of Health and Human Services in 2018 to communicate to a pluralised audience the complexity of the legislative

---

5   Foucault (n 4) 147.

6   Shai Lavi, 'How Dying Became a "Life Crisis"' (2008) 137(1) *Dædalus* 57, 64.

7   Wolfgang Schadewaldt, 'The Greek Concepts of "Nature" and "Technique"' in Robert C Scharff and Val Pusek (eds), *Philosophy of Technology: The Technological Condition: An Anthology* (John Wiley & Sons, Inc, 2nd ed, 2014).

framework of voluntary assisted dying is not only a legal technology in itself, but consists of a number of visual and textual signs and devices for attaching the dying to the institutional life of law.

In *Jurisdiction*, Shaunnagh Dorsett and Shaun McVeigh consider the *Rights of the Terminally Ill Act 1995* (NT), which was nullified by the *Euthanasia Laws Act 1997* (Cth), through the theoretical framework of a jurisdiction of persons. The legislative agenda in the Northern Territory, which temporarily rendered euthanasia lawful in Australia, created a new kind of person, the terminally ill, and a new type of jurisdiction, which lay between conscience and government. The person of the terminally ill arranged, according to Dorsett and McVeigh, new legal relations between the doctor and the patient for caring for the dying, while the creation of the jurisdiction of 'lawful killing', which also reshaped legal relations between the doctor and the state, suspended the operation of the criminal law. The *Rights of the Terminally Ill Act* functioned as a 'state-centred *ars moriendi*'[8], an institutional manual instructing individuals on how to prepare for their medically supervised death:

> What is established through the array of procedural, administrative and classificatory devices is an *ars moriendi* or preparation for death, that can be phrased in terms of an ethic and practice of civility, particularly social honour, suitable for medically assisted suicide and euthanasia. *It can also be phrased in terms of a government project.*[9]

This chapter examines an important aspect of the government project of taking care of the dying that is missing from Dorsett and McVeigh's analysis of the temporary legalisation of euthanasia in the Northern Territory. It considers how the discourse of neoliberal rationality is a vital component of the implementation of a voluntary assisted dying regime in Victoria. The chapter will focus on how legal technologies for taking care of the dying form part of a repertoire of governmental practices that economise relations between the living, the dying and the state. In *Undoing the Demos: Neoliberalism's Stealth Revolution*, Wendy Brown argues that '[w]idespread economization of heretofore noneconomic domains, activities, and subjects, but not necessarily marketization or monetization of them, then is the distinctive signature of neoliberal

---

8   Shaun McVeigh, 'Subjects of Jurisdiction: The Dying, Northern Territory, Australia, 1995–1997' in Shaun McVeigh (ed), *Jurisprudence of Jurisdiction* (Routledge, 2007) 206.
9   Shaunnagh Dorsett and Shaun McVeigh, *Jurisdiction* (Routledge, 2012) 87 (emphasis added).

rationality'.[10] In other words, neoliberalism is no longer simply defined by the accumulation of capital through exchange, cost–benefit analysis or entrepreneurialism, which are nonetheless still valued in the art of government. Rather, its distinctiveness lies in how it extends techniques of economisation – the creation of what Foucault calls '*homo oeconomicus*'[11] – into areas of life that were once thought of as non-economic. This chapter then questions how voluntary assisted dying is economised under neoliberalism, and how the dying themselves participate as 'decision-makers' in an economy of human capital.

The economisation of dying in the twenty-first century has been marginalised in critical responses to the legalisation of voluntary assisted dying around the world. This chapter aims to account for how the figure of *homo oeconomicus* extends into spheres of dying, but also what the effects of neoliberal rationality are for understanding transformations in the government of death in the twenty-first century. I will contend that first, it is important that we recognise how the language of economisation suffuses legal relations between decision-makers, medical practitioners and the state, and second, we need to examine how an economy of human capital, as a model for the conduct of government, but also the government of self, will lead to differential experiences of voluntary assisted dying. The problem of access to the administrative procedures for assisted dying is not separable from the *raison d'être* of neoliberalism, such as the replacement of exchange with competition, the substitution of labour with human capital and the augmentation of socio-economic inequality.

Dying as a matter of choice

In writing a history of euthanasia in the United States, Shai Lavi locates the genesis of discourse about medically hastening death in the nineteenth century, not the twentieth century. The medicalisation of the deathbed, which was shaped by the assumption of a 'duty to provide care in the absence of any possible cure', foreshadowed the doctor's usurpation of the traditional role assumed by the clergy in taking care of the dying.[12]

---

10   Wendy Brown, *Undoing the Demos: Neoliberalism's Stealth Revolution* (Zone Books, 2015) 31–2.
11   Michel Foucault, *The Birth of Biopolitics: Lectures at the Collège de France 1978–1979*, tr Graham Burchell, ed Arnold I Davidson (Picador, 2008).
12   Lavi (n 7) 61. See further, Shai J Lavi, *The Modern Art of Dying: A History of Euthanasia in the United States* (Princeton University Press, 2005).

The patient's cries of moribund suffering were no longer met with prayers, but posed a medical quandary that only a doctor could master. In debates from at least the 1870s, euthanasia emerged as a possible medical 'choice' among a limited range of options for the dying patient. What thus appeared in the late nineteenth century was that the manner of dying could become a matter of choice, liberty and autonomy.

The nineteenth-century ideal of an autonomous patient, who could decide whether to accept or refuse futile medical treatment, prefigured the emergence in the twentieth century of the consumer patient, where alongside the support of a discourse of right, the manner of dying became a commodified object. Medical advancements in the second half of the twentieth century extended life to such an extent that taking care of the dying materialised as an economic problem for medical, legal, financial and governmental institutions.[13] The invention of medication, machinery and surgical methods and treatments, to extend, sustain and support life, undoubtedly resulted in human beings living longer. However, they were only living longer because of the support of costly instruments and apparatuses as well as labour-intensive human resources. The technical mastery sought by doctors and longed for by patients about the time, place and quality of dying became increasingly contingent on the question of economic rationality. This is of course part of a repertoire of institutional practices that have sought to economise many aspects of death, ranging from health, life and funeral insurance, methods of disposal of human remains, management of estates and the transgenerational life of debt, production of mortality statistics and classification tables, public and private systems of registration and certification, delivery of social, psychological and spiritual services for the bereaved, and the provision of medical and legal advice for the dying.[14]

The question of where, when and how one dies is routinely subject to economic analysis in the twenty-first century. Hal Swerissen and Stephen Duckett from the Grattan Institute published a report in 2014 showing that while 60 to 70 per cent of Australians prefer to die in the comfort of their home, in reality 54 per cent die in hospitals and 34 per cent in

---

13   Lavi (n 7) 59.
14   On the link between the compilation of mortality statistics and the emergence of an insurance industry that accumulates profits by financialising the timing of death, see Zohreh Bayatrizi, 'From Fate to Risk: The Quantification of Mortality in Early Modern Statistics' (2008) 25(1) *Theory, Culture and Society* 121.

residential care.[15] The main reason for this discrepancy between 'demand and supply' is a lack of public funding for community-based palliative care services, and as they warn, 'the costs of dying are likely to increase dramatically in the near future as more people die each year'.[16] On the other hand, *The Economist* ranked Australia as offering the second best quality of dying in the world because of its '[h]igh levels of public spending on healthcare services' and '[g]enerous subsidies to reduce the financial burden of palliative care on patients'.[17] The problem here is not the veracity of these statements, but that dying is conceived of in economic terms and the question of choice is calculated on the basis of a cost–benefit analysis. Indeed, the costs of dying, as a matter of choice, are not simply a concern for the consumer patient but for governments themselves, for as *The Economist* extols, investment in community-based palliative care can offer savings in other health-related costs.[18]

Economic analysis on the manner of dying has been discursively framed since the twentieth century around the ideal of the consumer patient who has a choice about where, when and how they may die. The discourse of choice flows throughout debates about end-of-life care, from right-to-die activism to healthcare consumer advocacy, from public forums to parliamentary committees. When the Victorian Government asked the Legislative Council's Legal and Social Issues Committee, which recommended the enactment of a legislative framework for assisted dying in Victoria, to begin an inquiry into end-of-life care, it framed the

---

15 Hal Swerissen and Stephen Duckett, *Dying Well* (Grattan Institute Report No 2014-10, September 2014) 1, 4 <https://grattan.edu.au/wp-content/uploads/2014/09/815-dying-well.pdf>.

16 Ibid 21. See further, Martina Orlovic, Joachim Marti and Elias Mossialos, 'Analysis of End-of-Life Care, Out-of-Pocket Spending, and Place of Death in 16 European Countries and Israel' (2017) 36(7) *Health Affairs* 1201; Mette Asbjoern Neergaard et al, 'What Socio-Economic Factors Determine Place of Death for People with Life-Limiting Illness? A Systematic Review and Appraisal of Methodological Rigour' (2019) 33(8) *Palliative Medicine* 900.

17 The Economist Intelligence Unit, *2015 Quality of Death Index: Ranking Palliative Care Across the World* (Report, 2015) 7.

18 Ibid 8. See also, Stephen Duckett, 'Aligning Policy Objectives and Payment Design in Palliative Care' (2018) 17(42) *BMC Palliative Care* 1. In Canada, this has been taken further by medical practitioners who suggest that annual healthcare spending for patients nearing the end of their lives could be substantially reduced by 'between $34.7 million and $138.8 million' through the implementation of a medical assistance in dying regime. Though they are at pains to explain that they

> are not suggesting medical assistance in dying as a measure to cut costs. At an individual level, neither patients nor physicians should consider costs when making the very personal decision to request, or provide, this intervention.

Aaron J Trachtenberg and Braden Manns, 'Cost Analysis of Medical Assistance in Dying in Canada' (2017) 189(3) *Canadian Medical Association Journal* E101, E101 and E104.

discussion around the question of *choice*.[19] In addition, when the then Minister for Health introduced in parliament the second reading speech of the Voluntary Assisted Dying Bill 2017 (Vic), the language of choice was deployed to frame the government's support of voluntary assisted dying. The Act would provide a highly regulated opportunity for eligible Victorians to choose the time, place and manner of one's death. Not only does this discourse misrecognise how dying is always already relational and contingent,[20] but it underpins the extent to which dying as a matter of choice is governed through economic terms.

In the twenty-first century, neoliberal rationality has tended to redefine the question of choice as a problem of 'user experience' and, to this extent, the consumer patient has morphed into an 'end user' of healthcare. Portable's 2019 report on *The Future of Death & Ageing in Australia* identifies a number of 'pain points' of the 'user experience' of dying and proposes changes to make it more 'user friendly'.[21] The company writes that:

> [e]veryone is an end user and we will likely experience the death and ageing of others before our own. Each and every one of us has an interest in making the experiences more positive and less frustrating.[22]

Portable's solution to this problem is the 'appification' of dying. The company has designed prototype apps for digitally storing advanced care directives, a virtual deck of cards for catalysing end-of-life conversations and social networks for gathering together dying patients, carers and death doulas. The appification of end-of-life care is designed, as Portable notes, to '[p]ut the user in the centre of products and services'.[23]

The substitution of the consumer with the discourse of the user and the appification of dying further extends techniques of economisation into end-of-life care. While Portable's report does not analyse the implementation of voluntary assisted dying in Victoria, in a 2019 blog

---

19   Department of Health and Human Services, Government of Victoria, *Ministerial Advisory Panel on Voluntary Assisted Dying* (Final Report, 31 July 2017).

20   Ari Gandsman, 'Paradox of Choice and the Illusion of Autonomy: The Construction of Ethical Subjects in Right-to-Die Activism' (2018) 42(5) *Death Studies* 329.

21   Portable, *The Future of Death & Ageing in Australia: A Portable R&D Initiative* (Report, 2019) 9 <https://www.portable.com.au/reports/the-future-of-death-and-ageing>.

22   Ibid 10.

23   Ibid 94.

post, it employs the term 'UX', which has become slang for user experience, to discuss the question of access to the administrative procedures of the scheme. Portable opines that

> [i]t may be distasteful to evaluate ... VAD as 'consumer' experiences, but as the Government starts to take a human-centred, or customer-focussed approach to providing services, it's important to critique it. This service is likely going to be accessible mostly to those who can afford to think in terms of 'being consumers'. Those who, in a neoliberal economic sense, can participate, represent themselves in a complex system and have enough mobility to choose how they might like to die.[24]

The blog categorises voluntary assisted dying as a user experience to both identify its in-built 'pain points' (or what the government may call safeguards), but also to critique the neoliberal rationality that conditions the emergence of this discourse. Portable warns against the privatisation of end-of-life care in Australia, and yet when read together with its report on *The Future of Death & Ageing*, the blog reveals an interest in how relations between the living, the dying and the state can be optimised and enhanced in the pursuit of an user-friendly experience of voluntary assisted dying. However, as the next section shows, the language of economisation already permeates the legislated regime for voluntary assisted dying. In other words, it is not surprising that a company such as Portable, which specialises in 'human-centred' or 'user experience' design, conceptualises medically supervised dying through discourses of economic rationality, because the dying themselves already participate as decision-makers in an economy of human capital.

Dying as a matter of time

In *Files: Law and Media Technology*, Cornelia Vismann argues that filing is integral to the institutionalisation of law. She writes that law is 'a repository of forms of authoritarian and administrative acts that assume concrete shape in files'.[25] To put this differently, law and files are mutually constitutive. The former assumes its institutional form in the recording

---

24   'The UX of Voluntary Assisted Dying: Friction and Complexity as Safeguards', *Portable* (Blog Post) <https://www.portable.com.au/blog/the-ux-of-voluntary-assisted-dying>.
25   Cornelia Vismann, *Files: Law and Media Technology*, tr Geoffrey Winthrop-Young (Stanford University Press, 2008) xiii.

of its proceedings, yet files acquire their materiality in the institutional practices of law. This is most evident in how a patient may access medically supervised assisted dying in Victoria.[26] The administration of voluntary assisted dying requires that a patient prove that they have 'decision-making capacity',[27] they have a serious and incurable disease, illness or medical condition,[28] and that disease, illness or medical condition is causing intolerable suffering.[29] The patient must first request from a doctor access to assisted dying,[30] which formally commences the bureaucratic process, but they also must repeat that initial step if a doctor refuses.[31] If the doctor accepts the request, the patient must then undergo an assessment by that doctor and if they are deemed eligible to be a decision-maker, the doctor must within seven days submit a report in Form 1 to the Voluntary Assisted Dying Review Board.[32] The patient must then undergo a consulting assessment by a different doctor, which will result in the submission of another report in Form 1 to the Voluntary Assisted Dying Review Board.[33] Following the second assessment, both doctors need to make a 'written declaration' in Form 3 on behalf of the decision-maker, requesting access to lawful assisted dying.[34] The final request must then be made after the signing of the written declaration at least nine days after the first request was made.[35]

The administration of voluntary assisted dying undoubtedly assumes its legal form in an economy, a cascade of files, reports and forms. 'In our cultures "paper shuffling" is the source of an essential power', writes Bruno Latour, 'that constantly escapes attention since its materiality is ignored'.[36]

---

26   The administrative procedures are outlined in the *Voluntary Assisted Dying Act 2017* (Vic) s 6. They involve the following steps: first request; first assessment; consulting assessment; written declaration; final request; contact person appointment; final review and permit application.
27   *Voluntary Assisted Dying Act 2017* (Vic) s 9(1)(c).
28   *Voluntary Assisted Dying Act 2017* (Vic) s 9(1)(d).
29   *Voluntary Assisted Dying Act 2017* (Vic) s 9(1)(d)(iv).
30   *Voluntary Assisted Dying Act 2017* (Vic) s 11. This request can only be made to a 'registered medical practitioner' in person. The health practitioner must not initiate this discussion under section 8. They have seven days to decide whether to accept or refuse the request.
31   *Voluntary Assisted Dying Act 2017* (Vic) s 13. Medical practitioners can refuse to participate in the process because of a conscientious objection to voluntary assisted dying, because they are not able to perform duties under the Act or because they are not qualified to do so.
32   *Voluntary Assisted Dying Act 2017* (Vic) ss 16–21. Under section 19, the first doctor must provide the following information to the patient: diagnosis and prognosis; end of life options; risks of assisted dying; the effects of assisted dying; and the right not to continue with assisted dying at any time.
33   *Voluntary Assisted Dying Act 2017* (Vic) ss 22–30.
34   *Voluntary Assisted Dying Act 2017* (Vic) ss 34–36.
35   *Voluntary Assisted Dying Act 2017* (Vic) ss 37–38.
36   Bruno Latour, 'Drawing Things Together' in Michael Lynch and Steve Woolgar (eds), *Representation in Scientific Practice* (MIT Press, 1990) 55.

The copious amounts of paperwork produced by the implementation of *Voluntary Assisted Dying Act 2017* (Vic), coupled with the legislatively determined time delays between each step of the process, means not only that eligible decision-makers *may* die before a 'permit' is issued, but that the time of dying is figured in economic terms. This is most evident in the panoply of guidance manuals and instruction booklets for health services, medical practitioners and consumer patients, which fragment the administrative procedures, but also the experience of voluntary assisted dying, into discrete units of time that can be elongated or truncated.[37]

In *Undoing the Demos*, Brown develops a theory of neoliberalism as a 'governing rationality' that extends into all aspects of living: 'all spheres of existence are framed and measured by economic terms and metrics, even when those spheres are not directly monetized'.[38] Brown argues that in the twenty-first century a condition of possibility of human life is a historically specific form of economic rationality, which extols, for example, human beings to optimise the economic value of time. Her book builds upon both Michel Callon's performative concept of economisation, which he utilises to describe 'behaviours, organizations, institutions and, more generally, the objects in a particular society ... as "economic"',[39] and Michel Foucault's historical account of governmentality, or the transformations in the art of government, which he contends embedded the notion of the economy into the management of the population during the eighteenth century.[40]

If neoliberal rationality emerges in the twentieth century as a distinctive form of governance, it is due to the fact that it is both pervasive, yet disunified in constructing persons and states on the model of corporate firms and self-investing entrepreneurs competing against each other in an economy of human capital. Economisation is a model for the conduct of government, but also a model for the government of the self, where both

---

37   See for example, Department of Health and Human Services, Government of Victoria, *Voluntary Assisted Dying: Information for People Considering Voluntary Assisted Dying* (11 October 2019); Department of Health and Human Services, Government of Victoria, *Voluntary Assisted Dying: Guidance for Health Practitioners* (4 July 2019); Department of Health and Human Services, Government of Victoria, *Voluntary Assisted Dying: Managing Access to Voluntary Assisted Dying in Health Services* (18 April 2019).
38   Brown (n 11) 10.
39   Koray Çalışkan and Michel Callon, 'Economization, Part 1: Shifting Attention From the Economy Towards Processes of Economization' (2009) 38(3) *Economy and Society* 369, 370.
40   Michel Foucault, 'Governmentality' in Graham Burchell, Colin Gordon and Peter Miller (eds), *The Foucault Effect: Studies in Governmentality* (The University of Chicago Press, 1991).

persons and states transform every aspect of society into a market and in this process, they themselves are transformed into market actors. The *homo oeconomicus* that Foucault introduces in his lectures on biopolitics becomes then for Brown a market actor that 'takes its shape [everywhere] as human capital seeking to strengthen its competitive positioning and appreciate its value, rather than as a figure of exchange or interests'.[41]

The language of economisation suffuses relations between decision-makers, medical practitioners and the state, cultivated in the implementation of a voluntary assisted dying regime. It manifests in the bureaucratic procedures for determining whether a person has 'decision-making capacity' and also in the organisation of a permit system created to govern access to voluntary assisted dying for eligible decision-makers. The remainder of this chapter explores how decision-makers participate in an economy of human capital and it concludes that this model for the conduct of government will lead to differential experiences of voluntary assisted dying, particularly for patients who struggle to comport to the norms of, but importantly demonstrate their performance of themselves as, *homo oeconomicus*, or as Brown puts it, 'comport themselves in ways that maximize their capital value in the present and enhance their future value'.[42]

Dorsett and McVeigh explain that the temporary legalisation of euthanasia in the Northern Territory in the 1990s required 'terminally ill people' to demonstrate that they have a capacity to petition a medical practitioner to access physician-assisted dying. They had to show that they 'possess a set of competencies in the management of one's affairs'.[43] 'Decision-making capacity' is defined under section 4(1) of *Voluntary Assisted Dying Act 2017* (Vic) as the ability to understand information about the administration of voluntary assisted dying, retain that information to the extent of making a decision, use or weigh that information in the process of making a decision and communicate that decision through speech, gestures or other means. While the standard of proof for determining whether a person has capacity lies outside the legislation, which means a subjective assessment is to be made by medical practitioners, the Act points out that they should not make assumptions about how a person may understand the administration and especially, the consequences of

---

41   Brown (n 11) 33.
42   Ibid 22.
43   Dorsett and McVeigh (n 10) 87.

voluntary assisted dying – 'modified language, visual aids or any other means' may be required[44] – and they should not make an assessment based on a person's appearance or opinions.[45] Doctors must take into account that 'practicable and appropriate support' should be given for someone to make a decision, such as the use of specific technology, extended time to understand and deliberate, allowing someone to assist with communicating a decision or using information or formats tailored to the particular needs of a person.[46]

Notwithstanding the attempts by lawmakers to curtail the subjectivity of the assessment process, what Dorsett and McVeigh wrote about the administration of euthanasia in the Northern Territory applies equally to the implementation of voluntary assisted dying in Victoria. The state may presume that a person has a capacity to make a decision, if they can demonstrate that they can manage their affairs, or rather, that they can participate in a cost–benefit analysis regarding their own death. What I am suggesting here is that the subjective assessment of decision-making capacity by a medical practitioner and its affirmation by government officers is inextricable from a neoliberal rationality that has subjugated, normalised and measured all spheres of life and death according to economic terms. The patient in this context can only acquire the status of a decision-maker by performing *homo oeconomicus*:

> an intensely constructed and governed bit of human capital tasked with improving and leveraging its competitive positioning and with enhancing its (monetary and nonmonetary) portfolio value across all of its endeavors and venues.[47]

Whether this performance consists of theorising the economic consequences of the extension or reduction of one's life for oneself, another or the state, or conceptualising a prognosis in terms of time left to be maximised – that is, how can time be financialised for monetary or nonmonetary purposes – *homo oeconomicus*, as a performance and a status, increases the 'value' of the patient's life and death for the purposes of making an assessment on their competency. It may be strange to think of a person seeking access to voluntary assisted dying in relation to notions

---

44 *Voluntary Assisted Dying Act 2017* (Vic) s 4(3).
45 *Voluntary Assisted Dying Act 2017* (Vic) s 4(4)(c).
46 *Voluntary Assisted Dying Act 2017* (Vic) s 4(4)(d).
47 Brown (n 11) 10.

of economisation, value seeking and 'competitive positioning', but as I remarked in the previous section, neoliberal rationality has extended itself into all spheres of end-of-life care.

It could be noted further that doctors are assessing a patient's capacity through their own understanding and situatedness, which is determined by a constellation of power–knowledge relations, of what kind of human capital is required to understand and retain information, and deliberate and communicate a decision. Not only are the doctors fashioning themselves everywhere as *homo oeconomicus* – that is after all integral to their vocations – but they are assessing their patients' capacity to perform 'human capital' by reference to an economic rationality constituted as 'sophisticated common sense, a reality principle remaking institutions and human beings everywhere it settles, nestles, and gains affirmation'.[48] This means that while patients may not be subject to overt discrimination by medical practitioners, which is explicitly prohibited by the Act, they will nonetheless be assessed through an epistemological framework inextricable from the governing rationality of *homo oeconomicus*.

The economisation of dying does not only appear in the form and content for determining whether a person has 'decision-making capacity'. It also manifests in the permit system created to govern access to voluntary assisted dying for the decision-maker who has successfully made a final request to the coordinating doctor. The doctor may subsequently apply under *Voluntary Assisted Dying Act 2017* (Vic) for a self-administration permit,[49] which authorises a doctor to prescribe and supply a 'voluntary assisted dying substance'[50] to be self-administered by the decision-maker, or a practitioner administration permit,[51] which authorises a doctor to administer that substance themselves, particularly if the decision-maker is incapable of self-administration and requests the doctor to do so. These permits are crucial for understanding how time is economised by the Act, for the processing and issuing of permits is yet to be constrained within a specified limit. It can only be surmised that administrative time would

---

48   Ibid, 35.
49   *Voluntary Assisted Dying Act 2017* (Vic) ss 45, 47.
50   The ingredients of the 'lethal' substance remain shrouded in secrecy. It is clear though that the substance is hand-delivered by hospital pharmacists and placed in a prescribed locked box that can only be accessed by eligible decision-makers. The pharmacists are also directed to retrieve and dispose any unused medications from the contact person of the deceased decision-maker. See further, Department of Health and Human Services, Government of Victoria, *Voluntary Assisted Dying: Statewide Pharmacy Service FAQs* (January 2019).
51   *Voluntary Assisted Dying Act 2017* (Vic) ss 46, 48.

be subject to 'economic policy', however much individual bureaucrats would like to issue permits as soon as possible, in the same way that a corporation dictates metrics for processing life insurance claims after the death of a spouse or a parent and while the bereaved find themselves in an economically vulnerable position. Yet this is not all that can be said about how the Act understands the timing of dying, for while there are also no time limits enshrined in the Act for the use of the permits, expiry dates can be embedded in the lethal substances themselves. These substances, which are administered by the government through contracts with pharmaceutical corporations, must be destroyed by the coordinating doctor or returned to the dispensing pharmacy if not used (promptly).[52]

Voluntary assisted dying creates a bureaucratic apparatus for lawfully hastening the death of a particular type of person who has 'decision-making capacity'. While it transforms the government of death in the twenty-first century, it is important not to see this as a liberatory moment, a radical break from a past that prohibited suicide, assisted suicide and medically supervised dying. This new technology for governing death sits among a repertoire of institutional practices that have sought to economise many aspects of dying. The risk of course of failing to inquire into how voluntary assisted dying fits into and further enhances, rather than breaks from, the economisation of life and death under neoliberalism, is that only those who can harness their capital to demonstrate that they can manage their own affairs, that they can perform the role of *homo oeconomicus*, even if that is geared towards gaining a nonmonetary legal status of 'decision-maker', will be able to access lawful means of medically supervised assisted dying. Indeed, the integration of the government of death with neoliberal rationality will augment socio-economic inequality in creating differential experiences of voluntary assisted dying. But even for those eligible decision-makers that gain access to the voluntary assisted

---

52 The disposing of a lethal substance of course requires additional paperwork: the completion of a disposal form and records of disposal or return: *Voluntary Assisted Dying Act 2017* (Vic) ss 54–55, 57–63. It should be clear at this point that only those who can *afford* to wait for a permit to die may actually receive one. In the second report on the operations of the Act, the Voluntary Assisted Dying Review Board tabled that 19 people may have died during the application process from 'means other than voluntary assisted dying': Voluntary Assisted Dying Review Board, Safer Care Victoria, *Report of Operations June to December 2019* (Report, 2020) 3. By the third report, this number may have increased substantially as more people applied to access voluntary assisted dying in Victoria: Voluntary Assisted Dying Review Board, Safer Care Victoria, *Report of Operations January–June 2020* (Report No 3, 31 August 2020) 3.

dying regime, their deaths do not lie outside the spheres of economics, for the very substances that cause their deaths are designed to make the most efficient and value-oriented use of everyone's time.

Bibliography

A Articles/books/reports

Bayatrizi, Zohreh, 'From Fate to Risk: The Quantification of Mortality in Early Modern Statistics' (2008) 25(1) *Theory, Culture & Society* 121 doi.org/10.1177/0263276407085160

Brown, Wendy, *Undoing the Demos: Neoliberalism's Stealth Revolution* (Zone Books, 1st ed, 2015)

Çalışkan, Koray and Michel Callon, 'Economization, Part 1: Shifting Attention from the Economy towards Processes of Economization' (2009) 38(3) *Economy and Society* 369 doi.org/10.1080/03085140903020580

Department of Health and Human Services, Government of Victoria, *Ministerial Advisory Panel on Voluntary Assisted Dying* (Final Report, 31 July 2017)

Department of Health and Human Services, Government of Victoria, *Voluntary Assisted Dying: Guidance for Health Practitioners* (4 July 2019)

Department of Health and Human Services, Government of Victoria, *Voluntary Assisted Dying: Information for People Considering Voluntary Assisted Dying* (11 October 2019)

Department of Health and Human Services, Government of Victoria, *Voluntary Assisted Dying: Managing Access in Health Services* (18 April 2019)

Department of Health and Human Services, Government of Victoria, *Voluntary Assisted Dying: Statewide Pharmacy Service FAQs* (January 2019)

Dorsett, Shaunnagh and Shaun McVeigh, *Jurisdiction* (Routledge, 2012)

Duckett, Stephen, 'Aligning Policy Objectives and Payment Design in Palliative Care' (2018) 17(42) *BMC Palliative Care* 1 doi.org/10.1186/s12904-018-0294-4

The Economist Intelligence Unit, *The 2015 Quality of Death Index Ranking Palliative Care Across the World* (Report, October 2015)

Foucault, Michel, *The Birth of Biopolitics: Lectures at the Collège de France, 1978–1979*, ed Arnold I Davidson, tr Graham Burchell (Picador, 2008)

Foucault, Michel, 'Governmentality' in Graham Burchell, Colin Gordon and Peter Miller (eds), *The Foucault Effect: Studies in Governmentality* (University of Chicago Press, 1991)

Foucault, Michel, *The History of Sexuality, Volume 1: The Will to Knowledge*, tr Robert Hurley (Penguin, 1998)

Foucault, Michel, 'The Political Technology of Individuals' in Luther H Martin, Huck Gutman and Patrick H Hutton (eds), *Technologies of the Self: A Seminar with Michel Foucault* (University of Massachusetts Press, 1st ed, 1988)

Gandsman, Ari, 'Paradox of Choice and the Illusion of Autonomy: The Construction of Ethical Subjects in Right-to-Die Activism' (2018) 42(5) *Death Studies* 329 doi.org/10.1080/07481187.2017.1396646

Latour, Bruno, 'Drawing Things Together' in Michael Lynch and Steve Woolgar (eds), *Representation in Scientific Practice* (MIT Press, 1990)

Lavi, Shai, 'How Dying Became a "Life Crisis"' (2008) 137(1) *Dædalus* 57 doi.org/10.1162/daed.2008.137.1.57

Lavi, Shai J, *The Modern Art of Dying: A History of Euthanasia in the United States* (Princeton University Press, 2005)

McVeigh, Shaun, 'Subjects of Jurisdiction: The Dying, Northern Territory, Australia, 1995–1997' in Shaun McVeigh (ed), *Jurisprudence of Jurisdiction* (Routledge, 2007) doi.org/10.4324/9780203945483-21

Neergaard, Mette Asbjoern et al, 'What Socio-Economic Factors Determine Place of Death for People with Life-Limiting Illness? A Systematic Review and Appraisal of Methodological Rigour' (2019) 33(8) *Palliative Medicine* 900 doi.org/10.1177/0269216319847089

Orlovic, Martina, Joachim Marti and Elias Mossialos, 'Analysis of End-of-Life Care, Out-of-Pocket Spending, and Place of Death in 16 European Countries and Israel' (2017) 36(7) *Health Affairs* 1201 doi.org/10.1377/hlthaff.2017.0166

Portable, *The Future of Death & Ageing in Australia: A Portable R&D Initiative* (Report, 2019)

Schadewaldt, Wolfgang, 'The Greek Concepts of "Nature" and "Technique"' in Robert C Scharff and Val Pusek (eds), *Philosophy of Technology: The Technological Condition: An Anthology* (John Wiley & Sons, Inc, 2nd ed, 2014)

Swerissen, Hal and Stephen Duckett, *Dying Well* (Grattan Institute Report No 2014-10, September 2014) <https://grattan.edu.au/wp-content/uploads/2014/09/815-dying-well.pdf>

Trabsky, Marc, *Law and the Dead: Technology, Relations and Institutions* (Routledge, 2019)

Trachtenberg, Aaron J and Braden Manns, 'Cost Analysis of Medical Assistance in Dying in Canada' (2017) 189(3) *Canadian Medical Association Journal* E101 doi.org/10.1503/cmaj.160650

Vismann, Cornelia, *Files: Law and Media Technology*, tr Geoffrey Winthrop-Young (Stanford University Press, 2008)

Voluntary Assisted Dying Review Board, Safer Care Victoria, *Report of Operations January–June 2020* (Report No 3, 31 August 2020)

Voluntary Assisted Dying Review Board, Safer Care Victoria, *Report of Operations June to December 2019* (Report, February 2020)

B Legislation

Voluntary Assisted Dying Act 2017 (Vic)

C Other

'The UX of Voluntary Assisted Dying: Friction and Complexity as Safeguards', *Portable* (Blog Post) <https://www.portable.com.au/articles/the-ux-of-voluntary-assisted-dying>

6

Over the Rainbow Bridge: Animals and Euthanasia

Jessica Ison

Animal death 'is everywhere, and it is nowhere'.[1]

From the outset, it might be easy to wonder what animals have to do with the question of human voluntary assisted dying (VAD). On the surface, the two issues seem disparate. Surely the killing of animals by way of a supposedly good death has nothing to do with the debates of human VAD. However, this chapter argues that there are connections, starting with the definition of euthanasia itself, which often includes animals. For example, the Merriam-Webster dictionary definition is 'the act or practice of killing or permitting the death of hopelessly sick or injured individuals (such as persons or domestic animals) in a relatively painless way for reasons of mercy'.[2] In this definition animals can be individuals and euthanasia is extended to them, but only those who are domesticated. This definition begs the question, what about those animals who we do not deem eligible for, or worthy of, euthanasia? How do we decide who is allowed death by means of euthanasia?

---

1   Megan H Glick, 'Animal Instincts: Race, Criminality, and the Reversal of the "Human"' (2013) 65(3) *American Quarterly*, 645.
2   *Merriam-Webster Dictionary* (online at 24 June 2021) 'Euthanasia', <https://www.merriam-webster.com/dictionary/euthanasia>.

This chapter grapples with the questions that arise from euthanising animals and whether these can be related to humans, including the questions raised above. It begins with an overview of animal studies and a very brief history of animal–human relations in the Eurocentric context. The chapter reveals that the practice of euthanising animals demonstrates significant complexities, in particular, relating to the fact that only some animals are considered worthy of this intervention. The complexities of defining animal euthanasia is one of the critical issues raised in this chapter, which opens up the question of why humans only euthanise some animals when we control nearly all animals. What of those animals who are not eligible to be euthanised, who instead are killed or slaughtered? Regardless of this distinction, the increase in pet ownership means that we must manage a considerable number of pet animals and we must consider human emotion in this process, which makes up the next section. All of this will open the discussion for the final section, which considers if we can relate animal euthanasia to human VAD.

Before delving into this topic, it may be relevant to note that many who engage with this collection will primarily be interested in human VAD. Therefore, the author assumed that, in general, most of the readers have little – if any – knowledge of the broad field loosely called animal studies. Consequently, at points, the chapter offers some of the foundations for the animal studies field, and the footnotes make a variety of suggestions for further reading. This is not to say that this chapter will be of no use for scholars in animal studies because, as the reader will see, animal euthanasia is a topic with little scholarship and therefore this chapter also makes a contribution to the field of animal studies.

It must also be noted that the sheer extent of our relationship with animals means that not all animals are covered here. In general, this chapter makes comparisons between pet animals and those who humans kill to eat. The chapter does not discuss free-living animals in cities,[3] wild animals, animals exploited for entertainment[4] and animals experimented on in laboratories, though they too are animals who may – or may not – be euthanised, and the question of their eligibility or otherwise could be seen as an extension of the analysis below.

---

3   For an analysis of so-called 'feral animals' see Fiona Probyn-Rapsey, 'Five Propositions on Ferals' (2016) 6 *Feral Feminisms* <https://feralfeminisms.com/five-propositions-on-ferals/>.
4   A case study for further analysis could be the giraffe Marius who was euthanised by the Copenhagen zoo, which garnered international attention compared to, for example, the number of giraffes killed in order to procure animals for zoos.

Overview of animal and human relations

Animals are an ever-present part of human society. We have them as pets in our homes, some of us eat them, we have unwanted animals throughout our cities, we use them for experiments for medicine, we look at them for pleasure in nature (or on the television), and we interact with them in countless other scenarios. However, animals are often not seen as a legitimate consideration for study, policy or everyday acknowledgement. The academy neglected animals until the 'animal turn',[5] which resulted in animals becoming considered worthy as a subject of study in an expanding field called human–animal studies, animal studies or critical animal studies. This chapter is influenced by and uses the framework of critical animal studies.[6]

Within the broad field of animal studies, animals and death is the topic of various publications, most notably a collection by the Animal Studies Group titled *Killing Animals*.[7] This collection offers a diverse range of topics centred on the theme of animal killing, from Mad Cow Disease to hunting. Building on this is another notable collection titled *Animal Death*, which focuses on not just the killing but the death of animals.[8] The diverse chapters point out that animal death is a complicated and broad topic that throws up many varied ethical and moral dilemmas.

What both collections highlight is that by far the most extensive relationship people have with animals is through eating them or their bodily excretions. The number of animals whom humans kill for food are almost impossible to comprehend. Globally, they are in the billions, but numbers vary across the research because it is impossible to account for those who die in fields, in factories or at birth.[9] For a glimpse into this reality: 1,548,119 lambs were killed in Australia in June 2020 alone according to the Australian Bureau of Statistics.[10] It is hard to imagine those lambs, still trying to feed from their mothers, killed in industrial

5   Kari Weil, 'A Report on the Animal Turn', (2010) 21(2) *differences* 1.
6   For an introductory overview see: Anthony J Nocella II et al (eds), *Defining Critical Animal Studies* (Peter Lang Publishing, 2014); Nik Taylor and Tania Signal (eds), *Human-Animal Studies: Theorizing Animals: Re-Thinking Humanimal Relations* (Brill, 2011).
7   Animal Studies Group (ed), *Killing Animals* (University of Illinois Press, 2006).
8   Fiona Probyn-Rapsey and Jay Johnston, *Animal Death* (Sydney University Press, 2013).
9   Animal Studies Group (n 7).
10   Australian Bureau of Statistics, *Livestock and Meat, Australia, June 2020* (Catalogue No 7218. 0.55.001, 8 May 2020) <https://www.abs.gov.au/statistics/industry/agriculture/livestock-and-meat-australia/latest-release>.

slaughter at such a scale. Add to this cows, chickens, pigs, sheep and sea life – who humans kill at astounding rates – and others. The effects of our industrial slaughter of animals does not end at this loss of life. Beyond this, animal agriculture is one of the key contributors to the climate crisis, with the UN urging everyone to drastically lower meat consumption in multiple reports for both the climate and health reasons.[11] The impact of animal agriculture on our planet is devastating and defies the imagination.

Animal exploitation is pervasive. Indeed:

> It is not just the statistics [on animals killed by humans] that are staggering but the fact that almost all areas of human life are at some point or other involved in or directly dependent on the killing of animals.[12]

However, this death is often not considered, or even rendered 'death' at all. In Eurocentric countries, we are generally far removed from the slaughterhouse, with most people only encountering an animal dying in situations such as hitting an animal on the road or euthanising a pet. Given the extent of animal death, one would imagine more scholarship on the topic might exist. Across the literature, the subtopic of euthanasia concerning animals is mostly only found in veterinary articles and policies. Notable exceptions are the increasing research on the emotions experienced by humans when they euthanise a pet[13] and how euthanising healthy animals affects workers.[14] However, an analysis of the cultural phenomenon of animal euthanasia is currently lacking.

---

11   For an overview see: Kip Andersen, 'The Facts', *Cowspiracy: The Sustainability Secret* (Web Page) <http://www.cowspiracy.com/facts/>.

12   Animal Studies Group (n 7) 3.

13   For example: Cheri Barton Ross, *Pet Loss and Human Emotion: A Guide to Recovery*, ed. Jane Baron-Sorensen (Taylor & Francis, 2nd ed, 2013); Patricia Morris, 'Managing Pet Owner's Guilt and Grief in Veterinary Euthanasia Encounters' (2012) 41(3) *Journal of Contemporary Ethnography* 3337; Karyn McKinney, 'Emotion Work of Coping with the Death of a Companion Animal' (2019) 27(1) *Society & Animals* 109.

14   For example: Stephanie Frommer and Arnold Arluke, 'Loving Them to Death: Blame-Displacing Strategies of Animal Shelter Workers and Surrenderers' (1999) 7(1) *Society & Animals* 1.

History of animal and human relations

When talking about animals, people tend to make rather large claims. The history of euthanasia is no different. Indeed, most of the writing tells us more about how we perceive animals than any real historical truths – if this is even possible – about animal euthanasia. For example, Kleinfeldt claims that:

> Whereas euthanasia of humans has historically been prohibited, euthanasia of animals is not an emergence of the present age, but has been performed for centuries. In ancient Egypt, it was not uncommon that at the owner's death, if his [sic] pet was still alive, the pet would be euthanized to be reunited with its [sic][15] owner, so the pet could continue to be the deceased's companion in the afterlife.[16]

Here, Kleinfeldt frames these grand assumptions about Egyptian burial practices as euthanasia. It is worth noting that, embedded in these assumptions are views about what an animal wants and needs alongside the social and political context of burials from Ancient Egypt.

There is little else written on the history of animals and euthanasia. Therefore, to have a deep understanding of euthanasia today, we must turn to a broader analysis of animal–human relations to shed light on some of the changing attitudes that led to the euthanasia regulations we have today. As an illustrative case, a brief look at the history of animal cruelty laws provides insight into some of the ways that animal–human relations have changed with capitalism in Eurocentric countries. The prominent example that most readers will know is the Royal Society for the Prevention of Cruelty to Animals or the RSPCA.

The RSPCA started as the SPCA in 1824 and was focused primarily on vivisection and animal cruelty enacted by the working class, such as the treatment of ponies in coal mines and cockfighting.[17] That is, primarily the people organising for the SPCA were in the middle- to upper-class of

---

15   Throughout this chapter when animals are referred to as 'it' or 'its', this speciesist language is noted with a '[sic]'.

16   Alexandra Kleinfeldt, 'Brief Summary of Animal Euthanasia', *Animal Legal & Historical Center* (Web Page, 2017) <https://www.animallaw.info/article/brief-summary-animal-euthanasia>.

17   Josephine Donovan and Carol J Adams (eds), *The Feminist Care Tradition in Animal Ethics: A Reader* (Columbia University Press, 2007); Lyle Munro, *Compassionate Beasts: The Quest for Animal Rights* (Praeger, 2001).

British society. Queen Victoria decided to give patronage to the SPCA in 1937, which saw the addition of Royal to the name.[18] The formation of the RSPCA is a crucial moment in Eurocentric animal rights movements. In the Victorian era, society closely tied animals to moral and political issues, particularly concerning controlling the working class, which was also influenced by Christianity and the morals of the church.[19] The use of animals in moral crusades is still prevalent today, easily seen in the supposed care for animals in live export.[20] Humans use animals in every conceivable way, including politically.

Returning to earlier examples, a case in point of the earlier use of animals for political gains was in the 1800s when the first animal protection legislation begins to emerge in Europe. Indeed, the 'First [animal rights] bill to be brought in Parliament was introduced by Sir William Pulteney in 1800 to end bullbaiting'.[21] The Bill may seem like a positive development with regard to human concern for animals, but generally, it is understood that bullbaiting was something the working classes also enjoyed. The bill passed in 1822, titled *Prevent the Cruel Treatment of Cattle*, which was the first legal protection for animals in Britain.[22] Following this line of critique, it is significant to note that the cruelty that the upper classes called sport, such as fox hunting, was not on the agenda. Indeed, nor was the killing of cows or other animals for food.

The creation of the RSPCA and the various animal cruelty bills passed in British parliament show, on the surface at least, that there was care for animals and distaste for animal cruelty, albeit usually intertwined with the practices of the working class. Once who was being targeted by the different legislation is considered, it becomes clear that animals were a tool for control and criminalisation. Care for animals, as is shown throughout this chapter, is rarely about the animals themselves.[23] Victorian literature scholars Laurence Mazzeno and Ronald Morrison take this point further to argue that:

---

18   'Our History', *RSPCA UK* (Web Page) <http://www.rspca.org.uk/utilities/aboutus/history>.
19   Li Chien-Hui, 'An Unnatural Alliance? Political Radicalism and the Animal Defence Movement in Late Victorian and Edwardian Britain' (2012) 42(1) *EurAmerica* 1.
20   The uproar about these abused animals not only obscured the cruelty animals face in Australia but it was generally thinly veiled racism about how supposedly Australian animals were treated overseas. For further analysis see Nick Pendergrast, 'Live Animal Export, Humane Slaughter and Media Hegemony' (2015) 4(1) *Animal Studies Journal* 99.
21   David Perkins, *Romanticism and Animal Rights* (Cambridge University Press, 2003) 17.
22   Ibid, 16.
23   Jessica Ison, 'Animal Abuse and Advocating for the Carceral: Critiquing Animal Abuse Registries' (2019) 8(2) *Animal Studies Journal* 55.

At another level, these issues also became the means for Victorian culture to consider the shifting boundaries of social class, the expansion and maintenance of the British Empire, and the benefits and challenges created by the development of modern science, including ethical challenges posed by Darwinism.[24]

Mazzeno and Morrison support the argument that social class was a crucial factor in legislation concerned with animals. It is clear that how humans treat animals reflects changes in culture and social attitudes. Human–animal relations were arguably altered forever because of the English naturalist and founder of evolutionary theory, Charles Darwin.[25] People started to view the natural world in an entirely different way and, based on hitherto unimagined closeness between humans and other animals (such as apes), humanity began to develop a capacity for thinking about animals differently.[26] It follows that this impacted views on animal death.

With this as background, it is significant that alongside the creation of animal cruelty laws was the creation of the slaughterhouse. In the context of understanding the significance of the slaughterhouse for global capitalism, critical animal studies scholar Nicole Shukin draws our attention to the often-forgotten fact that Ford took his model for production lines from abattoirs. Shukin dates the slaughterhouse production line to at least the 1850s.[27] She points out that the slaughterhouse presents the first (dis)assembly line and questions the fact that analysis of capitalism often neglects this history. The rendering of a live animal into meat for consumption at such a fast pace would simply be impossible for a single worker, and so necessitates something like the slaughterhouse, that functions by breaking the work into specific tasks. This rendering of so many animals into meat also could not be tolerated psychologically by individuals, and so the production line took the onus of killing off any one person.[28]

---

24   Laurence W Mazzeno and Ronald D Morrison, 'Introduction' in Laurence W Mazzeno and Ronald D Morrison (eds), *Animals in Victorian Literature and Culture: Contexts for Criticism* (Palgrave Macmillan UK, 2017) 2.
25   Jed Mayer, 'Ways of Reading Animals in Victorian Literature, Culture and Science' (2010) 7(5) *Literature Compass* 348.
26   While out of scope for this chapter, the abuse of animals was also central to the colonial processes at the time and animals were (and are) used in a variety of ways to create discourses of white supremacy. The relationship of human to apes for example, played into racial hierarchies in some particularly heinous ways. See: Claire Jean Kim, *Dangerous Crossings: Race, Species, and Nature in a Multicultural Age* (Cambridge University Press, 2015).
27   Nicole Shukin, *Animal Capital: Rendering Life in Biopolitical Times* (University of Minnesota Press, 2009).
28   Timothy Pachirat, *Every Twelve Seconds: Industrialized Slaughter and the Politics of Sight* (Yale University Press, 2011).

Not only were these slaughterhouses places of intense animal cruelty, worker exploitation and pollution, they were also in fact places of entertainment:

> Tours of slaughterhouses, already a popular sideline of Chicago's Packing town as early as the 1860s, were designed to showcase the tremendous efficiency with which American culture managed its material nature. Slaughterhouse tourism also promised to fascinate and disturb tour-goers with the somatic sights, smells, and sounds – the 'physiological trials' – of doomed animals and gore covered laborers.[29]

As this analysis shows, there exists then an incredible tension between animals and humans, emerging from this period where people supposedly began to care about the wellbeing of animals. This closer look reveals a more complex combination of the interplay of interests, including providing a way to control the working class in a period of the sharp increase in the exploitation of animal's bodies.

This contradiction of animal welfare and animal exploitation that increased during industrialisation was also mirrored by the presence of animals in people's homes as pets.

> Since the nineteenth century, there has been a particular split between domesticated farm animals and domesticated house animals. Today, few Westerners have daily contact with working animals or those destined to be eaten.[30]

The increase in friendship between animals often obscures the realities of how many animals are killed by humans.

The shifting relationship with animals in the twentieth century saw the rise of the pet industry. To understand this shift, Bulliet argues that there is a domestic and a postdomestic era concerning animals, with the latter beginning in the 1970s:

> A postdomestic society emerging from domestic antecedents continues to consume animal products in abundance, but psychologically, its members experience feelings of guilt, shame,

---

29   Shukin (n 27) 94.
30   Matthew Wills, 'The Invention of Pets', *JSTOR Daily* (Blog Post, 28 January 2017) <https://daily.jstor.org/the-invention-of-pets/>.

and disgust when they think (as seldom as possible) about the industrial processes by which domestic animals are rendered into products and about how those products come to market.[31]

While the 1970s is perhaps a little late for this distinction – the turn of the century or even earlier seems to be more accurate given the above history – the separation between domestic and postdomestic is useful. In the postdomestic era, people somewhat contradictorily became close to their pets, even to the point of seeing them as part of their family, while being further separated from other animals.[32] In this way, pets become a kind of in-between animal, who we afford certain levels of care and treatment to that was hitherto unavailable to animals, and which expanded the discourse on animal cruelty for this group of animals. This closeness opened up the possibility of animals who could be euthanised, not just killed, which in turn needed regulation.[33]

What is animal euthanasia in the postdomestic era?

Currently, the killing of animals is regulated but not as strongly as one might imagine. Animal death depends on the type of animal in question.[34] The specific welfare of animals in Australia is state-based under *Prevention of Cruelty to Animals* Acts (POCTAs). Given that the vast majority of animals are raised to be killed in Australia, there is a Code of Practice for how to care for and kill these animals. Under POCTAs, killing an animal will in many circumstances constitute cruelty, and therefore POCTAs cannot relate to those animals humans eat because killing them would be illegal. To circumvent this problem, the POCTAs have exceptions. For instance, in the state of Victoria, the *Prevention of Cruelty to Animals*

---

31 Richard Bulliet, *Hunters, Herders and Hamburgers: The Past and Future of Human-Animal Relationships* (Columbia University Press, 2005) 3.
32 Amy J Fitzgerald, 'A Social History of the Slaughterhouse: From Inception to Contemporary Implications' (2010) 17(1) *Human Ecology Review* 59.
33 Other animals have deaths framed as euthanasia, such as racehorses who have an injury and animals for experimentation. Also, some 'pest' animals might be euthanised, though usually this will be called 'culling'. Pets are unique in their apparent position as part of the family.
34 This chapter has not touched on such issues as wild animals and the issue of culling or killing animals during a disease outbreak.

Act 1986 does not apply to '[a]ny act or practice with respect to the farming, transport, sale or killing of any farm animal which is carried out in accordance with a Code of Practice'.[35]

And further:

> the keeping, treatment, handling, transportation, sale, killing, hunting, shooting, catching, trapping, netting, marking, care, use, husbandry or management of any animal or class of animals ... which is carried out in accordance with a Code of Practice.[36]

Within the law, there are already specific differences between certain animals. Some animals fall under the need of protection and others are simply within the Code of Practice, which is generally regulated by the industry.

Pets fall under POCTAs and therefore are one of the only groups whose deaths we deem 'euthanasia' because it does not take place in a slaughterhouse. Generally, veterinary associations regulate this practice. The Australian Veterinary Association (AVA) outlines what is considered euthanasia for veterinary purposes in Australia:

> The attending veterinarian must recommend euthanasia for an animal if the animal is suffering and that suffering is not able to be adequately minimised or managed. Euthanasia is the act of inducing humane death with the minimum of pain, fear or distress to the animal involved. It is most often used with terminally unwell or injured animals, where the prognosis is considered hopeless, and should also be considered for animals with intractable behaviour problems.[37]

The use of the word 'suffering' is of interest because, in this outline, euthanasia is in the best interest of an animal who cannot speak for themselves.[38] Therefore, the vet consults with the 'owner' of the animal. Often those animals who are domesticated but who do not have an owner will be killed by euthanasia in pounds.

---

35 *Prevention of Cruelty to Animals Act 1986* (Vic) s 11.
36 Ibid.
37 'Euthanasia', *Australian Veterinary Association* (Web Page, 10 August 2007) <https://www.ava.com.au/policy/44-euthanasia>.
38 Writing about animals offers a range of issues relating to language, particularly when also avoiding gendering animals. 'Themself' or 'themselves' is one tactic for challenging the way that English creates animals as objects through the use of 'it' or similar.

The AVA also outlined some of the broad definitions of euthanasia for their purposes:

- 'the process of inducing a painless death'[39]
- 'the humane killing of an animal, in the interests of its [sic] own welfare, to alleviate pain and distress'[40]
- 'a gentle death … regarded as an act of humane killing with the minimum of pain, fear and distress'.[41]

There are definitive differences in these definitions, most notably that only one seems to outline that euthanasia is to 'alleviate pain and distress', whereas the other descriptions offered are about the process of euthanasia. Veterinary scientist Anne Fawcett questions these definitions and also highlights how the American Veterinary Medical Association's definition is specifically about the killing of the animals, not about the intentionality behind this killing, stating 'it seems that the term "euthanasia", where animals are concerned, is synonymous with any death effected by a veterinarian'.[42] There is a difference here between the laws in various countries, and how the death of the animal is understood. Fawcett voices this as a concern about 'what indeed euthanasia actually is, if animals who are not suffering are killed'.[43] In particular, Fawcett is referring to pet animals killed in pounds though this same observation could apply to pet animals whom a veterinarian euthanises because their owners can no longer look after them, or no longer wants them. Perhaps one of the critical issues is that there are so many different types of animals, here only some domesticated animals have been discussed.

---

39   JS Reilly (ed), *Euthanasia of Animals Used for Scientific Purposes*, ed JS Reilly (Australian & New Zealand Council for the Care of Animals in Research and Teaching, 2nd ed, 2001), cited in 'Euthanasia' (n 37).

40   National Health and Medical Research Council, *Australian Code of Practice for the Care and Use of Animals for Scientific Purposes* (Report, 7th ed, 2004), cited in 'Euthanasia' (n 37).

41   European Commission, *Euthanasia of Experimental Animals* (March 1997), cited in 'Euthanasia' (n 37).

42   Anne Fawcett, 'Euthanasia and Morally Justified Killing in a Veterinary Clinical Context' in Jay Johnston and Fiona Probyn-Rapsey (eds), *Animal Death* (Sydney University Press, 2013) 208.

43   Ibid, 209.

Not all perspectives on euthanasia come from the law or veterinarians. Some activists and scholars weigh in on this debate to generally outline an ideal situation for animals within a welfare or rights framework.[44] For example, animal studies scholar Tom Regan proposed the following rules:

1. Killing must be by the most painless means possible;
2. That it must be believed to be in the animal's best interests and this must be a true belief;
3. One who kills must be motivated by concern for the interest, good or welfare of the animal involved.[45]

This definition comes from a very different perspective to those writing from a veterinary or industry agenda because it does not relate to just pet animals, but to all animals. Regan is writing from a perspective where euthanasia is only in the service of helping the animal, and therefore killing of animals in pounds could perhaps not be euthanasia. For Regan, this is 'preference respecting euthanasia'.

Regan has some resonance with Catherine Tiplady, who writes about animal abuse, and in relation to euthanasia states that:

> Where there is uncertainty whether to attempt treatment, continue treatment or euthanize, it is advisable to arrange a meeting of all members of the animal care team so everyone can discuss the patient, express their concerns and reach a consensus about the options for this animal.[46]

---

44 There is a distinct difference between those who advocate for animal welfare and those who advocate for animal rights. To put it simply, welfare advocates would argue that chickens should have bigger cages and rights advocates would say no animals should ever be caged for human use. On top of this, abolitionist or total liberationists might argue that no animal should ever be used or harmed by humans. Total liberation might also be paired with other politics that advocate for intersectionality. For more information see: Sarat Colling, Sean Parson, and Alessandro Arrigoni, 'Until All Are Free: Total Liberation through Revolutionary Decolonization, Groundless Solidarity, and a Relationship Framework' in Anthony J Nocella II et al (eds), *Defining Critical Animal Studies: An Intersectional Social Justice Approach for Liberation* (Peter Lang Publishing, 2014); David N Pellow, *Total Liberation: The Power and the Promise of Animal Rights and the Radical Earth Moment* (University of Minnesota Press, 2014); Richard Twine, 'Intersectional Disgust? Animals and (Eco)Feminism' (2010) 20(3) *Feminism & Psychology* 397.

45 Tom Regan, *The Case for Animal Rights* (Routledge & Kegan Paul, 1983).

46 Catherine Tiplady, *Animal Abuse: Helping Animals and People* (CABI, 2013) 164.

Here the animal is to be spoken for, yet it is not clear how one consults the animal, a problem that is also present in Regan's argument. Tiplady then goes on to outline the method for euthanasia drawing from Wolfensohn and Lloyd's[47] rules for laboratory animals:

> 1. Death must occur without producing pain. 2. The time required to produce loss of consciousness must be as short as possible. 3. The time required to produce death must be as short as possible. 4. The method must be reliable and nonreversible. 5. There must be minimal psychological stress on the animal. 6. There must be minimal psychological stress to the operators and observers. 7. It must be safe for personnel carrying out the procedure. 8. Any drugs used should be readily available and have minimum abuse potential. 9. The method should be economically acceptable. 10. It should be simple to carry out, with little room for error.[48]

This outline is unique in that it takes into account the impact euthanising could have on the workers, surely a topic worthy of an entire paper.[49]

A more recent proposition, from a legal and animal protection perspective, is Janice H Cox and Sabine Lennkh's *Model Animal Welfare Act*,[50] which they specifically designed to be a 'basic template and guidance document for those interested in enacting new legislation or improving existing animal protection legislation'.[51] In this extensive document, there is no section on euthanasia. The closest they come to euthanasia is 'Section 20 Humane Killing and Slaughter of Animals' where they state:

> the killing of an animal has at all times to be carried out in compliance with the subject Act as well as in a humane way and in such a manner that the animal is spared any avoidable pain, suffering, injury, fear or distress.[52]

---

47   Sarah Wolfensohn and Maggie Lloyd, *Handbook of Laboratory Animal Management and Welfare* (Blackwell Science, 2nd ed, 1998) 49–51.
48   Tiplady (n 46) 166.
49   Veterinarians in fact have high rates of suicide that has been attributed to multiple issues, one being the high rates of having to euthanise healthy animals. For further information see: 'Suicide', *Australian Veterinary Association* (Web Page) <https://www.ava.com.au/member-services/vethealth/suicide/>.
50   Janice Cox and Sabine Lennkh, *Model Animal Welfare Act: A Comprehensive Framework Law* (World Animal Net, 2016).
51   Ibid.
52   Ibid, 57.

While this appears to be a reasonable argument, they still couch it within a section that is about the killing and slaughter of animals. There is little differentiation between animals and no critical engagement with why some animals are only killable because they will become food.

Many cases of euthanising animals would not fit any of the more animal welfarist or rights-based definitions of euthanasia. Fawcett goes so far as to claim:

> In reality, the killing of an animal is often not a case of 'euthanasia', no matter how painless, dignified and legally sanctioned that happens to be, because the interests of the animal are not served.[53]

Fawcett is specifically referring to the killing of animals in pounds, where euthanasia is most commonly associated. While these statistics of animals in pounds are hard to gather, Animals Australia claims that pounds in Australia kill hundreds of thousands of animals each year.[54] The RSPCA does not admit to killing any 'excess' animals; however, their statistics have a surprisingly high number killed for 'behavioural issues', which they do not explain.[55] There are more studies on pounds in the US and they tend to say that each year pounds kill millions of animals.[56] These numbers indicate a disconnect between those animals we say we love and their actual treatment. So as Palmer argues:

> alongside the social recognition of cats and dogs as companions and family members lies the social treatment of them as expendable individuals that can be killed en masse at human will – or even whim.[57]

The killing of so many dogs and cats brings in to question our supposed love for pets. How do we kill so many pet animals and yet we see some animals as a member of the family?

---

53   Fawcett (n 42) 208.

54   'Companion Animals', *Animals Australia* (Web Page, 13 August 2019) <https://www.animals australia.org/issues/companion_animals.php>.

55   RSPCA Australia, *RSPCA Australia National Statistics 2019–2020* (Report) <https://www.rspca. org.au/sites/default/files/RSPCA%20Australia%20Annual%20Statistics%202019-2020.pdf>.

56   'Statistics', *No Kill Advocacy Center* (Web Page) <https://www.nokilladvocacycenter.org/statistics. html>.

57   Clare Palmer, 'Killing Animals in Animal Shelters' in Animal Studies Group (ed), *Killing Animals* (University of Illinois Press, 2006) 171.

Humane killing

A growing part of euthanising animals concerns the single beloved pet, often framed in terms of compassion and love for the animal. Such as a popular website that notes, '[h]aving to make the decision to end a pets [sic] life is the ultimate act of love, however, this in turn brings enormous feelings of guilt'.[58] As a result of this guilt, there is increased awareness of human emotions. Therefore, part of the euthanising of animals is mitigating the human emotions by sanitising the death of the animal. For example, the large animal welfare service in the US is called The Humane Society and they refer to the procedure as 'End of life services'.[59] Here they are even shunning the word euthanasia, opting for a euphemism that obscures the death of a loved pet.[60] The process is also expensive. It could cost thousands of dollars when an animal is sick, and the euthanasia fee can be hundreds on top of this.[61] Death becomes a commodity that one must pay for, yet one might chose it as a more cost-effective intervention than other treatments for a sick animal. This sanitised and commodified approach to death is an interesting and confusing reality when billions of animals are killed every year by humans, and yet some are afforded a death in a clinic, or even a home visit from a vet, and given a burial.

A flow-on problem with so many pet animals is what to do with their bodies (which is a concern with humans too). In major cities, this is a problem because people might not have backyards in which to bury them.[62] However, a backyard burial can also be a problematic choice because of the chemicals used in euthanising animals, which can have an impact on the environment or could poison an animal who digs up and

---

58 'When is the Right Time for Euthanasia?', *Living With Pet Bereavement* (Web Page) <https://livingwithpetbereavement.com/is-the-time-right%3F>.
59 'End-of-Life Services', *Animal Humane Society* (Web Page) <https://www.animalhumanesociety.org/health/end-life-services>.
60 In fact, when this chapter was being finalised there was an article circulating on social media about euthanising kangaroos 'humanely' to make way for a development in Perth, which begs the question: is this really in the best interest of the animals? Lauren Pilat, '"Humanely Euthanised": Roos to Be Killed to Make Way for Development South of Perth', *WA Today* (online, 28 January 2019) <https://www.watoday.com.au/national/western-australia/humanely-euthanised-roos-to-be-killed-to-make-way-for-development-south-of-perth-20190128-p50u4u.html>.
61 The cost across a range of veterinary websites is from A$50–A$300 for euthanasia.
62 Yi Zhu and Min Liu, 'Discussion of the Metropolis Pet Funeral and Burial Service', in Ying Zhang (ed.), *Future Communication, Computing, Control and Management: Volume 2* (Springer Berlin Heidelberg, 2012) 267.

eats the body.[63] Another option is to have a pet buried in a pet cemetery. Archaeologists have found animal remains in what could be a burial ritual as far back as the Neolithic period.[64] Pet cemeteries as we have them today have their origin in the nineteenth century in Europe.[65] With the rise of the middle-class pet ownership and the increase in urbanisation, dealing with the body of pets became a problem.

> Not surprisingly, the first official establishment of this kind were created on the outskirts of two bustling metropolises of the world – New York (Hartsdale Pet Cemetery, est. 1896) and Paris (Cimetière des Chiens et Autres Animaux Domestiques, est. 1899).[66]

Yet again, when looking at pet cemeteries, we see this distinction between those who we supposedly love and those who are merely animals we use, because '[c]rucially, pet cemeteries are for pets, not for animals more generally'.[67] As noted above, often this way of expressing care for animals is not extended to all animals who can be pets because dogs and cats are killed in the millions every year in pounds. Perhaps there are parallels here with humans, where humans in death are clearly not treated equally. Money determines how we deal with a body after death.

This contradiction of an increased sanitised death and the burial of some animals in a world with industrial slaughterhouses raises many issues. Returning one last time to the AVA's description of euthanasia, they also state:

> The necessary killing of animals for other reasons [such as slaughterhouses, laboratories] should not be confused with euthanasia, although the methods used and the principles to apply are the same.[68]

---

63   Rachel Allavena, 'Why You Shouldn't Bury Your Pet in the Backyard' *ABC News* (online, 19 March 2019) <https://www.abc.net.au/news/2019-03-19/why-you-shouldn%E2%80%99t-bury-your-pet-in-the-backyard/10915772>.

64   Ivy D Collier, 'More Than a Bag of Bones: A History of Animal Burials' in Margo DeMello (ed), *Mourning Animals: Rituals and Practices Surrounding Animal Death* (Michigan State University Press, 2016).

65   Hilda Kean, 'Human and Animal Space in Historic "Pet" Cemeteries in London, New York and Paris' in Jay Johnston and Fiona Probyn-Rapsey (eds), *Animal Death* (Sydney University Press, 2013).

66   Michał Piotr Pręgowski, 'All the World and a Little Bit More: Pet Cemetery Practices and Contemporary Relations between Humans and Their Companion Animals' in Margo DeMello (ed), *Mourning Animals: Rituals and Practices Surrounding Animal Death* (Michigan State University Press, 2016).

67   Jane C Desmond, *Displaying Death and Animating Life: Human-Animal Relations in Art, Science, and Everyday Life* (University of Chicago Press, 2016).

68   'Euthanasia' (n 37).

The policy then outlines what supposedly necessary killings are. They make a specific distinction between those animals who are to be euthanised and those who are to be killed. With such a stark line drawn between those who are allowed to be euthanised and those who are killed, the ethics of euthanasia becomes even murkier.

What would it mean to euthanise a cow? Or to euthanise a chicken? Outside of animal liberation circles, this may seem preposterous as those animals are only allowed to live to be eaten.[69] Therefore, we draw a line where we deem some animals as not worthy of being euthanised because they are not enveloped within the circle of human concern and are rather a product to be consumed. Or perhaps it is that some animals are deemed worthy of being euthanised. If euthanasia really is just about giving a pleasant death (a contention debated throughout this collection), then we should also consider who can access this death. As we have seen through the consideration of animal euthanasia, a crucial consideration here is who – and who is not – deemed worthy of accessing a pleasant death, what criteria do we use to determine this, and who ultimately chooses.

Can this be related to humans?

This chapter does not intend to draw parallels between animals and humans in a crude sense; that has been done, and it has rarely been done well.[70] However, we can draw some analysis between those animals we euthanise and those we kill and how this can be related to the arguments around VAD for humans.

Animals and euthanasia is framed as offering comfort in death but often only given to those we supposedly love. And yet, in general, every facet of animal life is controlled, and their exploitation is infinite. Animal studies scholar Dinesh Wadiwel frames this point as a 'war against animals' that

---

69 There is not space here to talk about animals and mourning but this is also an important aspect; groups such as Animal Liberation Victoria hold public memorials for dead animals. Animal Rights, 'Animals Are Not Ours Memorial', *Vimeo* (Video, 7 October 2013) <https://vimeo.com/76382879>.
70 There are many animal studies scholars who have engaged with multiple issues in a critical and nuanced way, such as: Esther Alloun, '"That's the Beauty of It, It's Very Simple!" Animal Rights and Settler Colonialism in Palestine-Israel' (2018) 8(4) *Settler Colonial Studies* 559; Amie Breeze Harper (ed), *Sistah Vegan: Black Female Vegans Speak on Food, Identity, Health, and Society* (Lantern Books, 2010); Jessica Ison and JL Schatz, 'Introduction: Queering the Ecofeminist Tradition' (2016) 9(3) *Green Theory & Praxis Journal* 4; Kim (n 26).

is ever-present and total.[71] Critical race scholar Megan H Glick calls this ever-present control and death as 'normalizable' because the system is so pervasive.[72] When you consider animals, there are few – if any – who are not in some way controlled or managed by humans. We may frame euthanasia as care for animals, but the extent of those who we kill and the reasons for this killing shows that it is too a form of animal management. By talking sweetly of one's dog crossing the rainbow bridge, waiting for us in heaven as they drift off to sleep in the veterinary clinic, we forget those who we kill in pounds, the slaughterhouse rolls on and the less benign reasons for choosing euthanasia on behalf of a pet are ignored – such as the cost of keeping the pet or that they have become too burdensome.

Animals also show us that we presume to understand the subject who cannot speak for themself. Dying a good death is presumed to be the most desired outcome, after living a good life. However, the presumption of what a good death is, particularly concerning animals, is premised on knowing them in a relationship where humans have complete management and control. If we forgo the presumption that we know what a good death is for animals, we may have to begin to question what is a good life. Animal euthanasia happens so often, to such an unfathomable degree, that assurance of this being a 'good death' obfuscates the reality of the extent of these supposed good deaths. The animals who cannot speak for themselves, at least not in a language we bother to learn, have a good death forced on them. Inevitably, this is a concern for those humans who also cannot advocate for themselves. Who says what a good death is?

The crucial difference between the management of human death and animal death is that we do not – for the most part – eat humans.[73] Even further, we breed some animals to eat them. We bring them into this world for this purpose. Indeed, if they do not fulfil this purpose we kill them, such as roosters or bobby calves who are respectively thrown into macerators alive or taken from their mothers and kept in a tiny cage for a few weeks before slaughter. These animals show the stark cruelty of this industry and also the depths to which we wave our concern for

71   Dinesh Joseph Wadiwel, *The War Against Animals* (Brill Rodophi Press, 2015).

72   Megan H Glick, 'Animal Instincts: Race, Criminality, and the Reversal of the "Human"' (2013) 65(3) *American Quarterly*, 645.

73   Though an argument could be made that we do consume humans and human life through exploitation and the control of workers under the capitalist system. Could consumption be extended to slavery and indentured servitude? Or in a different vein, what of the woman consumed by a violent relationship? At what point is the human consumable even if they are not edible?

the vulnerable. A society that throws live chicks into plastic bags to die must surely not be one that has pet cemeteries. Nevertheless, this contradiction exists.

Due to this contradiction, our opinions on how they should die offer an interesting insight into how we conceive of life and who indeed we conceive of as living a life. If we have such stark separation between animals we love and animals we exploit, then perhaps we can question whether this relates to humans. However, what even constitutes the human? Indeed, 'the human as a category is frequently taken for granted, though it remains deeply tied to political and juridical notions of enfranchisement and belonging.'[74] Those who have access to being seen as fully human are a privileged few. With VAD will we see some people allowed to access a supposedly peaceful death and others left to suffer? The legal issues and access to knowledge will surely prohibit many humans from accessing VAD. What might the study of animals and their deaths, considerations of who and who is not enveloped in a circle of care, and the question of who determines what constitutes a 'peaceful death', how that is administered and by whom, teach us that may be relevant for human VAD? If nothing else, it shows us that we can construct elaborate layers of meaning that obfuscate cruelty and solidify a moral and ethical position that refuses to engage with the myriad inconvenient concerns.

Conclusion

VAD raises a slew of moral concerns, many of which this collection addresses. Yet people often believe it is simply a case of allowing someone to die painlessly. Even if it was this simple – which this collection definitively shows it is not – it is still a matter of who we see as worthy of having a good life. Over and again, whom we include and whom we exclude from available treatments obscures a series of social issues. Those animals left in pounds are not able to have a human speak for them, and for a variety of reasons, veterinarians often euthanise healthy animals. They are not able to access the wealth of those animals who get to live well because of their categorisation as 'pets'. In this society, it seems that only those who we extend care to in life are granted care in death. The debate then must shift away from the ethics of dying by choice, to the ethics of who is

---

74   Glick (n 1) 642.

deemed worthy of care in both death and life. Our complicated relations with animals can teach us that we have the capacity for great love and care but also for allowing death to become something that is managed within a system of exploitation that only allows some to die well, particularly when they were allowed to live well.

Bibliography

A Articles/books/reports

Alloun, Esther, '"That's the Beauty of It, It's Very Simple!" Animal Rights and Settler Colonialism in Palestine–Israel' (2018) 8(4) *Settler Colonial Studies* 559 doi.org/10.1080/2201473X.2017.1414138

Animal Studies Group, *Killing Animals* (University of Illinois Press, 2006)

Bulliet, Richard W, *Hunters, Herders, and Hamburgers: The Past and Future of Human-Animal Relationships* (Columbia University Press, 2005)

Collier, Ivy D, 'More than a Bag of Bones: A History of Animal Burials' in Margo DeMello (ed), *Mourning Animals: Rituals and Practices Surrounding Animal Death* (Michigan State University Press, 2016) 3

Colling, Sarat, Sean Parson and Alessandro Arrigoni, 'Until All Are Free: Total Liberation through Revolutionary Decolonization, Groundless Solidarity, and a Relationship Framework' in Anthony J Nocella II et al (eds), *Defining Critical Animal Studies: An Intersectional Social Justice Approach for Liberation* (Peter Lang Publishing, 2014)

Cox, Janice and Sabine Lennkh, *Model Animal Welfare Act: A Comprehensive Framework Law* (World Animal Net, 2016)

Desmond, Jane C, *Displaying Death and Animating Life: Human-Animal Relations in Art, Science, and Everyday Life* (University of Chicago Press, 2016) doi.org/10.7208/chicago/9780226375519.001.0001

Donovan, Josephine and Carol J Adams (eds), *The Feminist Care Tradition in Animal Ethics: A Reader* (Columbia University Press, 2007)

European Commission, *Euthanasia of Experimental Animals* (March 1997)

Fawcett, Anne, 'Euthanasia and Morally Justifiable Killing in a Veterinary Clinical Context' in Jay Johnston and Fiona Probyn-Rapsey (eds), *Animal Death* (Sydney University Press, 2013) 205 doi.org/10.2307/j.ctt1gxxpvf.18

Fitzgerald, Amy J, 'A Social History of the Slaughterhouse: From Inception to Contemporary Implications' (2010) 17(1) *Human Ecology Review* 58

Frommer, Stephanie S and Arnold Arluke, 'Loving Them to Death: Blame-Displacing Strategies of Animal Shelter Workers and Surrenderers' (1999) 7(1) *Society & Animals* 1 doi.org/10.1163/156853099X00121

Glick, Megan H, 'Animal Instincts: Race, Criminality, and the Reversal of the "Human"' (2013) 65(3) *American Quarterly* 639 doi.org/10.1353/aq.2013.0046

Harper, Amie Breeze (ed), *Sistah Vegan: Black Female Vegans Speak on Food, Identity, Health, and Society* (Lantern Books, 2010)

Ison, Jessica, 'Animal Abuse and Advocating for the Carceral: Critiquing Animal Abuse Registries' (2019) 8(2) *Animal Studies Journal* 55 doi.org/10.14453/asj.v8i2.7

Ison, Jessica and JL Schatz, 'Introduction: Queering the Ecofeminist Tradition' (2016) 9(3) *Green Theory & Praxis Journal* 4

Kean, Hilda, 'Human and Animal Space in Historic "Pet" Cemeteries in London, New York and Paris' in Jay Johnston and Fiona Probyn-Rapsey (eds), *Animal Death* (Sydney University Press, 2013) 21 doi.org/10.2307/j.ctt1gxxpvf.8

Kim, Claire Jean, *Dangerous Crossings: Race, Species, and Nature in a Multicultural Age* (Cambridge University Press, 2015)

Li Chien-hui, 'An Unnatural Alliance? Political Radicalism and the Animal Defence Movement in Late Victorian and Edwardian Britain' (2012) 42(1) *EurAmerica* 1

Mayer, Jed, 'Ways of Reading Animals in Victorian Literature, Culture and Science' (2010) 7(5) *Literature Compass* 347 doi.org/10.1111/j.1741-4113.2009.00697.x

Mazzeno, Laurence W and Ronald D Morrison, 'Introduction' in Laurence W Mazzeno and Ronald D Morrison (eds), *Animals in Victorian Literature and Culture: Contexts for Criticism* (Palgrave Macmillan UK, 2017) 1 doi.org/10.1057/978-1-137-60219-0_1

McKinney, Karyn, 'Emotion Work of Coping with the Death of a Companion Animal' (2019) 27(1) *Society & Animals* 109 doi.org/10.1163/15685306-12341586

Morris, Patricia, 'Managing Pet Owners' Guilt and Grief in Veterinary Euthanasia Encounters' (2012) 41(3) *Journal of Contemporary Ethnography* 337 doi.org/10.1177/0891241611435099

Munro, Lyle, *Compassionate Beasts: The Quest for Animal Rights* (Praeger, 2001)

National Health and Medical Research Council, *Australian Code of Practice for the Care and Use of Animals for Scientific Purposes* (Report, 7th ed, 2004)

Nocella, Anthony J II et al (eds), *Defining Critical Animal Studies: An Intersectional Social Justice Approach for Liberation* (Peter Lang Publishing, 2014) doi.org/10.3726/978-1-4539-1230-0

Pachirat, Timothy, *Every Twelve Seconds: Industrialized Slaughter and the Politics of Sight* (Yale University Press, 2011)

Palmer, Clare Alexandra, 'Killing Animals in Animal Shelters' in Animal Studies Group (ed), *Killing Animals* (University of Illinois Press, 2006) 170

Pellow, David Naguib, *Total Liberation: The Power and Promise of Animal Rights and the Radical Earth Movement* (University of Minnesota Press) doi.org/10.5749/minnesota/9780816687763.001.0001

Pendergrast, Nick, 'Live Animal Export, Humane Slaughter and Media Hegemony' (2015) 4(1) *Animal Studies Journal* 99

Perkins, David, *Romanticism and Animal Rights* (Cambridge University Press, 2003)

Pręgowski, Michał Piotr, 'All the World and a Little Bit More: Pet Cemetery Practices and Contemporary Relations between Humans and Their Companion Animals' in Margo DeMello (ed), *Mourning Animals: Rituals and Practices Surrounding Animal Death* (Michigan State University Press, 2016)

Probyn-Rapsey, Fiona, 'Five Propositions on Ferals' (2016) 6 *Feral Feminisms* <https://feralfeminisms.com/five-propositions-on-ferals/>

Probyn-Rapsey, Fiona and Jay Johnston, *Animal Death* (Sydney University Press, 2013)

Regan, Tom, *The Case for Animal Rights* (University of California Press, 1983)

Reilly, JS (ed), *Euthanasia of Animals Used for Scientific Purposes* (Australian & New Zealand Council for the Care of Animals in Research and Teaching, 2nd ed, 2001)

Ross, Cheri Barton, *Pet Loss and Human Emotion: A Guide to Recovery*, ed Jane Baron-Sorensen (Taylor & Francis, 2nd ed, 2013)

Shukin, Nicole, *Animal Capital: Rendering Life in Biopolitical Times* (University of Minnesota Press, 2009)

Taylor, Nik and Tania Signal (eds), *Theorizing Animals: Re-Thinking Humanimal Relations* (Brill, 2011) doi.org/10.1163/ej.9789004202429.i-294

Tiplady, Catherine, *Animal Abuse: Helping Animals and People* (CABI, 2013)

Twine, Richard, 'Intersectional Disgust? Animals and (Eco)Feminism' (2010) 20(3) *Feminism & Psychology* 397 doi.org/10.1177/0959353510368284

Wadiwel, Dinesh Joseph, *The War Against Animals* (Brill Rodopi, 2015)

Weil, Kari, 'A Report on the Animal Turn' (2010) 21(2) *differences* 1 doi.org/10.1215/10407391-2010-001

Wolfensohn, Sarah and Maggie Lloyd, *Handbook of Laboratory Animal Management and Welfare* (Blackwell Science, 2nd ed, 1998)

Zhu, Yi and Min Liu, 'Discussion of the Metropolis Pet Funeral and Burial Service' in Ying Zhang (ed), *Future Communication, Computing, Control and Management: Volume 2* (Springer, 2012) 267 doi.org/10.1007/978-3-642-27314-8_38

B Legislation

Prevention of Cruelty to Animals Act 1986 (Vic)

C Other

Allavena, Rachel, 'Why You Shouldn't Bury Your Pet in the Backyard', *ABC News* (online, 19 March 2019) <https://www.abc.net.au/news/2019-03-19/why-you-shouldn%E2%80%99t-bury-your-pet-in-the-backyard/10915772>

Andersen, Kip, 'The Facts', *Cowspiracy: The Sustainability Secret* (Web Page) <https://www.cowspiracy.com/facts>

Animal Rights, 'Animals Are Not Ours Memorial', *Vimeo* (Video, 7 October 2013) <https://vimeo.com/76382879>

Australian Bureau of Statistics, *Livestock and Meat, Australia, June 2020* (Catalogue No 7218.0.55.001, 8 May 2020) <https://www.abs.gov.au/statistics/industry/agriculture/livestock-and-meat-australia/latest-release>

'Companion Animals', *Animals Australia* (Web Page, 13 August 2019) <https://www.animalsaustralia.org/issues/companion_animals.php>

'End-of-Life Services', *Animal Humane Society* (Web Page) <https://www.animal humanesociety.org/health/end-life-services>

'Euthanasia', *Australian Veterinary Association* (Web Page, 10 August 2007) <https://www.ava.com.au/policy-advocacy/policies/euthanasia/euthanasia/>

Kleinfeldt, Alexandra, 'Brief Summary of Animal Euthanasia', *Animal Legal & Historical Center* (Web Page, 2017) <https://www.animallaw.info/intro/animal-euthanasia>

Merriam-Webster Dictionary (online at 24 June 2021) 'Euthanasia', <https://www.merriam-webster.com/dictionary/euthanasia>

'Our History', *RSPCA UK* (Web Page) <https://www.rspca.org.uk/whatwedo/whoweare/history>

Pilat, Lauren, '"Humanely Euthanised": Roos to Be Killed to Make Way for Development South of Perth', *WAtoday* (online, 28 January 2019) <https://www.watoday.com.au/national/western-australia/humanely-euthanised-roos-to-be-killed-to-make-way-for-development-south-of-perth-20190128-p50u4u.html>

RSCPA Australia, *RSPCA Australia National Statistics 2019–2020* (Report) <https://www.rspca.org.au/sites/default/files/RSPCA%20Australia%20Annual%20Statistics%202019-2020.pdf>

'Statistics', *No Kill Advocacy Center* (Web Page) <https://www.nokilladvocacycenter.org/statistics.html>

'Suicide', *Australian Veterinary Association* (Web Page) <https://www.ava.com.au/member-services/vethealth/suicide/>

'When is the Right Time for Euthanasia?', *Living With Pet Bereavement* (Web Page) <https://livingwithpetbereavement.com/is-the-time-right%3F>

Wills, Matthew, 'The Invention of Pets', *JSTOR Daily* (Blog Post, 28 January 2017) <https://daily.jstor.org/the-invention-of-pets/>

7

A Desire unto Death: The Warnings of Girard and Levinas against the Sanitisation of Euthanasia

Nigel Zimmermann

Introduction

In this chapter I make three propositions. First, a word on the nature of facing death; second, I propose that we have much to learn from the warnings of René Girard and Emmanuel Levinas against the false promise of euthanasia; third, we may view their warnings as a lesson for us facing the particular reality of voluntary assisted dying (VAD), what can be called a 'soft' version of euthanasia. VAD has been a reality in the State of Victoria since 19 June 2019 and other Australian jurisdictions are considering similar legislation. The Girard–Levinas critique of VAD issues us with a responsibility for those who suffer rather than the chilling prospect of a bureaucratic process of magnified autonomy resulting in the death of those most vulnerable to pressure and coercion.

Facing death

In Victoria's VAD legislation, a sanitising promise is made to those who suffer: your pain will be lessened and your autonomy increased. While the *Voluntary Assisted Dying Act 2017* (Vic) places bureaucratic restrictions upon those who can access VAD and under what circumstances, the promise is issued full of optimism about how a magnified individual autonomy can result in shared happiness among those involved in the exercise of desiring and enacting one's death. Campaigners for VAD suggest that the exercise of autonomy represents an overwhelmingly positive result for the happiness of Victoria residents, such as in a documentation of the process undertaken by the Ministerial Advisory Panel that ultimately drafted the legislation and made a case for its successful implementation. They advised:

> This change represents a major shift in exercise of individual autonomy over that of the state. In tolerant communities, it is noted that acceptance of control over dying links to other personal freedom-in-life choices.[1]

These kinds of positive connotations pepper the description by Margaret O'Connor and others: notions of tolerance, personal control and autonomy, personal freedom and, of course, choice.

However, René Girard argues for the opposite; contrary to making the end of life positive or easier, euthanasia places a heavy burden of responsibility on each person for his or her own death, and will make death harder, more painful and ultimately a heavier burden at the end of life. Those with fewer resources – spiritual, material, familial and social – will be at greater risk of harm. This question of the responsibility to die has been passed over by the supporters of VAD because the way that social relationships of mutual and complementary responsibility operate is an inconvenient obstacle to arguments in favour of steps towards euthanasia. Girard's ethical concerns, and the analysis of alterity in Emmanuel Levinas, provides a chilling warning that death, and therefore life, has now become more burdensome for health providers, family and loved ones. Violence is a logical and usually unintended correlate.

---

1   Margaret M O'Connor et al, 'Documenting the Process of Developing the Victorian Voluntary Assisted Dying Legislation' (2018) 42(6) *Australian Health Review* 621.

On 19 June 2019, a possibility opened up for patients who meet certain criteria to be able to embark on a complicated bureaucratic process to legally obtain access to a form of physician-assisted suicide, a 'soft' version of euthanasia, in the State of Victoria, under the *Voluntary Assisted Dying Act 2017*.[2] After the Act passed Victoria's Houses of Parliament, the Premier referred to that moment as 'a day of reform, a day of compassion, a day of giving control to those who are terminally ill'.[3]

Similar proposals are being considered in other jurisdictions around the world and are much advanced in places like the Netherlands and Canada, and in ethically dubious and less monitored contexts in China and other parts of South-East Asia. Legislation based on Victoria's VAD model are increasingly probable in states like Queensland and Western Australia, given how public sentiment seems to be reflected, representing a push to force all of us to face questions of death and the treatment of those who are dying or in conditions of pain and anxiety with a new urgency and in a new situation.

In the time following the introduction of VAD the situation has not become less problematic. For example, a Voluntary Assisted Dying Review Board exists for the purposes of reporting to parliament every six months for the first two years of VAD, but it has not proven to be transparent in its own processes. In its report for the period January–June 2020 the Board utilised anonymous quotes from patients, family and doctors who had been involved with a VAD assessment or process.[4] Some quotes are negative but most are overwhelmingly positive, referring to VAD as providing for a 'beautiful, peaceful death', a 'beautiful passing' and a supportive pharmacy team who were 'so kind and understanding'.[5] Negative comments were all related to the bureaucratic processes that are built into the VAD process in Victoria, such as references to the length of time it can take or the inconvenience of paperwork, disappointment at a doctor not wishing to facilitate VAD and frustration at having trouble finding a doctor willing to do likewise.[6] The implication is that there

---

2   *Voluntary Assisted Dying Act 2017* (Vic).

3   Jean Edwards, 'Euthanasia: Victoria Becomes First Australian State to Legalise Voluntary Assisted Dying' *ABC News* (online, 29 November 2017) <https://www.abc.net.au/news/2017-11-29/euthanasia-passes-parliament-in-victoria/9205472>.

4   Voluntary Assisted Dying Review Board, Safer Care Victoria, *Review of Operations January–June 2020* (Report No 3, 31 August 2020).

5   Voluntary Assisted Dying Review Board (n 4) 10, 12.

6   Voluntary Assisted Dying Review Board (n 4) 2, 7, 10.

are too many obstacles to assisted suicide and that it can take too long. Disappointingly the VAD Review Board, across its first three reports, failed to address any of the following: what proportion of VAD applicants undertook palliative care assessment before taking their lives in this way; how many doctors were actually involved in VAD; what supports and information were available to family and loved ones; and were mental health assessments conducted for patients seeking VAD? The document reads less like a sober and transparent report than it does an advertising brochure for assisted suicide.

We are not dealing simply with death, but a *desire unto death*.

First, a word on the title of this chapter. The term, 'a desire unto death' is taken from an article published in 2008 by Jason Wardley titled, 'A Desire Unto Death: The Deconstructive Thanatology of Jean-Luc Marion', in the *Heythrop Journal*.[7] It is a play on the words of Soren Kierkegaard's 1849 work, *A Sickness Unto Death*, under his pseudonym Anti-Climacus.[8] Kierkegaard's book is a powerful work of existential thought within a Western Christian context. It pioneered a way of philosophical reflection that foreshadowed the subjective turn of modern philosophy without simply turning in on itself in pure self-referentiality, and considered questions of religious conviction in their radical bareness, critiquing easy bourgeois attitudes and practices that operated under the guise of respectability and neoliberal material comfort. Kierkegaard's account of despair was both human and relatable, and he drew on the long biblical tradition of Original Sin as a way of giving meaning to what we would now call depression, and the anxious seeking after that which gives us pleasure amid false promises and securities.

Death is ever-near in the work of Kierkegaard, and Wardley took his cues from the Danish writer when studying the thought of Jean-Luc Marion, heavily influenced by Emmanuel Levinas. Wardley wrote that phenomenology, and the most interesting philosophy of late modernity, draws us towards the strangeness of the other – the incarnate and visible stranger before us – which under careful reflection can appear in the horizon of death, because it is strangeness that pulls us out of ourselves in such a way that enables us to better understand the human condition

---

7   Kenneth Jason Wardley, '"A Desire Unto Death": The Deconstructive Thanatology of Jean-Luc Marion' (2008) 49(1) *The Heythrop Journal* 79.
8   Soren Kierkegaard, *The Sickness Unto Death: A Christian Psychological Exposition of Edification and Awakening by Anti-Climacus*, tr Alastair Hannay (Penguin, 2004).

in which we inhabit. Death places before us limits and the horizon of finitude, raising numerous questions about the life we live. For Wardley, we encounter in death a stranger that calls attention to ourselves, which is why questions of religious conviction, and of God, always hover so near to ethical questions around the end of life. Both the notion of limits and the subject of God can make us uncomfortable in a late modern, secular liberal democracy, but being uncomfortable can be an aid to the telling of truth. Wardley finds Jean-Luc Marion's phenomenology of death perplexing in this regard, and not without its difficulties, but ultimately he argues that a phenomenology of death unnerves us in our relationship to death, to God and to those who are dying. He writes:

> The God of Marion's Christian revelation is the God whom no-one can see without dying, a look that we desire unto death.[9]

In other words, the perplexing search for God, even at a non-theological level, meets its conclusion in the face of death, regardless of one's religious commitments.

In 2014 Jason Wardley published *Praying to a French God: The Theology of Jean-Yves Lacoste*.[10] Jason passed away after his book was published, but days before he could have held it in his hands, facing the horizon of death of which he had written much. A young man, having faced a two-year battle with a malignant neoplasm upon his brain that was already forming malignant metastases at the time of its discovery and diagnosis, Jason's mental functioning had gone into serious decline, his good judgment becoming uneven, and his intellectual prowess becoming sporadic in the midst of physical deprivations; and as such Jason was forced to face death. He was my friend, and while he faced his death with a cheerful countenance, he also felt his own loss deeply, but at no time did he wish to sanitise its meaning, nor did he wish to avoid his sufferings for the sake of an early suicide. Jason never entertained such a thought, largely because he had learned from Lacoste and Marion that to do so is not actually to meet death, but to avoid its face and the lessons it teaches. That is not an argument in itself against euthanasia, but I learned much from Jason, in both his philosophical reflections on death, and the way that he faced it when it arrived. What it does, however, is remind us that dying is not

---

9   Wardley (n 7) 93.
10 Kenneth Jason Wardley, *Praying to a French God: The Theology of Jean-Yves Lacoste* (Routledge, 2016).

merely a discrete moment in the course of life, a fragment at the end, or a prologue, but includes the whole process of facing one's own death as a continuum in development in the course of a human life.

René Girard and the burdens of euthanasia

The French literary theorist René Girard (1923–2015) is best known for developing his theory of mimetic desire, the drama by which narratives in Western history cast light on the way in which a community becomes a crowd, mimics particular behaviours and desires of others, and can become a mob, seeking to locate upon an individual, or a particular community, or a caste of persons, blame for some form of suffering. According to Girard, violence is exercised upon the scapegoat so that salvation in one form or another can be obtained for the community. He finds this in literature of all descriptions and genres, and views it as the fundamental story at the heart of biblical literature and of Christian faith. The Christ is that figure of perfect suffering, torn and bloody because of the judgment of the mob, and whose death is hurried with salvific promise.

Girard has often turned his work to contemporary problems of death and suffering, and argues that Western cultures have been progressing through a forgetfulness of the scapegoating narrative, and a propensity to tell ourselves we are building paradise, all the while casting blame upon vulnerable people at the edges of our cities and suburbia for any suffering we still endure.[11] Inasmuch as we blame others, according to this approach, we eschew our own responsibility.

In an interview with James Williams, published in 2000, Girard was asked his thoughts on increased calls for euthanasia. He answered:

> The experience of death is going to get more and more painful, contrary to what many people believe. The forthcoming euthanasia will make it more rather than less painful because it will put the emphasis on personal decision in a way which was blissfully alien

---

11   See Girard's books *Violence and the Sacred*, tr Patrick Gregory (Johns Hopkins University Press, 1st ed, 1977); *The Scapegoat*, tr Yvonne Freccero (Johns Hopkins University Press, 1986); and *Oedipus Unbound: Selected Writings on Rivalry and Desire*, ed Mark Rogin Anspach (Stanford University Press, 2004).

to the whole problem of dying in former times. It will make death even more subjectively intolerable, for people will feel responsible for their own deaths and morally obligated to rid their relatives of their unwanted presence. Euthanasia will further intensify all the problems its advocates think it will solve.[12]

Girard identifies a change that takes place when euthanasia, even a soft version such as VAD, is made legal. Advocates argue that autonomy is the sovereign value, and only by it can compassion be realised in our care for those who experience serious and prolonged suffering.[13] However, the values of a society in which euthanasia is legal and one in which euthanasia is illegal must necessarily be different, and for Girard such a change in the law also results in increased capacities for social pressure and expectations that people will not just be responsible for their own death, but irresponsible when not enacting it at the appropriate time. The moral obligation of which Girard speaks does not lighten the burden upon the elderly, the sick and the disabled; it shifts the burden onto their shoulders in an intense way, such that we add to their pain instead of decreasing it. While Premier Daniel Andrews and his health minister used the language of compassion to appeal to the people of Victoria, Girard's warning goes unheeded, allowing us to liaise dangerously with a sanitised view of euthanasia that paints over the threats to those most vulnerable, most under pressure and with the most to lose.

Emmanuel Levinas and the demands of the Other

Emmanuel Levinas (1906–1995) was a Lithuanian Jewish philosopher who migrated to Paris and adopted French culture with the fervour of the convert, was largely responsible for bringing the thought of Edmund Husserl (1859–1938) to France, and crafted a radical philosophy of alterity – *otherness* – in response to Martin Heidegger (1889–1976). For Levinas, ethics is first philosophy, and phenomenology opens a way of describing the overwhelming ethical demand in the face of the other

---

12   René Girard, 'Epilogue: The Anthropology of the Cross: A Conversation with René Girard' in James Williams (ed), *The Girard Reader* (The Crossroad Publishing Company, 2000) 262, 277.
13   Similar arguments have been made against the primacy or adequacy of 'autonomy', such as J David Velleman's essay 'Against the Right to Die' (1992) 17(6) *The Journal of Medicine and Philosophy: A Forum for Bioethics and Philosophy of Medicine* 665. Velleman makes his argument from a Kantian perspective, but it has resonances with Girard on this point.

person, the Other, for our responsible care and attention towards them. This is most effective in the demand issued forth from those in particular vulnerability and need.

Levinas had a complicated relationship with his own religious tradition, and although he was a Jewish adherent in a strong intellectual sense, matters of faith were private to him and he was shy of public religion or indeed public political commitments. During World War II his wife and daughter were spared death (despite later deportation) through the protection of a Catholic cloister, for which Levinas expresses gratitude and a painful joy.[14] He comments upon his development of a view, largely taken from Franz Rosenzweig (1886–1929), that in Christianity and Judaism can be found a common measure of the (ethical) *kenosis* of God, as well as the necessity that God demands an incarnate servant-hood to the weak, hungry and the oppressed.[15] According to Levinas the ethical demand of the Other, including the dying and those in great suffering, arrives pre-philosophical reflection, naked of political intrigue and without a religious identity. We are responsible for the Other not despite philosophy, politics and religion, but without appeal or reliance upon those commitments.[16]

Coming from the Polish philosophical school of Thomistic thought in dialogue with Husserlian phenomenology, Karol Wojtyla, better known as John Paul II, wrote of Emmanuel Levinas in an essay 'The Defence of Every Life':

> I cannot dwell here on *contemporary thinkers*, but I must mention at least one name – *Emmanuel Levinas*, who represents a particular school of contemporary *personalism* and of the *philosophy of dialogue*. Like Martin Buber and Franz Rosenzweig, he takes up the personalistic tradition of the Old Testament, where the relationship between the human 'I' and the divine, absolutely sovereign 'THOU' is so heavily emphasized.
>
> God, who is the supreme legislator, forcefully enjoined on Sinai the commandment 'Thou shalt not kill,' as an absolute moral imperative. Levinas, who, like his co-religionists, deeply

---

14 Emmanuel Levinas and Jill Robbins, *Is It Righteous to Be? Interviews with Emmanuel Levinas* (Stanford University Press, 2001) 257.
15 Levinas (n 14) 256.
16 The use of other or Other can be a complicated business in commentary on Levinas. Here, I try to use the capitalised 'Other' when using the other person in the conceptual sense of Levinas, with its overwhelming connotations of difference and distance. I use the 'other' when simply referring to the other person in a more perfunctory or less abstract sense.

experienced the tragedy of the Holocaust, offers a remarkable formulation of this fundamental commandment of the Decalogue – for him, the face reveals the person. This *philosophy of the face* is also found in the *Old Testament*: in the Psalms, and in the writings of the Prophets, there are frequent references to 'seeking God's face' (cf. Ps 26[27]:8). It is through his face that man speaks, and in particular, every man who has suffered a wrong speaks and says the words 'Do not kill me!' *The human face and the commandment 'Do not kill' are ingeniously joined in Levinas, and thus become a testimony for our age*, in which governments, even democratically elected governments, sanction executions with such ease.

Perhaps it is better to say no more than this about such a painful subject.[17]

John Paul's reading of Levinas weaves together the strangeness of the Other with the dark episodes of history, in which, including in the present, there are regimes that kill the Other, committing acts of violence that deny the unique significance of every human face, devoid of a moral awareness of what is being trampled upon and disfigured.

The Levinasian injunction of the face is an interruption of both personal comfort and any attempt to view our relation to other persons in an ethically sanitised manner. It is not merely an invitation but a demand, and in a peculiar kind of way the Victorian Government has forced us to look at the face of the other with a new intensity, while at the same time legislating for their death.

Levinas's work has been described as the 'phenomenology of alterity'.[18] This is in evidence from his earliest works. In the early 1930s, Levinas became the French translator of Husserl's *Cartesian Meditations*, thus forging an important bridge between German phenomenology and its French descendants that blossomed in Paris throughout the latter part of the twentieth century.[19] This translation was followed by *The Theory of Intuition in Husserl*.[20] Nevertheless, it was not until *Totality and Infinity* was published in 1961 that his original contribution to phenomenology

---

17   John Paul II, *Crossing the Threshold of Hope*, ed Vittorio Messori, tr Jenny McPhee and Martha McPhee (Jonathan Cape, 1994) 210–11 (emphasis in the original).

18   Dermot Moran, *Introduction to Phenomenology* (Routledge, 2000) 320.

19   Moran (n 18) 320.

20   *La théorie de l'intuition dans la phénoménologie de Husserl* (1930): Emmanuel Levinas, *The Theory of Intuition in Husserl's Phenomenology*, tr André Orianne (Northwestern University Press, 2nd ed, 1995).

was made manifest.[21] In that book he introduces a radicalised appreciation of alterity in terms of ethics, contra Heidegger, for whom ethics was not a branch of fundamental ontology.[22] This was developed further with *Otherwise than Being or Beyond Essence*, in the declaration that Western philosophy has, at heart, treated difference and the other with disdain by giving primary significance to being as the fundamental category.[23] Levinas's idea was not a rejection of being per se, but rather understanding it 'on the basis of *being's other*'.[24] Unlike Wojtyla, for whom metaphysics in the tradition of Aristotle and Thomas provides a necessary corrective to the limitations of phenomenology, Levinas draws on Plato as a self-inversion of the Western philosophical tradition.[25] For him, Plato's prioritisation of the good beyond being challenges the prioritisation of ontology, so reinterpreting the whole philosophical tradition from Plato onwards. Levinas insists that the going out of the self for the sake of the other – absolute responsibility – places the self in the role of 'hostage', restless and 'gnawing away at oneself', both 'inspired' and taken up completely in one's psyche for the sake of the good of the other.[26] The body of the other is taken up into the self's own ethical practice, just as it is infinitely distant. Levinas says:

> The psyche can signify this alterity in the same without alienation in the form of incarnation, as being-in-one's-skin, having-the-other-in-one's-skin.[27]

---

21   Emmanuel Levinas, *Totality and Infinity: An Essay on Exteriority*, tr Alphonso Lingis (Duquesne University Press, 1969).

22   Throughout *Sein und Zeit* (1927), Heidegger is concerned with the nature of authenticity and does not develop an ethics as such, nor clearly describe the role ethics might play in his philosophy. See Martin Heidegger, *Being and Time*, tr John Macquarrie and Edward Robinson (SCM Press, 1962). The Levinasian critique has been contested by Heidegger interpreters such as Laurence Paul Hemming who rejects Levinas' argument that *Being and Time* instrumentalises the other for the sake of the self. See Laurence Paul Hemming, 'A Transcendental Hangover: Lévinas, Heidegger and the Ethics of Alterity' (2005) 18(2) *Studies in Christian Ethics* 45.

23   *Autrement qu'être ou au-delà de l'essence* (1978): Emmanuel Levinas, *Otherwise Than Being: Or Beyond Essence*, tr Alphonso Lingis (Duquesne University Press, 1998).

24   Levinas (n 23) 16.

25   See for example, Sarah Allen, *The Philosophical Sense of Transcendence: Levinas and Plato on Loving Beyond Being* (Duquesne University Press, 2009); Tanja Staehler, *Plato and Levinas: The Ambiguous Out-Side of Ethics* (Routledge, 2010); Mary-Ann Webb, 'Eros and Ethics: Levinas's Reading of Plato's "Good Beyond Being"' (2006) 19(2) *Studies in Christian Ethics* 205.

26   Levinas (n 23) 114.

27   Levinas (n 23) 114–15.

Here, Levinas makes use of his phrase 'the same' as denoting that which is not just the self, but all that lies close to the self; that which we associate with ourselves in some intimate and comfortable sense. According to Levinas, the psyche has a capacity to enfold within itself difference at the same time as sameness, a complicated event that is never stable and always undergoing a paradoxical challenge from the Other. The key is that even when enfolded in an unclear and ambiguous relationship, the Other holds the self to account and maintains a relationship of utter responsibility towards that which is different. Such a relationship is both beyond and prior to all our professional relationships, including that of the doctor and the patient.

The God of the Hebrews marked an unambiguous ethical boundary: 'Thou shalt not kill'. For Levinas the command is not only a verbal or literary command; it is inscribed in the humanity of the other person: *do not kill me*. Such a demand derives from the experience of human community in which difference is honoured and respected, regardless of whether one believes the command is uttered by the Creator or not.

For Marion, what Levinas draws our attention to, past the loud voice of the state or of personal investment or the incursions of bureaucracy, is the ethical 'call' or even better, the 'appeal'.[28] In the appeal of the face, we are addressed in a singular demand. One receives the address as a demanding excess of meaning in which both a summons and a command are issued without hesitation. Marion takes this up in his phenomenological analysis of what he describes as 'saturated phenomena' (the event, the idol, flesh and the icon).[29] The call and the appeal, which is received in a presence that exceeds all understanding and containment, which 'saturates' one's intentionality, relies very much on the notion of an event that speaks personally to us. Levinas's critique of Western philosophy and its compulsion to circumvent all thought into Being, and the ethical signification of alterity in the face of the Other, create the means by which human nature can speak to us and call us away from easy answers designed to release us from simple questions. The otherness of the Other, who is thought beyond Being, is present in a way that so saturates one's ethical relationship with its subjective constitution that

28   See Jean-Luc Marion, 'The Final Appeal of the Subject', in John D Caputo (ed), *The Religious* (Blackwell, 2002); also Marion, *The Erotic Phenomenon*, tr Stephen E Lewis (University of Chicago Press, 2007).
29   See especially Jean-Luc Marion, *In Excess: Studies of Saturated Phenomena*, tr Robyn Horner and Vincent Berraud (Fordham University Press, 2002).

it, in effect, envelopes and overcomes oneself. This effectively denies the possibility of reducing the Other in any way, even if in practical terms the Other may be diminished in its phenomenal experience. At the bedside of the dying, Levinas says we have to listen and watch more intensely, and this will mean that we must sometimes answer on behalf of the Other in their vulnerability, issuing a demand for better care, for more resources, for an investment of attention and even of love and friendship, and to mark a line in the sand so that our ethical commitments are not trampled through the soothing and sanitising language of a false compassion.

The appearing of another person in this way is the event of concrete human experience. It must not be interpreted as a mystical experience in any overtly religious sense, but as the ethical content that rises in the subjectivity of the most urbane human encounters. It is a radicalisation of human sociality. Marion takes this human moment – seemingly banal in its domestic sensibility – and interprets it to allow for the possibility of revelation. As Robyn Horner describes, revelation can have a content, although as an excessive content it is marked as holding an 'inevitably hermeneutical supplement to phenomenology'.[30] In other words, the excess has a boundary experience in which interpretation is necessitated.

For Levinas, death is the circumstance in which ethical action is possible. This is so because death makes us intrinsically vulnerable creatures, and so ethics has a very serious life-threatening gravity to it. A readiness to die for the Other proves the sincere disinterest of the ethical gesture, thus precluding the will to power. Levinas also assumes that we become self-aware and aware of other people through the cry of the vulnerable and the consequence that one must sacrifice oneself to meet the need indicated by that cry. The Other therefore is greater than us and places the demand for ethical attention upon us; it is not derived from our own natural disposition or commitments. It carries an objectivity that, for Levinas, has to remain absolute because our humanity demands it, and the command not to kill is unalterable.

---

30   Robyn Horner, *Jean-Luc Marion: A Theo-logical Introduction* (Routledge, 2005) 133.

For or against the other? Against the sanitisation of euthanasia

In January 2019, *The Guardian*, whose editors have advocated for euthanasia, ran a story on how doctors are critically pushing back on physician-assisted suicide.[31] Christopher de Bellaigue identifies two factors that are complicating the legal situation for euthanasia in Belgium, where it has been legal since 2002: autonomy and dementia. At least one euthanasia malpractice case is now in process in a situation in which a dementia patient's advance directive, which had instructed euthanasia to be administered in certain circumstances, has been called into question because of the changed mental state of the patient once they had an advanced form of dementia. Dementia is an uneven and complicated process and its advent does not necessarily mean that 'unbearable suffering' is being experienced. As Bellaigue explains:

> The underlying problem with the advance directives is that they imply the subordination of an irrational human being to their rational former self, essentially splitting a single person into two mutually opposed ones. Many doctors, having watched patients adapt to circumstances they had once expected to find intolerable, doubt whether anyone can accurately predict what they will want after their condition worsens.[32]

Even if one argues that euthanasia adequately respects personal autonomy and is a means for showing genuine compassion for the other, who exactly can be said to have sovereignty over their own healthcare – the earlier rational self or the later self who is experiencing dementia? In the case of dementia, it is not always clear that the patient experiences the condition as a form of suffering per se. This helps to explain why review boards in Holland are finding it more difficult to reach consensus on particular requests for euthanasia, and a tension between increased societal pressure to keep euthanasia available on the principle of autonomy, and expectations of thoughtful ethical deliberation for those called to make the final decision. We have here an example of Girard's prediction about the new expectations to conform to the pressures of a legal-euthanasia

---

31 Christopher de Bellaigue, 'Death on Demand: Has Euthanasia Gone Too Far?' *The Guardian* (online, 18 January 2019) <https://www.theguardian.com/news/2019/jan/18/death-on-demand-has-euthanasia-gone-too-far-netherlands-assisted-dying>.
32 Bellaigue (n 31).

context. Doctors are pushing back on such pressures, and showing signs of resentment for the expectation that they are simply there to sign off on every such request. Those advocating for increased liberalisation of euthanasia often represent interests more aligned to neoliberal principles of autonomy and material gain, as Bellaigue observes:

> At any meeting organised by the NVVE [Dutch Voluntary Euthanasia Society], you will look in vain for poor people, pious Christians or members of the Netherlands' sizeable Muslim minority. Borne along by the ultra-rational spirit of Dutch libertarianism (the spirit that made the Netherlands a pioneer in reforming laws on drugs, sex and pornography), the Dutch euthanasia scene also exudes a strong whiff of upper-middle class entitlement.[33]

It is no wonder that pressures around euthanasia as an entitlement have become pronounced as baby boomers reach the end of their lives; the generation that won the battle for access to contraception, pornography and abortion as teens and young adults, are the same who now wish to exercise control over their death. However, like contraception and abortion, the long-term implications are never known in the immediate aftermath of a new change in legislation, but only after a generation or two have lived with that change of values. While the Netherlands and other jurisdictions are just beginning to give us a glimpse of the results of euthanasia, we are still a long way to go from having a full picture, but at the very least we should avoid sanitised narratives about the good that euthanasia or VAD will achieve, and be more attentive to others in their suffering, without the loud voices of campaigners shouting us down.

Conclusion

The call of the Other in Levinas, and the grim predictions of Girard, constitute a warning for us in jurisdictions in which euthanasia, even along the lines of 'voluntary assisted' dying in Victoria, is being liberalised and endorsed. There is a seduction in the language of compassion and the cessation of suffering, even if it is ill-informed, and it can hide a sinister denial of the vulnerability and fragility of the Other, especially given the complexities of mental and physical decline. We have opened ourselves

---

33   Bellaigue (n 31).

up not to a magnification of autonomy, but increased pressures to be responsible for one's own death to not be a burden, and to suppress intense fears and anxieties that are better worked out in dialogue and friendship. As Girard puts it:

> The increasing subjective power of death converges with the fact that people are living longer lives. It is an enormous religious and ethical issue, to my mind. In the Netherlands, where I gather assisted suicides have become commonplace, there are claims that some of the assisted suicides are not suicides at all. Even if they are, the suspicion will linger that they are not, and the fear of being murdered is going to merge once again with the fear of dying. Our supermodern utopia looks very much at times like a regression to archaic terror.[34]

Bibliography

A Articles/books/reports

Allen, Sarah, *The Philosophical Sense of Transcendence: Levinas and Plato on Loving Beyond Being* (Duquesne University Press, 2009)

Girard, René, 'Epilogue: The Anthropology of the Cross: A Conversation with René Girard' in James Williams (ed), *The Girard Reader* (The Crossroad Publishing Company, 2000) 262

Girard, René, *Oedipus Unbound: Selected Writings on Rivalry and Desire*, ed Mark Rogin Anspach (Stanford University Press, 2004)

Girard, René, *The Scapegoat*, tr Yvonne Freccero (Johns Hopkins University Press, 1986)

Girard, René, *Violence and the Sacred*, tr Patrick Gregory (Johns Hopkins University Press, 1st ed, 1977)

Hart, David Bentley, *The Beauty of the Infinite: The Aesthetics of Christian Truth* (Eerdmans, 2003)

Heidegger, Martin, *Being and Time*, tr John Macquarrie and Edward Robinson (SCM Press, 1962)

---

34 Girard (n 12) 277.

Hemming, Laurence Paul, 'A Transcendental Hangover: Lévinas, Heidegger and the Ethics of Alterity' (2005) 18(2) *Studies in Christian Ethics* 45 doi.org/10.1177/0953946805054804

Horner, Robyn, *Jean-Luc Marion: A Theo-Logical Introduction* (Routledge, 2005)

John Paul II, *Crossing the Threshold of Hope*, ed Vittorio Messori, tr Jenny McPhee and Martha McPhee (Jonathan Cape, 1994)

Kierkegaard, Soren, *The Sickness Unto Death: A Christian Psychological Exposition of Edification and Awakening by Anti-Climacus*, tr Alastair Hannay (Penguin, 2004)

Levinas, Emmanuel, *Otherwise than Being, or Beyond Essence*, tr Alphonso Lingis (Duquesne University Press, 1998)

Levinas, Emmanuel, *The Theory of Intuition in Husserl's Phenomenology*, tr Andre Orianne (Northwestern University Press, 2nd ed, 1995)

Levinas, Emmanuel, *Totality and Infinity: An Essay on Exteriority*, tr Alphonso Lingis (Duquesne University Press, 1969)

Levinas, Emmanuel and Jill Robbins, *Is It Righteous to Be? Interviews with Emmanuel Levinas* (Stanford University Press, 2001)

Marion, Jean-Luc, *In Excess: Studies of Saturated Phenomena*, tr Robyn Horner and Vincent Berraud (Fordham University Press, 2002)

Marion, Jean-Luc, *The Erotic Phenomenon*, tr Stephen E Lewis (University of Chicago Press, 2007)

Marion, Jean-Luc, 'The Final Appeal of the Subject' in John D Caputo (ed), *The Religious* (Blackwell, 2002)

Milbank, John, 'The Ethics of Self-Sacrifice' [1999] (91) *First Things: A Monthly Journal of Religion & Public Life* 33

Moran, Dermot, *Introduction to Phenomenology* (Routledge, 2000)

O'Connor, Margaret M et al, 'Documenting the Process of Developing the Victorian Voluntary Assisted Dying Legislation' (2018) 42(6) *Australian Health Review* 621 doi.org/10.1071/AH18172

Staehler, Tanja, *Plato and Levinas: The Ambiguous Out-Side of Ethics* (Routledge, 2010)

Velleman, J David, 'Against the Right to Die' (1992) 17(6) *The Journal of Medicine and Philosophy: A Forum for Bioethics and Philosophy of Medicine* 665 doi.org/10.1093/jmp/17.6.665

Voluntary Assisted Dying Review Board, Safer Care Victoria, *Report of Operations January–June 2020* (Report No 3, 31 August 2020)

Wardley, Kenneth Jason, '"A Desire Unto Death": The Deconstructive Thanatology of Jean-Luc Marion' (2008) 49(1) *The Heythrop Journal* 79 doi.org/10.1111/j.1468-2265.2007.00358.x

Wardley, Kenneth Jason, *Praying to a French God: The Theology of Jean-Yves Lacoste* (Routledge, 2016)

Webb, Mary-Ann, 'Eros and Ethics: Levinas's Reading of Plato's "Good Beyond Being"' (2006) 19(2) *Studies in Christian Ethics* 205 doi.org/10.1177/0953946806066151

B Legislation

Voluntary Assisted Dying Act 2017 (Vic)

C Other

Bellaigue, Christopher de, 'Death on Demand: Has Euthanasia Gone Too Far?', *The Guardian* (online, 18 January 2019) <http://www.theguardian.com/news/2019/jan/18/death-on-demand-has-euthanasia-gone-too-far-netherlands-assisted-dying>

Edwards, Jean, 'Euthanasia: Victoria Becomes the First Australian State to Legalise Voluntary Assisted Dying', *ABC News* (online, 29 November 2017) <https://www.abc.net.au/news/2017-11-29/euthanasia-passes-parliament-in-victoria/9205472>

8

Gosport Hospital, Euthanasia and Serial Killing

Penny Crofts[1]

Introduction

In many jurisdictions euthanasia remains illegal. In part, this is in order to reiterate the sanctity of human life, but also due to fears around changing the central ethos of health institutions and medical practitioners from saving lives to that of causing death. Despite the apparent severity of law, it is recognised that medical practitioners currently provide criminal assistance to patients to die and that this is sometimes without the patients' consent.[2] There is a certain legal tolerance – in terms of investigations, prosecutions, jury findings and sentencing.[3] The recent *Report of the Gosport Hospital Independent Panel* provides a meditation upon homicides without patient consent within the health system.[4] *The Gosport Report* found that 456 patients died where opioids were prescribed by Doctor

---

1   This research was funded by the Australian Government through a Discovery Early Career Researcher Award ('DECRA'), project number DE180100577 'Rethinking Institutional Culpability: Criminal Law, Philosophy and Horror'.
2   Legislative Council, Legal and Social Issues Committee, Parliament of Victoria, *Inquiry into End of Life Choices: Final Report* (Parliamentary Paper No 174, June 2016) 207, 181–3.
3   Police and prosecutors pursue criminal proceedings where there is evidence to support that cause of action. However, for those who are convicted, sentences tend to be very low in terms of what is possible for these offences. Lorana Bartels and Margaret Otlowski, 'A Right to Die? Euthanasia and the Law in Australia' (2010) 17 *Journal of Law and Medicine* 532. See also *Justins v The Queen* (2010) 79 NSWLR 544, which distinguishes between aiding and abetting a suicide and manslaughter.
4   Henceforth, *The Report of the Gosport Hospital Independent Panel* will be referred to in text as *The Gosport Report*.

Barton and then administered by nursing staff without appropriate clinical justification. The Panel also found that there may have been a further 200 such deaths, bringing the overall total to more than 650 patients dying as a consequence of this treatment.[5] As shown in *The Gosport Report*, killing patients is a real but occult practice that occurs in the absence of clear and enforced legal norms. There are contradictions within the current legal categories – patients cannot make a free and conscious choice to die but can refuse treatment. Doctors may provide palliative care that has the effect of causing death, on the proviso that this care is given with the intention to relieve suffering and not to shorten life. The absence of established and applied legal norms undermines a clear and debated distinction between unlawful and lawful homicides. This obscure legal framework, coupled with a reluctance to enforce existing laws, provides a veil to homicides occurring within the health system – whether consensual or not.

One of the fears associated with the decriminalisation of euthanasia is that of doctors 'playing God' or worse – killing patients without their consent. There is a developing academic literature of health professionals as serial killers; however the idea remains unusual. Hesketh (2003) has argued that:

> The notion of the individual deviance of doctors and other health professionals is so novel that it is sufficient to limit this discussion of the need for a police-health professions' protocol to only those crimes committed by health professionals. That is, this introductory discussion concentrates for the time being on general crime committed by health professionals, which happen to be committed in the course of their employment, not on wider systems failures that might also be regarded by the critical criminologist as crime.[6]

This chapter extends Hesketh's analysis in two ways. First, I take up Hesketh's invitation to extend analysis beyond individual culpability to highlight group culpability and systemic failure in the homicides of patients at Gosport Hospital. Second, I relate serial killer analysis to provide insight into euthanasia – almost a taboo topic. I will consider legal regulation of euthanasia in light of this analysis. This approach is

---

5   House of Commons, *Gosport War Memorial Hospital: The Report of the Gosport Independent Panel* (Report, June 2018) ('*Gosport War Memorial Hospital Report*') graph, 37.
6   Wendy Hesketh, 'Medico-Crime: Time for a Police-Health Professions Protocol' (2003) 76(2) *Police Journal* 121, 127.

suggested in part by the timing of events at Gosport Hospital. The earliest police investigations into Doctor Barton occurred soon after Doctor Harold Shipman was convicted of murdering 15 elderly patients with lethal injections of morphine in January 2000.[7] Shipman was arrested for murder on September 1998. A public inquiry was launched in June 2001 to investigate the extent of his crimes, how they went undetected for so long and what could be done to prevent the repeat of the tragedy. Although Shipman was regarded as an isolated example of serial killing by a medical professional, the killings at Gosport Hospital occurred across the same time period. *The Gosport Report*, published in 2018, revealed that the same concerns about investigation and prevention of mass homicides by the medical profession remained unresolved.

Part one of this chapter highlights vagueness in law and lexicon distinguishing between unlawful homicides and euthanasia reflected and reinforced in *The Gosport Report*. Part two focuses on the use of the broad category of palliative care to veil unlawful homicides at Gosport Hospital. Part three draws upon the insights of medical practitioner serial killer literature to provide insight into how so many patients were killed at Gosport Hospital over such a long period of time. Part four then considers the implications of serial homicides for the legal regulation of euthanasia.

Lexicon and legal context

There is a lack of clarity and consistency around the meaning and use of various words in this area, and these definitions are also not necessarily mirrored in law. The word 'euthanasia' dates from the 1640s and is from the Greek 'an easy or happy death' – *eu* 'good' and *thanatos* 'death'. In 1869, the sense of 'legally sanctioned mercy killing' was recorded in English. The literature differentiates between 'voluntary euthanasia' – where euthanasia is performed at the request of the person whose life is ended and that person is competent – and non-voluntary euthanasia – which is performed without request and/or the person is not competent.[8] In New South Wales currently, and in England at the time of Gosport

---

7   Throughout the chapter, I will refer to Doctor Barton using her title, as she was never stripped of her title and retired without being deregistered.

8   For more detail see Lindy Willmott et al, '(Failed) Voluntary Euthanasia Law Reform in Australia: Two Decades of Trends, Models and Politics' (2016) 39 *University of New South Wales Law Journal* 1, 6.

Hospital, neither of these 'types' of euthanasia were legal. Palliative care is described as providing end-of-life care with the intention to relieve pain and not to cause or hasten death, although this may be foreseen.[9]

The literature enunciates a clear distinction between euthanasia and palliative care.[10] In the majority of countries, including Australia, even where euthanasia remains criminalised, palliative care is legal. The provision of appropriate palliative care is lawful even if it may hasten death:

> In the case of PS [palliative care], a physician is generally seen as performing an act that relieves intractable suffering; the outcome of death is not perceived as a physician having 'caused harm' to a patient, but rather as having helped that patient by relieving suffering and distress.[11]

This legal protection arose in response to fears that palliative care might accelerate death, although many argue that palliative care usually does not alter the timing or mechanism of patient's death.[12] While the law may (ostensibly) be clear in relation to palliative care, in practice the line between palliative care and unlawful slayings is less clear. However, as shown in Gosport Hospital, the line is frequently drawn in favour of characterising care as palliative (and thus legal), rather than as criminal.

The ambiguities in this area arise in part due to a preference for softened and euphemistic language that is framed in terms of health discourse rather than criminal legal discourse. This is reflected in *The Gosport Report* in quoting witnesses and in the analysis of *The Gosport Report* itself. Rather than speaking of unlawful homicide (whether murder or manslaughter), *The Gosport Report* referred to 'end of life care',[13] 'end of life pathway',[14] 'terminal care', 'palliative care', or 'the end'. It was noted that the treatment led patients to 'die sooner rather than later'.[15]

---

9   Benjamin White and Lindy Willmott, 'How Should Australia Regulate Voluntary Euthanasia and Assisted Suicide?' (2012) 20 *Journal of Law and Medicine* 410.

10   For an early case see *Dr Adam's Case*: which held that a doctor may do 'all that is proper and necessary to relieve pain, even if the measure … may incidentally shorten life'. Quoted in Alan W Norrie, *Legal Form and Moral Judgment: The Problem of Euthanasia* (SSRN Scholarly Paper No ID 1577163, Social Science Research Network, 23 March 2010) <https://papers.ssrn.com/abstract=1577163>.

11   Silvana Barone and Yoram Unguru, 'Should Euthanasia be Considered Iatrogenic?' (2017) 19(8) *American Medical Association Journal of Ethics* 802.

12   Ibid.

13   *Gosport War Memorial Hospital Report* (n 5) 73.

14   Ibid 71.

15   Ibid 61.

A 2003 review of deaths of patients at Gosport examined Dr Barton's medical records and found that she had a conservative rather than active attitude toward clinical management and preferred palliative care rather than recovery. This finding included 'palliative care' for people who were admitted with fractures for rehabilitation. Very few people in *The Gosport Report* plainly labelled the actions in Gosport Hospital as homicides, and *The Gosport Report* itself preferred 'foreshortening of life'. The conclusion of *The Gosport Report* asserted that 'there was a disregard for human life and a culture of shortening the lives of a large number of patients'.[16]

Throughout *The Gosport Report*, there are suggestions that the 'shortening' of the lives of patients was a form of euthanasia. For example, in 2001, during one of the many investigations, one of the experts, Professor Donaldson, asked the Commission of Health Investigation 'for reassurance that in the context of an allegation of a *"culture of euthanasia"* … the hospital is providing safe care'.[17] In his expert's report to police, which was then given to the General Medical Council (GMC), Professor Gary Ford stated that the 'routine use of opiate and sedative drug infusions without clear indications for their use would raise concerns that a culture of *"involuntary euthanasia"* existed on the ward'.[18] A nursing auxiliary at Daedalus Ward, Pauline Spilka told police in 2001 that Daedalus Ward was better termed 'Dead Loss', and described 'the regime of [the nurse] as being geared towards *euthanasia*'. She asserted that '*euthanasia* was practiced by the nursing staff'.[19] Similarly, an internal police report in 2001 stated that '[T]he allegations being made by the families are effectively that the hospital was guilty of *institutionalised euthanasia*'.[20] However, the conclusion of *The Gosport Report* emphasised that the practices at Gosport Hospital were not euthanasia:

> It may be tempting to view what happened at the hospital in the context of public debate over end of life care, what a 'good death' is, and assisted dying. That would be a mistake. What happened at the hospital cannot be seen, still less justified, in that context. The patients involved were not admitted for end of life care but

---

16   Ibid viii.
17   Ibid 87 (emphasis added).
18   Ibid 171 (emphasis added).
19   Ibid 122 (emphasis added).
20   Ibid 134 (emphasis added).

often for rehabilitation or respite care. The pattern of prescribing and administering drugs was excessive and inappropriate in the ways explained in this Report.[21]

The disagreement over terminology within *The Gosport Report* reflects the lack of clarity at law and in society about different forms of medical homicide. This labelling is significant because it is confusing, reflects ambiguities in the law, and in turn hampers the possibility of a criminal legal response.[22] One of the few experts who spoke plainly was Doctor Simon Tanner in 2002 who labelled the actions as 'unlawful killing'.[23] This use of an accurate label facilitated Tanner recommending action, including a full investigation and corresponding action in terms of clinical governance.

Palliative care and unlawful homicide

The unlawful homicides at Gosport Hospital were primarily placed within the amorphous and vague category of palliative care. The deaths were caused with a method closely associated with palliative care – the prescription by Dr Barton of drugs used in palliative care, administered by the nursing staff. Dr Barton was a clinical assistant at the hospital for 12 years until she tendered her resignation in April 2000. This was a new post of five sessions a week, worked flexibly to provide 24-hour medical cover. She visited the two wards, Daedalus and Dryad, at 7:30am before arriving at her surgery at 9:00am. Dr Barton would prescribe diamorphine (often in combination with Midazolam and Hyoscine) for patients to be administered by nursing staff using a syringe driver. Dr Barton's method was the same as Shipman's – a swift injection of diamorphine – pharmaceutical heroin.[24] Although these drugs are the kinds of drugs that

---

21   Ibid 319.

22   The difficulties in labelling the offences at Gosport Hospital is in part due to the group element of the offence. The homicides were not committed by only one person acting alone, but by groups of people. While this makes it difficult to point to the murderer at law, it should not be taken to mean that the homicides were lawful. The difficulties of attributing criminal liability to any particular actor, including Dr Barton, is the subject of another paper with David Carter.

23   *Gosport War Memorial Hospital Report* (n 5) 88.

24   Shipman has been labelled the most prolific serial killer in British history, and arguably the most prolific modern serial killer worldwide, claiming at least 215 victims. John Gunn, 'Dr Harold Frederick Shipman: An Enigma' (2010) 20(3) *Criminal Behaviour and Mental Health* 190. However, the deaths at Gosport Hospital far exceeded Shipman's murders. The difficulty is that Dr Barton did not act alone, but relied upon the nurses to administer the lethal drugs.

are used in palliative care, the patients for whom Dr Barton prescribed these drugs were not in this situation. Very few patients who received this treatment at Gosport Hospital survived for more than three days.[25] The underlying cause of death for the majority of these patients was recorded as bronchopneumonia. This treatment breached national and local guidelines at the time – the 'analgesic ladder' – 'start low and go slow' with opioids both in prescription and administration. There was a 'systemic failure to adopt the principles of the analgesic ladder' leading to 'dangerous doses' administered.[26]

The primary way of distinguishing between illegal homicide and palliative care is through the 'intention' of the medical practitioner. To be lawful, palliative care must be provided with the intention to relieve unbearable suffering and not to cause or hasten death, although that death may be foreseen.[27] This is labelled the doctrine of double effect. In the four Australian states that have enshrined this protection in statute, regard must also be had to other factors such as good medical practice.[28]

The Gosport Report indicates that Dr Barton and the nurses would have foreseen that death upon administration of the drugs was almost certain. For example, despite expressing concerns the nurses continued to administer the drugs 'although the link with the pattern of deaths would have been apparent to them'. Legal principle asserts that where knowledge of an outcome is virtually certain, then this certain knowledge can be equated with intention.[29] Criminal law asserts that it is interested only in intention and not motive, however criminal law theorists have long highlighted that the question of motive is significant to attributions of culpability.[30] Motive is the home of moral substance – while intention

---

25 *Gosport War Memorial Hospital Report* (n 5) 38.
26 Ibid 20, 316.
27 'What Is Palliative Care?', *QUT* (Web Page) <https://end-of-life.qut.edu.au/?a=548149#548149>.
28 For example, under the *Consent to Medical Treatment and Palliative Care Act 1995* (SA), a medical practitioner or someone supervised by a medical practitioner who hastens a person's death through medical treatment or care is not liable in civil or criminal law for the person's death if it is consented to, administered without negligence and in good faith with the intention of relieving pain or distress; is provided in accordance with professional standards of palliative care; and the person is in the terminal phase of a terminal illness. See also the *Criminal Code Act 1899* (Qld) s 282A; the *Criminal Code Act Compilation Act 1913* (WA) s 259; the *Medical Treatment (Health Directions) Act 2006* (ACT); and the *Powers of Attorney Act 2006* (ACT). See also 'What Is Palliative Care?' (n 27).
29 A classic example is the intention to blow up a plane in order to collect insurance. The primary intention is to collect insurance, however the perpetrator would recognise that death of all on the plane would be virtually certain. Accordingly, intention to kill would be imputed to the perpetrator.
30 Guyora Binder, 'The Rhetoric of Motive and Intent' (2002) 6(1) *Buffalo Criminal Law Review* 1.

is a formal question. This is highlighted in relation to palliative care. The issue is not whether the treatment is likely to result in death, but the motive of administering the drugs – was it to alleviate painful symptoms or to cause death?[31]

Given the length of time that had passed between the homicides and *The Gosport Report* it is difficult to ascertain motive. This is exacerbated by poor and inadequate record keeping, a practice that is not uncommon in the medical profession, and is also a feature in Shipman's murders.[32] I will consider first Dr Barton's motives and then the motives of the nurses.

There are limited indications in Dr Barton's notes of her motives in prescribing these drugs. Her language is consistent with that of palliative care. Her catchphrases in (poorly recorded) notes include: 'please make comfortable', and even more disturbing 'not obviously in pain please make comfortable'.[33] *The Gosport Report* asserts that 'make comfortable' was a 'euphemism for embarking on the pattern of prescribing which would lead to death in almost every case'.[34] Dr Barton would provide these anticipatory prescriptions when patients were admitted to the hospital – even if it was for respite or rehabilitation. Even more disturbing was a comment she frequently wrote, 'I am happy for nursing staff to confirm death' – for patients admitted for respite or rehabilitation. Doctor Barton defended this by stating:

> That was a routine entry I made into the notes of patients who might at some time in the future die on the ward [so that] … nursing staff … did not have to bring in an out of hours duty doctor to confirm death … it did not signify at that time I felt that she was close to death; it was a fairly routine entry in the notes.[35]

The tendency by medical practitioners to present homicide in palliative care terms is so common that researchers have adopted techniques to guard against it. For example, Yorker et al in their analysis of serial murder by healthcare professionals stated:

---

31 Alan Norrie, *Crime, Reason and History: A Critical Introduction to Criminal Law* (Cambridge University Press, 2001). Norrie makes this argument specifically in relation to euthanasia arguing that motive animates the discretionary decision not to prosecute: Norrie, *Legal Form and Moral Judgment* (n 10).
32 Hesketh (n 6) quoting one of the medical expert witnesses who provided an opinion to police in the earlier Shipman investigation.
33 *Gosport War Memorial Hospital Report* (n 5) 60.
34 Ibid 74.
35 Doctor Barton (2009), quoted in ibid 61.

We did however include some cases in which the healthcare provider claimed to be engaged in euthanasia as a defense against murder charges. To differentiate between *authentic euthanasia* and *serial murder*, we correlated the provider's justification of their actions as euthanasia with patient histories. If a caregiver claimed he or she was engaging in euthanasia, but the patients had been admitted for routine procedures … and postmortem examinations indicated they died from toxic levels of unauthorized medication, we considered it a case of murder.[36]

No post-mortem examinations took place in relation to the patients who died at Gosport Hospital, however the records indicate Doctor Barton's practice of prescribing palliative care drugs was not based on patient need.[37] Dr Barton prescribed the drugs to patients who arrived at the ward for respite care and rehabilitation.

News reporting about Gosport Hospital accepts the absence of intention to kill (possibly for fear of a civil suit): 'there is no suggestion that Dr Barton intentionally took lives'.[38] Like Shakespeare's Iago, there is no apparent motive for her actions, but the consequences were extremely

36   Beatrice Crofts Yorker, Kenneth Kizer and Paula Lampe, 'Serial Murder by Healthcare Professionals' (2006) 51(6) *Journal of Forensic Sciences* 1362, 1363 (emphasis in original).
37   For example, *The Gosport Report* notes the Internal Review Panel that was convened to consider complaints by Ann Reeves of the death of her mother Elsie Devine:

Although no guidance at the time or subsequently would support the use of opioids for confusion without pain, the IRP took a different view, and concluded that the clinical response was appropriate. The documents show no basis for the IRP's different view. When the complainant remained dissatisfied with the IRP report, a member of the IRP produced a further report:

She was wandering, agitated, acutely confused, disorientated and frightened. In a frail elderly person this is a very serious medical condition and may be as dangerous as a heart attack but it does not form part of the public perception of a serious or life-threatening illness. For this reason she clearly required a large dose of strong medication, as she was a danger to both herself and people around her.

The Panel can find no basis in the documents or from its wider experience to justify this conclusion, which explicitly condones the use of large doses of diamorphine simply to control symptoms of confusion and agitation. The Panel notes that this conclusion was contrary to all relevant evidence.

Gosport War Memorial Hospital Report (n 5) 76.
38   'Gosport Hospital Deaths: Who Is Jane Barton, the Doctor at the Heart of a Scandal that Claimed Hundreds of Lives?', *The Independent* (online, 20 June 2018) <https://www.independent.co.uk/news/uk/home-news/gosport-hospital-deaths-dr-jane-barton-independent-inquiry-gmc-a8408886.html>; same quotation also in Alexandra Topping, 'Profile: Dr Jane Barton, GP and the Gosport Hospital Scandal', *The Guardian* (online, 21 June 2018) <http://www.theguardian.com/society/2018/jun/20/profile-dr-jane-barton-gp-gosport-hospital-scandal-gmc-panel-2010>.

harmful. Her consistent claim is that she practised anticipatory prescribing and wrote 'the nurses can confirm the death' due to lack of resources. Her husband also defended her in these terms:

> 'Instead of trying to find a new Harold Shipman, it might be more constructive to ask why a part-time GP was looking after 48 beds' the husband told *The Sunday Times* in 2002.[39]

Her husband asserted that Doctor Barton had been 'overworked and was under a huge amount of pressure'.[40] Doctor Barton resigned from Gosport Hospital in April 2000 citing concerns over 'staffing levels that do not provide safe and adequate medical cover or appropriate nursing expertise'.[41] Although she claimed to be overworked she had not complained at the time. Upon her resignation the elevated deaths at Gosport Hospital radically dropped.[42]

The absence of any clear motive for Dr Barton is likewise reflected in the homicides by Dr Shipman. Various motives were suggested for Dr Shipman including that he was playing God, avenging his mother, easing the burdens on NHS and, a more recent suggestion, sexual excitement.[43] Thunder has researched the motives suggested for homicides in medical facilities – the slaying of the frail, injured or sick of any age to relieve a burden, for profit, for malice or revenge, to pretend to be a saviour, and/or acting out sexual fantasies.[44] In the absence of any response by Dr Barton, it is unclear why she prescribed the lethal drugs.

Unlike Dr Shipman, Dr Barton delegated authority to the nurses to administer the drugs, to determine the quantity of drugs and to establish death. In criminal law, the nurses who administered the drugs would be

---

39 'Gosport Hospital Deaths' (n 38); Topping (n 38). Dr Barton started work and had responsibility for the patients in Redclyffe Annex, with approximately 20 beds classified as continuing care. She then had responsibility for an additional 11 beds from the main hospital site until 1993–94 – with a total of 31 beds. From 1993–94 onwards, she was responsible for Dryad and Daedalus wards with a total of 44 beds.
40 'Gosport Hospital Deaths' (n 38).
41 *Gosport War Memorial Hospital Report* (n 5) 85.
42 Ibid.
43 Shipman refused to co-operate in investigations, refused to speak with professionals, refused a psychiatric defence, and maintained that he was not guilty. He committed suicide in 2004, 'his case remains somewhat of an enigma'. Sarah Hodgkinson, Herschel Prins and Joshua Stuart-Bennett, 'Monsters, Madmen ... and Myths: A Critical Review of the Serial Killing Literature' (2017) 34 *Aggression and Violent Behaviour* 282, 286.
44 James Thunder, 'Quiet Killings in Medical Facilities: Detection & Prevention' (2003) 18(3) *Issues in Law & Medicine* 211.

regarded as operating and substantial causes of the deaths of patients.[45] The nurses were definitely not innocent agents – they knew that patients would die within three days of administration of the drugs. The failure of nursing staff to challenge the drugs and refuse to administer them was in breach of standards that applied at the time: 'the nursing staff also had a responsibility to intervene and challenge the prevailing practice on the wards'.[46] Accordingly, their actions were voluntary acts of independent parties. This would sever the causal nexus between Doctor Barton's original prescriptions and the deaths of patients (although it is arguable that Doctor Barton could be charged as an accessory before the fact or instigator). Given that the nurses knew that the drugs were lethal and contrary to medical practice and the law, why then did they administer the drugs?

One argument is that they were simply obeying doctor's orders.[47] The impact of the hierarchy was demonstrated in 1988 and 1991 when the nurses expressed concern to hospital management and the Royal College of Nurses about Barton's practice of anticipatory prescription of drugs.[48] These concerns were shut down by management and not followed up. *The Gosport Report* notes:

> A prevailing culture dominated by the clinical assistant and the consultants which overshadowed any understanding that the nurses could or should exercise their autonomous professional status.[49]

---

45 *Royall v The Queen* (1991) 172 CLR 378.

46 *Gosport War Memorial Hospital Report* (n 5) 45.

47 Stanley Milgram, *Obedience to Authority: An Experimental View* (Harper & Row, 1974).

48 In Shipman's case, no-one complained or raised concerns about a single death until 1998, by which time he had killed more than 200 patients over a period of 20 years. Eventually, two funeral directors became suspicious about the circumstances of the deaths. Prior to 1998 two non-professionals had concerns – but were advised by friends and family to do nothing – especially due to fear of being sued for defamation. A taxi driver of elderly patients and a warden of sheltered accommodation where several of Shipman's patients lived and died were wracked by guilt and regret. They believed that because they were not professionals if they had tried to make a report it would have fallen on deaf ears. Unlike Doctor Barton, Shipman was unusually isolated. Doctors at the practice adjacent to Shipman's became suspicious around the same time as the funeral directors, when they noticed they were signing an abnormally large number of cremation certificates for him. The doctors reported their joint concerns to the coroner. The police, to whom the coroner passed *The Gosport Report*, made a very superficial job of the investigation and concluded that there was nothing amiss. The detective inspector in charge thought the concerns were unfounded from the start because Shipman was well respected. His mind was not really open to the possibility that what was being suggested might be true.

See, Janet Smith, 'Public Interest Responsibilities of Professionals: Lecture Given for Public Concern at Work on 13 October 2005' (2006) 46(2) *Medicine, Science and the Law* 93.

49 *Gosport War Memorial Hospital Report* (n 5) 49.

A nurse stated that despite 'considerable disquiet amongst ... staff' 'you can only be told so many times that you don't know what you are talking about'.[50] Nurses were concerned 'they would be sacked or moved ... wouldn't be supported ... would be named a trouble maker'.[51]

> The Panel found a picture of care which fell well below the expected standards of nursing practice at that time. It is a picture which demonstrates a lack of care for individuals' assessed needs, as well as a lack of challenge to the prevailing practice at the hospital. It also illustrates the bravery of the nurses who raised concerns in 1991.[52]

This reflects the insights of medical research. There has been a great deal of literature about the ways in which medical hierarchies undermine any possibility of nurses challenging doctors.[53]

There is, however, a darker motive for the nurses administering drugs – the removal of 'troublesome' patients.[54] *The Gosport Report* notes that 'opioids already prescribed in this way could be used as an inappropriate response to a patient's agitation or challenging behaviour'.[55] *The Gosport Report* suggests that patients may not have been given food or water, which may have led to 'troublesome' behaviour. The lethal drugs were administered to patients with dementia or incontinence, or who were just plain thirsty or hungry. Nurse Spilka claimed that she had argued with Nurse Marion Berry about administering drugs to a patient. The patient was lazy and quite tearful. Nurse Berry said if he wasn't careful he would 'talk himself onto a syringe driver'. Accordingly, staff had foresight that administration of the drugs would lead to death and their motive may have been to reduce workload or get rid of 'irritating' patients.

The idea that nurses were killing 'troublesome' patients reflects and reinforces fears of legalising euthanasia. That is, it is believed that presently the criminalisation of euthanasia retains the sanctity of human life, a protection against the utilitarian rationale of the health system, which is that limited resources and time must be allocated in a way that is

---

50   Ibid 41. For a sociological analysis of literal denial of atrocities by institutions see Stanley Cohen, *States of Denial: Knowing About Atrocities and Suffering* (Polity Press, 2001).
51   *Gosport War Memorial Hospital Report* (n 5) 91.
52   Ibid 48.
53   Marie M Bismark et al, 'Mandatory Reports of Concerns about the Health, Performance and Conduct of Health Practitioners' (2014) 201(7) *Medical Journal of Australia* 399.
54   *Gosport War Memorial Hospital Report* (n 5) 85.
55   Ibid 29.

most beneficial to the most people. According to this approach, it is more rational to kill than to care for problematic, high-maintenance patients who are expensive in an overcrowded and overworked health system.[56] It is feared that legalising euthanasia could lead to dystopian futures and social inequalities.[57] However, the killings in Gosport Hospital epitomised fears of dystopian futures and took place while euthanasia was criminal. The killings at Gosport Hospital were facilitated in part by the amorphous category of palliative care and the central role of motive in differentiating between whether a 'treatment' is legal or criminal. As Gosport Hospital showed, a doctor's intentions when providing certain treatments are easy to obscure or can be ambiguous. The same act can be done, namely hastening a patient's death, with radically different intentions.[58] Serial killers are able to take advantage of the ambiguous legal distinction between palliative care and unlawful homicide to reduce the likelihood of being detected and stopped.

Medical practitioners as serial killers

The notion of considering the vagueness of law about euthanasia and palliative care through the prism of serial killing may seem farfetched, especially as it is believed that killings like those at Gosport Hospital and by Dr Shipman are isolated and rare. However, there are numerous examples internationally of 'caregiver associated killing',[59] and increasing

---

56   Examples of motives that have been prosecuted and criminalised include Megan Haines, a nurse in an elderly nursing home, who was found guilty of two counts of murder in NSW in 2016. She murdered the residents several days after they made a complaint about the standard and quality of care she delivered. Haines was sentenced to 36 years imprisonment. Garling J: 'Her conduct was deliberate and calculating. It was a gross breach of trust and a flagrant abuse of her power … She clearly abused that position of trust. I consider this to be a significant aggravating factor.' (*R v Haines* [2016] NSWSC 1824). Dr Crickitt killed his wife with a lethal dose of insulin. The court was satisfied that he did this because he increasingly disliked his wife and was infatuated with another woman (*R v Crickitt* [2016] NSWSC 1738). Barbara Salisbury, a nurse on a geriatric ward in Crew was convicted of the attempted murder of two patients and acquitted with regard to two more. She was obsessed with unblocking beds in the ward. The judge said that she had broken her duty of care and abused her position of trust 'by attempting to hasten death'. She also administered diamorphine to patients. A question in the case was whether she was 'easing the passing' of patients or breaching her duty of trust (Helen Carter, 'Nurse Gets Five Years for Seeking to Kill Two Patients', *The Guardian* (online, 19 June 2004) <https://www.theguardian.com/society/2004/jun/19/health.uknews>).
57   Norrie (n 10).
58   White and Willmott (n 9); Lindy Willmott, Benjamin White and S Then, 'Withholding and Withdrawing Life-Sustaining Medical Treatment' in Benjamin White, F McDonald and Lindy Willmott (eds), *Health Law in Australia* (Thomson-Reuters, 2010) [13.280–13.290].
59   Crofts Yorker, Kizer and Lampe (n 36).

recognition that serial homicides by doctors are not unique to people such as Dr Shipman (and Dr Barton).[60] In fact, Kinnell has argued that medicine has arguably thrown up more serial killers than all the other professions together, with nursing a close second.[61] There is a tendency to avoid thinking about homicides by medical practitioners. It challenges our feelings of safety and the trusted position of doctors in society. This tendency to avoid thinking of homicidal medical practitioners is reflected in the history of investigations and in *The Gosport Report* itself. Through the long history of intermittent queries raised by staff and family members, investigations by police, the GMC, and internal and external medical and nursing committees regarding the 'treatment' at Gosport Hospital, it was almost unthinkable to consider the deaths as unlawful homicides. This is reflected in *The Gosport Report's* preference for the euphemistic phrase, noted above, of 'shortening of life' rather than the more accurate labels of 'killing', 'slaying' or 'unlawful homicide'.

In part, the relative ignorance about medical practitioners as serial killers is because they do not reflect popular culture understandings of serial killers. Hodgkinson et al argue that cases such as Shipman challenge our belief 'that we can readily identify a serial killer, that they are not people in positions of trust, or people we know, and that they can be easily apprehended by law enforcement'.[62] Gosport Hospital exacerbates this discomfort – because it was not the act of one isolated, malevolent individual but included other staff – whether actively administering lethal drugs and/or failing to prevent the homicides over the many years. Academic analysis highlights why doctors are the most prolific serial killers. Doctors are trusted, hence the phrase 'doctor knows best'. They have access to vulnerable and unwell people.[63] They have no difficulties in disposing of bodies. The treatment by Dr Barton was largely unquestioned by the majority of family members, consulting physicians, the GMC, police, coroners and the Council of Nurses. Systems in place to protect vulnerable patients failed abysmally. On the rare occasions when Doctor Barton was questioned by staff and/or family members, the questions were undermined by management and police, who suggested that they were

60   Thunder (n 44).
61   Herbert Kinnell, 'Serial Homicide by Doctors: Shipman in Perspective' (2000) 321(7276) *BMJ* 1594. See also Clare Dyer, 'Police Investigate Deaths of Terminally Ill Patients' (2000) 321(7267) *BMJ* 981; Katherine Ramsland, *Inside the Minds of Healthcare Serial Killers: Why They kill* (Praeger, 1st ed, 2007); Crofts Yorker, Kizer and Lampe (n 36).
62   Hodgkinson, Prins and Stuart-Bennett (n 43).
63   Alec Samuels, 'Editorial: Doctor Harold Shipman' (2000) 68(2) *Medico-Legal Journal* 37, 37.

not coping with their grief or were being unprofessional. When family members (nursing staff and eventually police) questioned 'treatments', the hospital responded in a hierarchical fashion that protected Dr Barton.

Hodgkinson et al argue that the dominant approach to the study of multiple killings, advanced by the FBI as well as other sources of highly influential information within the realms of mass media, supports an understanding and response that is principally fixed at the individual level.[64] This approach focuses on the killer's disposition or character, but fails to consider the 'wider social, cultural and historical contexts that may generate, shape and facilitate such behaviours, and that problematises the reductionist "traditionalist" approach'.[65] That is, there is a tendency to regard serial killers as acontextual and ahistorical. In contrast, Hodgkinson et al have argued that it is necessary to place these crimes within their own particular context. They have focused on the regard and value of the victim group, arguing that serial killers operate within the context of cultures of denigration and marginalisation of particular social groupings lacking protection and becoming vulnerable to predation.[66]

> Those who want to kill repeatedly can only achieve this objective when the social structure in which they operate allows them to do so by placing value on one group to the detriment of others.[67]

The elderly patients killed at Gosport Hospital (and by Dr Shipman) fit within the category of denigrated and marginalised.[68] There is an insidious presumption that old people will die soon anyway, with the consequence that abuse, neglect and consequent suffering is inadequately or not responded to at all in terms of detection, treatment, intervention and prosecution.[69]

The analysis of the context of serial killings can be extended to the regard of the medical profession. Medical homicides are less likely to be investigated and prosecuted because of the hierarchy both within the medical profession and outside. I have already noted that nurses were

---

64 Hodgkinson, Prins and Stuart-Bennett (n 43).
65 Ibid 288.
66 Ibid.
67 David Wilson, *Serial Killers: Hunting Britons and Their Victims 1960 to 2006* (Waterside Press, 2007) 23.
68 Concerns about the cultural denigration of the elderly and their vulnerability to predation is reflected in the current Australian Royal Commission into Aged Care.
69 Thunder (n 44).

actively discouraged from reporting their concerns about 'the treatment' at Gosport Hospital. This absence of reporting extends to the peers of doctors. Doctors are unlikely to report wrongdoing or incompetence because of fears of reprisals and detriments of various kinds.[70] Likewise, Rosenthal has noted that the profession will tend to cover up incompetence and misconduct committed by individuals.[71] This may in part be a form of institutional narcissism, with the aim of protecting the reputation of the medical profession generally. But it may also be due to a perception of the need to protect the health profession from the intervention of the criminal legal system.[72] *The Gosport Report* is clear that the doctors 'supervising' Dr Barton should have been aware of and challenged Dr Barton's prescription of lethal drugs. However, due to the passing of time it is unclear what the doctors did or did not know. The only thing that is clear is that they maintained professional solidarity and did not report the chronic overprescription and administration of lethal drugs.

The hierarchy extends beyond those within the medical profession to how the criminal legal system relates with the medical profession – both powerful professions. The medical profession is treated as a special case in criminal law. Medical professionals are able to touch and cut bodies, handle and administer drugs, and document as lawful acts that, outside the medical context, are regarded as the greatest of crimes.[73] The police are dependent on the medical profession to explain treatments and reasonable practices. The hierarchical relationship was shown in Gosport Hospital with police asking and then accepting Doctor Barton's reassurances that this was appropriate treatment and that using diamorphine 'is not any form of euthanasia'.[74] Police then also kept Gosport Hospital informed and even assisted the hospital in writing a press release about investigations,[75] despite recognition that the institution itself could

---

70   Smith (n 48). Smith compares the tribal nature of the medical profession to that of the legal profession. High standards are required for admission to the profession, but once admitted, the professional was within a society of like-minded people who understood each other and shared common interests. Smith refers to the example of the Bristol Royal Infirmity case, in which Dr Steve Bolsin had tried to draw attention to the problem in the paediatric cardiac surgery department but no-one listened for a long time and he was treated as an outcast.

71   Marilynn M Rosenthal, *The Incompetent Doctor Behind Closed Doors* (Open University Press, 1995).

72   David J Carter, 'HIV Transmission, Public Health Detention and the Recalcitrant Subject of Discipline: *Kuoth, Lam v R* and the Co-Constitution of Public Health and Criminal Law' (2016) 25(2) *Griffith Law Review* 172.

73   Hesketh (n 6).

74   *Gosport War Memorial Hospital Report* (n 5) 107.

75   Ibid 116.

potentially be liable for medical negligence. There is no clear protocol for police liaison with health authorities to prevent, detect or investigate medico-crime.[76] It is believed that the medical profession will police itself, a 'usurpation of the police role'.[77] Professional bodies such as the GMC and Nursing and Midwifery Council have a 'monopoly on the technical knowledge of medicine and, because of the intricacies of the unique medical environment, it can be expected to act responsibly'.[78] They are responsible for entry into the professions, monitoring standards and disciplining members for misconduct. However, in the case of Gosport Hospital none of these professional bodies fulfilled their policing roles. No-one was punished. No-one lost their jobs or registration. Specifically, Dr Barton has never been charged with any criminal offences. In addition, she kept her medical license until voluntary retirement many years later.[79]

The analysis of the context of serial killings at Gosport Hospital also extends to resource implications. A constant theme throughout *The Gosport Report* is that of limited resources. This was not only in terms of the capacity to treat patients in the hospital system (argued by Dr Barton), but also to the ability of regulatory bodies to investigate and prosecute. For example, the police and coroner eventually recognised that there may have been many more homicides at Gosport Hospital, but lacked the resources to pursue this further – both in terms of individual and institutional culpability.

Safeguards against homicides

The serial killer literature detailed above highlights that we should analyse not only the killer, but also the context in which the killings occur. The killings at Gosport Hospital occurred at an institution that was perceived to be safe and trusted, against victims who were vulnerable and elderly, in a professional hierarchy that is expected to police itself and is unlikely to report malfeasance. The killings occurred in the context of a systemic failure to prevent serial homicides by the medical profession. There are many safeguards that could be imposed to protect against

---

76   Hesketh (n 6).
77   Ibid 124.
78   Ibid 122.
79   'Gosport Hospital Deaths' (n 38).

unlawful homicides of the kind that occurred at Gosport Hospital.[80] This includes tracking the rate of death for individual doctors, wards and hospitals. Another simple safeguard would be to monitor drug prescribing habits of doctors. *The Gosport Report* provides stark graphs of rates of death and prescription of which even a cursory monitoring should have sounded alarm bells. Doctors are already required to keep notes of patient treatment but many do not do so, including serial killers such as Doctors Barton and Shipman, who rely upon the brevity of records to veil malfeasance. Doctors should be required to keep full computer records that are open to confidential audits. There should be procedures in place that encourage and respond appropriately to concerns and suspicions by staff – including nurses.

The Gosport Report also highlights that legal regulation should specify the ways in which family members are communicated with and how their concerns are treated. Note that much of the literature in this area is focused on protection of the elderly *from* their family and undue influence.[81] However, the homicides at Gosport Hospital highlights the other side – how family members attempted to protect their family from harmful treatments. Families were marginalised by professional staff at Gosport Hospital. Conversations were 'often brief, cursory and dismissive'. For example, a son reported that:

> [w]hen he was told his mother was unwell and 'we would like your permission to administer the necessary drugs to assist her through to the end.' Naturally I was very distressed by this, and tearful, and expressed my amazement that I was being asked to sanction what appeared to be euthanasia. When we left the meeting room, [the doctor] commented to the nursing staff 'we've got another weeper here'.[82]

Concerns about treatment, hydration and nutrition were treated as sadness about death, rather than recognition of a general problem with the 'treatment', despite management handling the same complaints over and over again. Family members who reported concerns outside the institution were treated in the same manner. Police responded to Mrs MacKenzie, the woman who persevered for decades by continuing

---

80   Crofts Yorker, Kizer and Lampe (n 36).
81   Anne PF Wand et al, 'The Nexus Between Elder Abuse, Suicide, and Assisted Dying: The Importance of Relational Autonomy and Undue Influence' (2018) 18 *Macquarie Law Journal* 79.
82   *Gosport War Memorial Hospital Report* (n 5) 74.

to raise questions about the death of her mother, by classifying her as a 'trouble maker'.[83] Accordingly, reforms to protect against serial killings by medical professionals should include the development of procedures to encourage and respond appropriately to concerns by family members.

An additional safeguard against unlawful homicides would be to clarify the law. Currently, medical professionals can hide homicides behind the vague and amorphous category of 'palliative care', confident in their protection within the medical hierarchy. Part of the clarification of law would include decriminalising euthanasia. Questions have been raised about whether unlawful homicides by medical practitioners can be relied upon to justify legalisation of euthanasia. For example, Keown has argued that the experience internationally is that legalisation does nothing to reduce the opportunity for abuse of the law. Keown asks, if medical practitioners already break the law why would this change if it was legalised?[84] He asserts that far from decreasing homicides, the practice is likely to increase if euthanasia is legalised. However, international quantitative studies have found the contrary. The Queensland University of Technology (QUT) summarised deaths due to voluntary euthanasia, assisted suicide and involuntary euthanasia since 1990 in the Netherlands and showed a decrease in life-terminating acts without explicit request of the patient, while voluntary euthanasia and assisted suicide stayed stable.[85] In other words, slayings without the consent of the victim decreased in a framework of legalised euthanasia. Similarly, Kuhse et al found that Australia had a higher rate of intentional ending of life without the patient's request than the Netherlands where euthanasia is openly practiced. The prohibition of euthanasia has not prevented doctors from practising euthanasia or making medical end-of-life decisions explicitly intended to hasten the patient's death without the patient's request.[86] What it does mean is that doctors are making these decisions in the absence of a clear legal framework of the standards required for lawful homicides in the health system. The experience in Belgium suggests that legalisation would bring with it its own regulatory issues and concerns

83   Ibid 107.
84   John Keown, '"Voluntary Assisted Dying" in Australia: The Victorian Parliamentary Committee's Tenuous Case for Legalization' (2018) 33(1) *Issues in Law & Medicine* 55.
85   Willmott, White and Then (n 58).
86   Helga Kuhse et al, 'End-of-Life Decisions in Australian Medical Practice' (1997) 166(4) *Medical Journal of Australia* 191.

surrounding unethical medical practices.[87] The law reform process would include debates about eligibility criteria (eg only terminally ill, adults with capacity, broader cohort?), what safeguards would be constructed (eg involving only the treating doctor or other specialists?) and the kinds of state oversight (eg independent review of each death? Prospective or retrospective?).[88] Legalisation would include safeguards and standards that are currently absent in a criminalised environment.[89]

Conclusion

Some of the worst fears about euthanasia are doctors and/or the health system killing expensive and/or troublesome patients in a time of limited resources. In those jurisdictions that criminalise euthanasia, a decision has been made to communicate that killing of human beings is wrong and the hope that criminal law will provide a deterrence to homicide. However, this chapter has argued that doctors and nurses are already covertly involved in making end-of-life decisions.[90] Voluntary euthanasia and assisted suicide occur despite being unlawful.[91] Worse, as events at Gosport Hospital show, decisions are made that would not be consistent with any modern form of legalised euthanasia.[92] Gosport Hospital involved the non-consensual, institutional slaying of patients. Although serial killer literature appears to be an extreme case through which to consider practices of euthanasia,

---

87   Tinne Smets et al 'Reporting Euthanasia in Medical Practice in Flanders, Belgium: Cross Sectional Analysis of Reported and Unreported Cases' (2010) 341 *BMJ* c5174.

88   Willmott, White and Then (n 58).

89   For example, the *Voluntary Assisted Dying Act 2017* (Vic) requires a person to have lived in Victoria for a minimum of one year; be over the age of 18; have decision-making capacity in relation to voluntary assisted dying; to have a condition that is incurable, advanced, progressive and will cause death; to have six months to live; and experience suffering that cannot be relieved in a manner perceived as tolerable to the individual. There must be two independent medical assessments and a written declaration from the person requesting assisted dying. There are also safeguards to protect vulnerable people from coercion and abuse. Requests will be subject to a dedicated board. A person whose primary reason for requesting assisted dying is a mental illness or a disability alone is ineligible. Keown has pointed to ethical questions within this legislation. Why should assisted dying be limited to only those who will die within the year? Why also is it only available for those sufficiently competent to request it? He notes that in Belgium and the Netherlands there has been 'bracket creep'; see Keown (n 84).

90   See Diaconescu, who notes cases such as Dr J Kevorkian's charge of murder for carrying out euthanasia in 130 cases. Amelia Mihaela Diaconescu, 'Euthanasia' (2012) 4(2) *Contemporary Readings in Law and Social Justice* 474.

91   Charles D Douglas et al, 'The Intention to Hasten Death: A Survey of Attitudes and Practices of Surgeons in Australia' (2001) 175(10) *Medical Journal of Australia* 511. Willmott, White and Then (n 57).

92   I am leaving aside euthanasia in Nazi Germany. Involuntary euthanasia was practised on tens of thousands of mentally sick people in Germany between the years of 1933 and 1945. Diaconescu (n 90).

it highlights that medical practitioners are able to kill behind the veil of ambiguous and rarely enforced laws and also demonstrates the need to implement and maintain effective safeguards. The medical practitioner serial killing literature challenges our preconceptions of serial killers *and* the medical profession. These slayings by the medical profession are not anomalous. Ultimately, the events at Gosport Hospital raise questions about the medical professional monopoly on regulation in relation to medico-crime.[93] Legal regulation of euthanasia will not solve all problems in relation to end-of-life decisions in the health system, but it will go some way towards addressing some of the ways in which medical professionals can take advantage of their roles to kill patients. It will give an opportunity to articulate and justify reasons for killing, rather than leaving it to covert, private decisions by medical professionals.

Bibliography

A Articles/books/reports

Barone, Silvana and Yoram Unguru, 'Should Euthanasia Be Considered Iatrogenic?' (2017) 19(8) *American Medical Association Journal of Ethics* 802 doi.org/10.1001/journalofethics.2017.19.8.msoc1-1708

Bartels, Lorana and Margaret Otlowski, 'A Right to Die? Euthanasia and the Law in Australia' (2010) 17 *Journal of Law and Medicine* 532

Binder, Guyora, 'The Rhetoric of Motive and Intent' (2002) 6(1) *Buffalo Criminal Law Review* 1 doi.org/10.1525/nclr.2002.6.1.1

Bismark, Marie M et al, 'Mandatory Reports of Concerns about the Health, Performance and Conduct of Health Practitioners' (2014) 201(7) *Medical Journal of Australia* 399 doi.org/10.5694/mja14.00210

Carter, David J, 'HIV Transmission, Public Health Detention and the Recalcitrant Subject of Discipline: *Kuoth, Lam v R* and the Co-Constitution of Public Health and Criminal Law' (2016) 25(2) *Griffith Law Review* 172 doi.org/10.1080/10383441.2016.1238563

Cohen, Stanley, *States of Denial: Knowing About Atrocities and Suffering* (Polity Press, 2001)

---

93   Hesketh (n 6).

Diaconescu, Amelia Mihaela, 'Euthanasia' (2012) 4(2) *Contemporary Readings in Law and Social Justice* 474

Douglas, Charles D et al, 'The Intention to Hasten Death: A Survey of Attitudes and Practices of Surgeons in Australia' (2001) 175(10) *Medical Journal of Australia* 511 doi.org/10.5694/j.1326-5377.2001.tb143704.x

Dyer, Clare, 'Police Investigate Deaths of Terminally Ill Patients' (2000) 321(7267) *BMJ* 981

Gunn, John, 'Dr Harold Frederick Shipman: An Enigma' (2010) 20(3) *Criminal Behaviour and Mental Health* 190 doi.org/10.1002/cbm.768

Hesketh, Wendy, 'Medico-Crime: Time for a Police-Health Professions Protocol?' (2003) 76(2) *The Police Journal* 121 doi.org/10.1177/0032258X0307600203

Hodgkinson, Sarah, Herschel Prins and Joshua Stuart-Bennett, 'Monsters, Madmen … and Myths: A Critical Review of the Serial Killing Literature' (2017) 34 *Aggression and Violent Behavior* 282 doi.org/10.1016/j.avb.2016.11.006

House of Commons, *Gosport War Memorial Hospital: The Report of the Gosport Independent Panel* (Report, June 2018)

Keown, John, '"Voluntary Assisted Dying in Australia": The Victorian Parliamentary Committee's Tenuous Case for Legalization' (2018) 33(1) *Issues in Law & Medicine* 55

Kinnell, Herbert G, 'Serial Homicide by Doctors: Shipman in Perspective' (2000) 321(7276) *BMJ* 1594 doi.org/10.1136/bmj.321.7276.1594

Kuhse, Helga et al, 'End-of-Life Decisions in Australian Medical Practice' (1997) 166(4) *Medical Journal of Australia* 191 doi.org/10.5694/j.1326-5377.1997.tb140074.x

Legislative Council, Legal and Social Issues Committee, Parliament of Victoria, *Inquiry into End of Life Choices: Final Report* (Parliamentary Paper No 174, June 2016)

Milgram, Stanley, *Obedience to Authority: An Experimental View* (Harper & Row, 1974)

Norrie, Alan, *Crime, Reason and History: A Critical Introduction to Criminal Law* (Cambridge University Press, 2001)

Norrie, Alan W, *Legal Form and Moral Judgment: The Problem of Euthanasia* (SSRN Scholarly Paper No ID 1577163, Social Science Research Network, 23 March 2010) <https://papers.ssrn.com/abstract=1577163> doi.org/10.2139/ssrn.1577163

Ramsland, Katherine, *Inside the Minds of Healthcare Serial Killers: Why They Kill* (Praeger, 1st ed, 2007)

Rosenthal, Marilynn M, *The Incompetent Doctor: Behind Closed Doors* (Open University Press, 1995)

Samuels, Alec, 'Editorial: Doctor Harold Shipman' (2000) 68(2) *Medico-Legal Journal* 37 doi.org/10.1258/rsmmlj.68.2.37

Smets, Tinne et al, 'Reporting of Euthanasia in Medical Practice in Flanders, Belgium: Cross Sectional Analysis of Reported and Unreported Cases' (2010) 341 *BMJ* c5174 doi.org/10.1136/bmj.c5174

Smith, Janet, 'Public Interest Responsibilities of Professionals: Lecture Given for Public Concern at Work on 13 October 2005' (2006) 46(2) *Medicine, Science and the Law* 93 doi.org/10.1258/rsmmsl.46.2.93

Thunder, James M, 'Quiet Killings in Medical Facilities: Detection & Prevention' (2003) 18(3) *Issues in Law & Medicine* 211

Wand, Anne PF et al, 'The Nexus between Elder Abuse, Suicide, and Assisted Dying: The Importance of Relational Autonomy and Undue Influence' (2018) 18 *Macquarie Law Journal* 79

White, Ben and Lindy Willmott, 'How Should Australia Regulate Voluntary Euthanasia and Assisted Suicide?' (2012) 20(2) *Journal of Law and Medicine* 410

Willmott, Lindy et al, '(Failed) Voluntary Euthanasia Law Reform in Australia: Two Decades of Trends, Models and Politics' (2016) 39 *University of New South Wales Law Journal* 1

Willmott, Lindy, Benjamin White and S Then, 'Withholding and Withdrawing Life-Sustaining Medical Treatment' in Benjamin White, F McDonald and Lindy Willmott (eds), *Health Law in Australia* (Thomson-Reuters, 2010)

Wilson, David, *Serial Killers: Hunting Britons and Their Victims 1960 to 2006* (Waterside Press, 2007)

Yorker, Beatrice Crofts et al, 'Serial Murder by Healthcare Professionals' (2006) 51(6) *Journal of Forensic Sciences* 1362 doi.org/10.1111/j.1556-4029.2006.00273.x

B Cases

Justins v The Queen (2010) 79 NSWLR 544

R v Crickitt [2016] NSWSC 1738

R v Haines [2016] NSWSC 1824

Royall v The Queen (1991) 172 CLR 378

C Legislation

Consent to Medical Treatment and Palliative Care Act 1995 (SA)

Criminal Code Act 1899 (Qld)

Criminal Code Act Compilation Act 1913 (WA)

Medical Treatment (Health Directions) Act 2006 (ACT)

Powers of Attorney Act 2006 (ACT)

Voluntary Assisted Dying Act 2017 (Vic)

D Other

Carter, Helen, 'Nurse Gets Five Years for Seeking to Kill Two Patients', *The Guardian* (online, 19 June 2004) <https://www.theguardian.com/society/2004/jun/19/health.uknews>

'Gosport Hospital Deaths: Who Is Jane Barton, the Doctor at the Heart of a Scandal that Claimed Hundreds of Lives?', *The Independent* (online, 20 June 2018) <https://www.independent.co.uk/news/uk/home-news/gosport-hospital-deaths-dr-jane-barton-independent-inquiry-gmc-a8408886.html> Topping, Alexandra, 'Profile: Dr Jane Barton, GP and the Gosport Hospital Scandal', *The Guardian* (online, 21 June 2018) <http://www.theguardian.com/society/2018/jun/20/profile-dr-jane-barton-gp-gosport-hospital-scandal-gmc-panel-2010>

'What Is Palliative Care?', *QUT* (Web Page) <https://end-of-life.qut.edu.au/?a=548149#548149>

9

A Criminal Legal Biopolitics: The Case of Voluntary Assisted Dying

David J Carter[1]

Introduction

Voluntary assisted dying ('VAD') marks a distinct shift in the governance of death in Australia. One aspect of this shift is a movement away from a governance of death dominated in juridical terms by the criminal law and its practices. Instead, deaths brought about according this new regime are framed as belonging to the domain of medical and health law and its practices. This characterisation of VAD as involving a shift from criminal law to medical and health law, however, fails to fully capture the vital and ongoing role that the criminal law plays in the establishment and operation of VAD itself. For this reason, this chapter approaches the *Voluntary Assisted Dying Act 2017* (Vic) ('the Act') as an instrument of the criminal law. It attends to the legal material of the legislation enabling VAD – the very 'black letter' of VAD law – and argues that it remains fundamentally criminal in nature, despite its reception as a regime that belongs to the

1   Senior Lecturer in Law, Faculty of Law, University of Technology Sydney. National Health and Medical Research Council ('NHMRC') Early Career Fellow (Grant ID: 1156520). The contents are solely the responsibility of the individual author and do not reflect the views of NHMRC. Visiting Fellow, Brocher Foundation, Switzerland. This research was supported by the Law | Health | Justice Research Centre at the University of Technology Sydney and the Brocher Foundation where much of the writing was completed as a Visiting Fellow.

domain of medical and health law and its attendant normative and other practices. This analysis of the legal 'machinery' of VAD is not undertaken for the sake of legal classificatory ends alone. Rather, acknowledging that VAD and the new biopolitical configuration it brings about remains deeply reliant upon the criminal law renders visible the 'biopolitics of criminal law'; that is, how criminal law achieves a rationing of life by its organisation of a differential distribution of death within a population to be governed. Building on Ben Golder's articulation of the *criminal sanction* as a tactic of biopolitics, I describe how criminal law achieves its biopolitical work in the domain of VAD.

Voluntary assisted dying: From criminal law to healthcare

Voluntary assisted dying ('VAD') marks a shift in the governance of death in Australia. Assisted dying of the sort now legal in Victoria[2] – and soon elsewhere[3] – has been neither legal nor an openly acknowledged part of the management of death. For this reason, the legalisation and bureaucratisation of this form of dying represents an immediate change to the landscape of death and its governance, with impacts not only on the availability of VAD itself, but also upon other practices from palliative care and other medical specialties, end-of-life planning, religious organisations' provision of state-funded healthcare services, and health services planning. In these ways, VAD represents a profound reshaping of the governance of death, including in areas beyond the immediate bounds of this new way of seeking assistance to die that VAD ushers in.

Among the various changes that the advent of VAD brings about is a shift in the specifically juridical and regulatory aspects of the governance of death. Primarily, this has been characterised as a shift in the locus of the legal regulation of death from the criminal law and its institutions to that of healthcare law and practice.[4] This is achieved, in legal terms at least, by way of the *Voluntary Assisted Dying Act 2017* (Vic) ('the Act'). The Act aims to provide 'Victorians with the genuine choices they need,

---

2   See *Voluntary Assisted Dying Act 2017* (Vic).
3   *Voluntary Assisted Dying Act 2019* (WA).
4   Compare Kenneth Veitch's analysis in the same assisted dying context in the United Kingdom ('the movement from medicalisation to legalisation'): Kenneth Veitch, 'Medical Law and the Power of Life and Death' (2006) 2(2) *International Journal of Law in Context* 137.

in line with their preferences, to have a good end of life and death'.[5] To achieve this, the Act makes two 'moves', juridically speaking. The first is to reform the multiple layers of criminal liability that had prevented both patients and their families, carers and health practitioners from legally engaging in, or cooperating with, assisted dying. The second is to establish a range of practical matters for the provision and governance of VAD by the state through the medical and healthcare professions and associated bureaucracy. With the advent of VAD, then, the longstanding practical and symbolic dominance of the criminal law, its knowledges and institutions, its normative content and practices is diminished – or some might say 'overcome' – replaced by a state-managed process that places medical knowledge and healthcare systems at its centre.

This progression from the centrality of criminal law to a greater role of medical and healthcare authorities and knowledges is no accidental outcome of the Act. Rather, this transition from criminal law to the medical disciplines is the purpose of these reforms. Shepherded by the Minister for Health, administered by the government department responsible for healthcare and human services provision, and entirely reliant upon health and medical expertise and systems, VAD is designed to bring about an almost total transition from governance by the criminal law to the health and social care domain in both rhetorical, practical and juridical terms.

VAD's reliance upon the complex apparatus of medicine and healthcare knowledges, institutions and practices means that not only is there a shift from a governance dominated by the criminal law to that of healthcare, it also places us in biopolitical 'territory'. The hallmarks of the biopolitical, as articulated by Foucault and those who follow in that tradition, are central to the character of VAD as constructed in Victoria: the Act establishes, authorises and mobilises an array of medical and state authorities who are authorised to interpret a set of 'truth discourses'[6] about the vital character of living human beings while it establishes the legal, regulatory, practical and supportive biopower interventions that will be applied to

---

5   Victoria, *Parliamentary Debates*, Legislative Assembly, 21 September 2017, 2949 (Jill Hennessy, Minister for Health).
6   Ben Golder, 'The Distribution of Death: Notes towards a Bio-Political Theory of Criminal Law' in Matthew Stone, Illan rua Wall and Costas Douzinas (eds), *New Critical Legal Thinking: Law and the Political* (Taylor & Francis, 2012) 91, 110.

the emergent biosocial collectivity of 'the dying'[7]. This characterisation of VAD as a largely biopolitical exercise of power is further reinforced by the 'periodization' of VAD as emerging in contrast to – and as an 'overcoming' of – a now outmoded, troubled and 'unsettled'[8] governance of death dominated by the criminal law and its institutions.

Naming VAD an exercise of biopolitical power is not controversial.[9] Rather, many others have named various forms of assisted dying regimes as biopolitical in nature.[10] Want I want to pursue in this chapter, however, is an examination of how the juridical and regulatory aspects of VAD – its legal 'machinery' – forges and partakes in this exercise of biopower. Such a focus is unusual in terms of biopolitical analyses of assisted dying regimes, and even rare in biopolitical analyses mounted outside of assisted dying contexts. This is because biopolitical analyses understand techniques other than law as (more) central to the formulation and operation of biopower. Not only this, the dominant view of this particular tradition reads law and legal techniques as progressively less central to the operation of power in modernity. This is an established reading of Foucault's articulation of power that interprets him as describing a shift from a time of law's ascendency to one of law's subordination to newer technologies of power – namely discipline and biopower – and thus a receding of the importance of legal technologies as elements in the exercise of power today.[11]

---

7   Courtney Hempton and Catherine Mills, 'Constitution of "the Dying": Voluntary Assisted Dying Law Reform in the Australian State of Victoria' (Conference Paper, Australasian Association of Bioethics and Health Law, 2 July 2018); Courtney Hempton and Catherine Mills, 'Constitution of "the Already Dying": The Emergence of Voluntary Assisted Dying in Victoria' (2021) 18(2) *Journal of Bioethical Inquiry* 265 doi.org/10.1007/s11673-021-10107-1.

8   Thomas Faunce, 'Justins v The Queen: Assisted Suicide, Juries and the Discretion to Prosecute' (2011) 18 *Journal of Law and Medicine* 706, 110.

9   There is, however, some controversy or tension regarding the implications of naming assisted dying in this way – or in alternate ways, like 'thanatopolitics'. See Braidotti for a concise overview of the differing conceptions of biopolitics and their varied implications for naming VAD in this way: Rosi Braidotti, 'The Politics of "Life Itself"and New Ways of Dying' in Diana Coole and Samantha Frost (eds), *New Materialisms: Ontology, Agency, and Politics* (Duke University Press, 2010) 204–6.

10   To name but a few works that engage with the varied relationship between euthanasia/assisted dying and a biopolitical frame, see Gürhan Özpolat, 'Between Foucault and Agamben: An Overview of the Problem of Euthanasia in the Context of Biopolitics' (2017) 7(2) *Beytulhikme An International Journal of Philosophy* 15; Todd F McDorman, 'Controlling Death: Bio-Power and the Right-to-Die Controversy' (2005) 2(3) *Communication and Critical/Cultural Studies* 257; Anna E Kubiak, 'The Discourse of Biopower against Disturbances of the Boundary between Life and Death' (2011) 15(Special) *Annales Universitatis Apulensis Series Historica* 481; Anna E Kubiak, 'Assisted Dying in the Context of Biopower' (2015) 21(1) *Anthropological Notebooks* 13; Brett Neilson, 'Anti-Ageing Cultures, Biopolitics and Globalisation' (2006) 12(2) *Cultural Studies Review* 149.

11   For an overview and critique of this view, see Ben Golder and Peter Fitzpatrick, *Foucault's Law* (Routledge-Cavendish, 2009).

With my focus on law, then, I am pursuing an unusual and perhaps even controversial position that sees not only law, but the criminal law in particular, as central to the establishment and exercise of biopower. This follows in the footsteps of Ben Golder in particular, who has used the Homosexual Advance Defence of the criminal law to 'illuminate the "tactical" bio-political role of law'[12] in aid of his formulation of a biopolitical theory of criminal law. In that analysis, Golder has been able to demonstrate that the criminal law itself has an important biopolitical role, in contradistinction from the body of writing that sees law – and the criminal law perhaps most particularly – as playing a much diminished role in the operation of biopolitical regimes.

So too am I developing my own intellectual project that attempts to render visible the fundamental and abiding relations between healthcare, medicine, and public health and the criminal law. This is a relation that I have worked to demonstrate and critique – often in the face of a body of scholarship and practice that disavows healthcare and public health's relation to the criminal law, attempting to define its very nature and practice as specifically separate and independent from that of the criminal law.[13]

VAD provides another moment to exercise and extend both of these analyses. Following Golder's lead, I want to 'illuminate the "tactical" bio-political role of law'[14] through a criminal legal reading of the Act. In so doing, I ask whether the Act really represents an overcoming of the criminal law and its role in the governance of death. In response, I argue that, in fact, it does not; rather than an overcoming of governance by the criminal law, VAD is achieved by use of the criminal law. Indeed, the raw 'legal machinery' of VAD is, as I demonstrate in the following pages, fundamentally criminal in nature and so its biopolitical effects are – in large part – produced by the criminal law, and in particular the ordering of criminal sanctioning found within the Act.

---

12   Golder (n 6) 110.
13   See, for example, David J Carter, 'The Use of Coercive Public Health and Human Biosecurity Law in Australia: An Empirical Analysis' (2020) 43 *University of New South Wales Law Journal* 117; David J Carter, 'Transmission of HIV and the Criminal Law: Examining the Impact of Pre-Exposure Prophylaxis and Treatment-as-Prevention' (2020) 43(3) *Melbourne University Law Review* 937; David J Carter, 'HIV Transmission, Public Health Detention and the Recalcitrant Subject of Discipline: *Kuoth, Lam v R* and the Co-Constitution of Public Health and Criminal Law' (2016) 25(2) *Griffith Law Review* 172.
14   Golder (n 6) 110.

To begin to unpack how the ordering of criminal sanctioning found within the Act operates as a biopolitical tactic, I first outline – briefly – the nature of biopower and the biopolitical in the work of Foucault and those who write in his wake. I focus especially upon the difficult relationship that characterises criminal law and biopolitics in that literature. I then engage with Ben Golder's articulation of the criminal sanction as a tactic of biopolitics, moving, finally, to describe how criminal law achieves its biopolitical work in the domain of VAD by way of its structuring of the field, its production of this new form of 'voluntary assisted' dying, and the use of VAD to expand and entrench criminal law's reach with greatly expanded, rather than contracted, criminal offences.

Biopolitics, the role of criminal law and the distribution of death

Adding to his conception of 'disciplinary' power, Foucault introduced the concept of biopower/biopolitics in the mid-1970s. Emerging in 1976 in the first volume of Foucault's study of sexuality, known in English as *The History of Sexuality*,[15] this new paradigm did not focus upon the drive towards adherence to the norm by individuals, as is the signal feature of disciplinary power. Instead, it focused upon a political rationality and associated technologies that are focused upon the governance of a population using technologies of power that address the management of, and control over, the *life* of the population. At the most elemental level, biopower is the bringing to bear upon life, the body and the population a series of rational attempts to foster and manage life. Marked by methods that focus on mortality and morbidity, birth and indicators of relative health or of behavioural risk of a population, biopower is concerned with the '"vital" character of living human beings'[16] enacted through the imposition of an *anatamo-politics* of the individual body, and *bio-politics* of the collective/population.[17]

VAD regimes like that in Victoria place us in 'biopolitical territory'. Most obviously, VAD regimes are an exercise of governance focused, perhaps in the most raw or direct way, upon life through the management of

---

15   Michel Foucault, *The History of Sexuality. Volume 1: The Will to Knowledge*, tr Robert Hurley (Penguin, 1998) ('*History of Sexuality*').
16   Paul Rabinow and Nikolas Rose, 'Biopower Today' (2006) 1(2) *BioSocieties* 195, 197.
17   Foucault, *History of Sexuality* (n 15) 139.

vitality and maximisation of (a certain kind of) life: two elements that are hallmarks of so much biopolitically inflected activity.[18] Paul Rabinow and Nikolas Rose propose what is now a classic threefold 'test' for identifying biopower, which is helpful in clarifying how, in more specific terms, VAD is an exercise of biopower. For them, fundamental signals as to its operation are the presence of 'truth discourses'[19] and a competent authority to speak the truth regarding the vital character of living human beings. This is joined by a collection of interventions that flow from this discursive apparatus, which are exercised in the name of life; which are addressed to populations; which may or may not be territorialised upon the nation, society or pre-given communities; and, important for our purposes, which may also be specified in terms of emergent biosocial collectivities.[20] Finally, they note that the working of biopower includes modes of subjectivisation where individuals are enjoined to engage in various practices of the self, directed by the competent authorities and discursive regimes.[21] The VAD regime performs these very moves. It constructs, authorises and mobilises an array of medical and state authorities who together are the only authorities empowered to decide who qualifies and who may access VAD.[22] The permit system established by the Act requires such interpretation, with medical practitioners called upon to confirm that a person has six or 12 months to live in order to proceed through the permit issuing process.[23] It develops and implements legal, regulatory, practical and supportive interventions like the institution of 'VAD Navigators'[24] and the complex logistical system of medication provision, storage, management and re-collection, all applied in the name of life and health to the emergent biosocial collectivity of 'the already dying'.[25] Finally, it enjoins people to engage in practices of the self that might be helpfully described as 'living and dying well', where practices of care are expressed in and through the exercise of a new freedom to choose death.

---

18   Braidotti (n 9) 201.
19   Rabinow and Rose (n 16) 197.
20   Ibid.
21   Ibid.
22   See for example the *Voluntary Assisted Dying Act* (n 2) s 10 (minimum qualifications for those acting as co-ordinating medical practitioners), and see ss 26–7.
23   Ibid ss 16, 18(4).
24   Kristian Silva, 'Voluntary Euthanasia Patients Caught in Red-Tape Bottleneck', *ABC News* (online, 18 July 2019) <https://www.abc.net.au/news/2019-07-18/voluntary-euthanasia-patients-caught-in-red-tape-bottleneck/11320626>.
25   Hempton and Mills, 'Constitution of "the Dying"' (n 7).

Despite VAD being clearly in 'biopolitical terrain', a challenge arises in relation to a biopolitical analysis of VAD due to the regime's intense and uniform focus upon 'death' rather than 'life'. A focus on life makes more immediate sense for a biopolitical regime or analysis, for, with a focus upon death, power could be said to have lost its object of its governance. Death could be seen, in this sense, as 'beyond ... power',[26] and potentially 'outside the power relationship ... Death is beyond the reach of power, and power has a grip on it only in general, overall, or statistical terms'.[27] For this reason, VAD sits somewhat awkwardly with relation to the theorisation of biopolitics most present in the literature, where *life* and the governance of living beings has been the touchstone of biopolitical analysis and theory.

Death and the power over death have a place within a biopolitical regime or analysis. Foucault's own theorisation of these questions admits as much, where he explained that biopolitics stood for the 'break between what must live and what must die'. And other thinkers have noted the connection between the two, within a biopolitical paradigm, where:

> new practices of 'life' mobilize not only generative forces but also new and subtler degrees of extinction ... [ushering in a] type of vitality, unconcerned by clear-cut distinctions between living and dying.[28]

As Ben Golder puts it, biopower operates not only with a concern for 'making provision for the protection of life', but in this vein 'precisely as a mechanism for the [differential] distribution of death'.[29] To understand the central place of death within biopower – a form of power concerned primarily with life and its governance – we must return to Foucault's own formulation of biopower.[30]

Having established the biopolitical tenor of the operation of power in modernity, Foucault remained troubled by the state's continued use of death after the emergence of this and other new(er) technologies of power.

---

26   Özpolat (n 10) 21.

27   Michel Foucault, *'Society Must Be Defended': Lectures at the Collège de France, 1975–1976* (Picador, Reprint ed, 2003) 247–248 (*'Society Must Be Defended'*), cited in Özpolat (n 10) 21.

28   Braidotti (n 9) 203.

29   Golder (n 6) 94.

30   Rosi Braidotti, 'Biomacht und nekro-Politik. Uberlegungen zu einer Ethik der Nachhaltigkeit [Bio-Power and Necro-Politics. Reflections on an Ethic of Sustainability]' (2007) 13(2) *Springerin: Hefte fur Gegenwartskunst* 18. For a clear explication see Braidotti's work here, including her synthesis of the differing interpretations following Foucault present at the time of writing.

For example, after describing the emergence of discipline and biopower and demonstrating their firm establishment and dominance as forms of power in modernity, Foucault asked how it was that power continued to 'exercise its highest prerogatives by putting people to death, when its main role was to ensure, sustain, and multiply life, to put this life in order?'[31]

There are a range of ways by which responses to this question have been forged, such that death and dying are seen to take their place as a part of the exercise of biopower in modernity as 'a power to foster life or disallow it to the point of death'.[32] Much of this debate centres on whether the concept of biopolitics can 'accommodate' death, and if so in what ways. In this chapter I draw on Ben Golder's response,[33] whereby he is able to demonstrate that biopolitics and biopower accommodate death – in fact, that they necessarily must. This is not the only approach to death and biopolitics. Anna Kubiak, for example, has written carefully about this question in the specific domain of assisted dying and biopolitics, concluding that the conceptual apparatus of biopolitics proves insufficient to account for the 'subjugation of death'[34] that assisted dying presents. She prefers 'thanatopolitics'[35] – a politics of death – that is made up of 'strategies of biopower in contemporary industrialised societies' to the use of biopolitics in the domain of assisted dying/euthanasia. I feel an affinity for the notion that assisted dying presents us with a 'special' case. However, I think that Golder's alternate/re-emphasis on death as a part of biopolitics allows for the continued use of biopolitics but without the need for renaming it or developing another theoretical apparatus. For these reasons, I provide a recapitulation of Golder's approach in the following paragraphs.

In Golder's engagement with this question of death and biopolitics, he draws upon the celebrated discussion of the 'repressive hypothesis' by Foucault in order to answer the question posed by him; a question posed in pages immediately after he deals with the repressive hypothesis.[36] As is well known, Foucault's reflection on silence and speech in relation to the

31   Foucault, *History of Sexuality* (n 15).
32   Ibid 138.
33   Golder (n 6).
34   Kubiak, 'Assisted Dying in the Context of Biopower' (n 10) 24.
35   Ibid 24 ('As Achille Mbembe … reveals, "the notion of biopower is insuffcient to account for contemporary forms of subjugation of life" … and, I would add, subjugation of death. For this, I refer to the concept of "thanatopolitics"').
36   Foucault, *History of Sexuality* (n 15) 138.

repressive hypothesis describes a significant explosion of speech about sex by way of counteracting the accepted understanding of the Victorian relationship to sex thought to have been marked primarily by widespread repression expressed as silence about the topic. On the contrary, Foucault argued, the rise of repression that is generally believed to begin in the seventeenth century leads not to silence but to 'a veritable discursive explosion'[37] where a 'a discursive ferment that gathered momentum'[38] by way of a 'steady proliferation of discourses concerned with sex'.[39] This abundance of speech about sex, however, was *accompanied* by silences. These silences were not an absence or censorship of 'sex talk', but were instead integral parts of an overarching discursive structuring and practice of the discourse itself:

> Silence itself—the things one declines to say, or is forbidden to name, the discretion that is required between different speakers— is less the absolute limit of discourse, the other side from which it is separated by a strict boundary, than an element that functions alongside the things said, with them and in relation to them within over-all strategies ... . There is not one but many silences, and they are an integral part of the strategies that underlie and permeate discourses.[40]

Indeed, for Foucault, censorship regarding sex is not exercised most effectively by way of enforced silence, but by way of continual encouragement or demand to speak about sex – to the disciplinary professions – in order to better regulate it.

Golder draws a parallelism between the interplay between silence/speech in relation to Foucault's treatment of the repressive hypothesis and the interplay between death/life in the operation of biopower in modernity. In the same way that speech about sex and silence about sex are intimately bound together, so too are the relations of death/life similarly structured. Golder is here extending the same structure of silence/speech into the domain of death/life claiming that 'just as in the midst of speech there is a necessary silence, so too in the midst of life there are necessary deaths'.[41]

---

37   Ibid 17.
38   Ibid 18.
39   Ibid.
40   Ibid 27.
41   Golder, (n 6) 100.

But what are these 'necessary' deaths of biopolitics? What are the sites within which (bio)power exercises its role of ensuring, sustaining and multiplying life by way of killing? The examples Golder provides are those that Foucault himself uses: war and the death penalty.[42] Both reveal for Foucault the disciplinary imperative to 'correct (and in default of this to delete) the aberrant individual'[43] by way of killing. For Foucault and Golder this is how the power concerned with enhancing the vital character of human beings comes to kill, '[o]ne had the right to kill those who represented a kind of biological danger to others'.[44]

VAD regimes are, I claim, another site where biopower comes to kill. Naturally enough, the characterisation of VAD-like regimes as biopolitical has been made by a number of scholars. However, no-one has yet engaged the specifically *legal* nature of these regimes in specifically biopolitical terms. That is, how the formal juridical instantiation of VAD law – that is, its 'black letter', doctrinal and associated institutional apparatus – operates in a 'bio-political register'.[45]

This challenge of how law – particularly in its 'black letter' form – can be integrated into a biopolitical analysis requires work to resolve. Perhaps the most significant difficulty of integrating law into a biopolitical analysis is the theoretical terrain itself. As analytics of power, Foucauldian approaches are understood to be interested in tracing the development of *new* technologies of power like discipline and biopower. Because of their 'recentness' in Foucault's historical rendering of them, the 'newness' of these technologies of power are contrasted with 'older' forms of sovereign/deductive power that operate through what Foucault usually referred to as 'juridical power' or, as we would term it, 'formal law' and its institutions (the court, judge etc). This chronology as embedded within Foucault's body of work structures a contrast between premodern forms of power that utilise techniques of juridical power, like criminal law, with technologies of power like biopower that do not find their primary expression through law but through various extra-legal strategies.

This chronological narrative structure provides a sense of historical progression between these forms of power, with newer forms of power being understood to overtake and replace older technologies of power and

---

42   Foucault, *History of Sexuality* (n 15) 137.
43   Golder (n 6) 101.
44   Foucault, *History of Sexuality* (n 15) 138; and see Golder (n 6) 101.
45   Golder (n 6) 95.

their attendant strategies. Moreover, these newer forms of power we see below were described variously by Foucault as 'counter-law', as 'alien to that of the law',[46] further building the sense that law was to be replaced by these newer technologies of power. Given this structuring of power in Foucault's body of work, interpreters of Foucault have generally received his description of power according to a template of law's expulsion from the general economy of power in modernity. This 'expulsion thesis' in the post-Foucault literature, is based on the reading of Foucault that sees him regard law – perhaps especially in its criminal guise – as:

> essentially negative (and violent) in its mode of operation; historically tied to monarchical sovereignty; and, finally, with the transition to modernity, overtaken by more productive and effective technologies of power which invest it and instrumentally subordinate it to their operations.[47]

As to biopower specifically, there Foucault writes '[o]ne might say that the ancient right to *take* life or *let* live was replaced by a power to *foster* life or *disallow* it to the point of death'.[48]

This quasi-'Whiggish' view of a progressive supplanting of technologies of power that rely on law over time is not the only challenge to an analysis that attends to the specifically legal nature of biopolitical regimes like VAD. So too is the attempt to isolate 'law' for analysis a significant challenge – rather than a version of law as enmeshed in extrajuridical discourse of discipline and the sciences. For when writers do engage law on its own, a 'good Foucauldian' (!) would plainly reject any engagement with such 'formal law' (ie juridical power) if divorced from the numerous extrajuridical technologies of power. This would be a too-partial and false separating out of the workings of power.[49] While this strategy is orthodoxy within Foucauldian scholarship, and I believe a broadly correct view of law, it has also resulted in an inattention to the specifics of law and thus a partial analysis of law and legal materials, as well as misreadings of its operation at times. For this reason, attentiveness to law in some detail – even if artificially isolated from its enmeshing in other forms of rule and technologies of power – is a useful prolegomena to broader analyses of the operation of power in modernity.

---

46   Michel Foucault cited in Golder and Fitzpatrick (n 11) 23.
47   Golder and Fitzpatrick (n 11) 15.
48   Foucault, *History of Sexuality* (n 15) 138.
49   This is a point that Golder grapples with well: see Golder (n 6) 93.

The criminal sanctions of voluntary assisted dying

In this section I will claim that the criminal sanction remains at the heart of VAD. To do so, I will briefly review the construction of the Act to demonstrate the centrality of the criminal sanction to its operation. I will claim that the criminal sanction shapes the landscape of the Act and of VAD, and is the fundamental legal mechanism through which the Act comes to produce voluntary assisted dying. Finally, this leads to a claim made in the following section that the criminal legal/juridical sanction is the mechanism by which the criminal law performs its distributive biopolitical role. There I conclude by noting how strange this continued and even expanded position of criminal law is within this domain – given the construction of VAD as explicitly a transition away from – perhaps also a 'rejection' of – a governance of this form of death as dominated by the criminal law.

The Act was passed by the Victorian parliament in November 2017. An implementation period followed its enactment, and the regime came into force in mid-2019.[50] The Act permits an adult with decision-making capacity who is resident in Victoria to seek assistance from a medical practitioner to die. It permits medical and other health practitioners, as well as other persons, to participate in the request to access VAD and its implementation. It permits these two processes where they conform to a strictly defined process established in large part by the Act itself.

In the following paragraphs I establish how the Act is an instrument of criminal sanction: in its use of criminal sanctions to give structure to the Act itself, through its establishment of detailed processes to administer VAD that are given authority and 'grip' in their identity by the criminal law and, finally, in the Act's affirmation not only of existing homicide sanctions, but its enactment of a number of new serious criminal sanctions. These three movements come together to produce VAD as death that takes place within the space of a limited and complex mixture of status and process that the criminal law constructs and from which the criminal law offers its protection.

---

50   For more detail, see the Introduction to this volume.

First as to the structuring of the Act itself. The structure to which I refer is of the 'legal ordering' of the Act. By this I do not mean the Act/Part/Section structure of the legislative text as such. Rather, I mean how it is that 'legal machinery' is arranged and mobilised by the Act, ordered so as to give meaning and effect to its provisions. This, I claim, is achieved in legal terms by way of the criminal sanctioning regime established in the Act.[51] The criminal sanctioning regime upon which the Act is based is found in a series of sections in Parts 7 and 8 of the Act.[52] These are structured as both imposition(s) of liability and confirmation of where liability will not be found. The Act, for example, defines participation in particular processes as that which will provide protection or 'safe-harbour' from criminal liability: for persons who assist or facilitate requests for access to VAD, for health practitioners who act in accordance with the Act or who do not apply resuscitation following administration of the voluntary assisted dying substance and for those who do not attempt to use justified force to prevent suicide in these circumstances.[53] This is, however, not a decriminalisation move. The Act does not decriminalise as such, but instead engages in a strategy of making explicit – by way of detailed description of VAD process and relevant status questions – the *boundaries of criminal illegality.* At the level of doctrinal and legislative detail, it simply (re)describes and thus establishes the circumstances where homicide or other criminal offences will be committed or not, leaving the criminal offence(s) untouched.

---

51 By 'criminal sanction', I am here following Ben Golder – again – by embracing the 'semantic and juridical ambiguity of the *sanction* as that which both allows and disallows'. However, I am not fully convinced that this is necessarily the best way of describing what the criminal law is doing in the instance of VAD. The VAD regime is one that operates in and through criminal law – and specifically by criminal law's strategic withdrawal from the scene of VAD, that is from specific instances of death delivered by the healthcare system. While the language of *sanction* can name both allowing and disallowing, I wonder if it fails to highlight how in criminal law's choosing to sanction/allow VAD it also cedes territory or jurisdiction over death to discipline's jurisdiction. By seeing criminal law's work being at the *boundary* of discipline's jurisdiction, we see criminal law allowing healthcare as a disciplinary power to make and maintain a claim of 'jurisdiction' over the supervision and correction of normality (by deciding who may access VAD), unchallenged in its authority by criminal law. On the other hand, the language of sanction can also be supplemented by a sense of criminal law's *supervision* or *oversight* of this space of disciplinary power carved out from criminal law's jurisdiction, which may also achieve the same end.

52 *Voluntary Assisted Dying Act* (n 2) ss 75–82 and ss 83–91 respectively.

53 Ibid ss 79–82.

Not only does the Act establish by (re)description when an offence will have been committed, it also establishes an entire set of *new* criminal offences – many of which are punishable by a gaol term of life imprisonment.[54] These offences include offences not to comply with a practitioner administration permit,[55] or to knowingly administer to another person a voluntary assisted dying substance that has been dispensed according to a self-administration permit.[56] This represents a major widening (in the sense of 'net widening') of the terrain now covered by criminal offences. So too does it represent an increase in the raw number of homicide offences in the jurisdiction, including those of the most serious nature. This widening of the jurisdiction of criminal law and the concomitant increase in the number of serious offences is, it should be recalled, all performed in aid of establishing VAD; a process that was to see the *falling away* of the criminal law's dominance of the governance of death has resulted instead in a net expansion of the criminal law in the field.

But what of the complex and lengthy set of processes that the Act creates? Like those relating to the issuing of permits or management of the VAD substance? Certainly, the bulk of the legislative text of the Act is taken up with describing medical and administrative processes for the request, assessment, granting of permits and governance of the VAD regime. However, despite appearances, these process elements are best understood as a form of 'superstructure' erected on and reliant upon a foundation of criminal sanction. They are given legal meaning and effect only in and through their establishment upon a criminal foundation.

How does this work in practice? In short, each of the processes is tethered to a criminal sanction that provides legal effect to the provisions. For example, where VAD processes are followed, those requesting and those executing VAD processes are sanctioned by the criminal law – they will not be subject to criminal liability for having done so.[57] Alternately, where VAD processes are not followed, persons failing to do so will be subject to both criminal sanctions found outside of the Act – notably homicide offences – but also new and significant criminal offences, punishable in many instances by life imprisonment, created by the Act. Viewed in this way, criminal law provides the impetus to VAD processes: it renders

---

54   Ibid ss 83, 84.
55   Ibid s 83.
56   Ibid s 84.
57   Ibid ss 79–82.

the provisions, including VAD processes, active and is the mechanism through which VAD is therefore enacted.[58] The criminal sanction regime found in the Act is that which gives authority and 'grip' to VAD processes, and in so doing is that which, legally speaking, produces VAD. It is in and through this sanctioning regime that the Act comes into being.

It is not only the presence of the criminal sanctioning regime, and its action as a 'tether' that gives effect to the Act, which renders visible how criminal law remains at the heart of VAD. So too does the way in which the criminal law is used to produce this new form of death – a 'voluntary assisted death' – itself, through its strategic withdrawal and deployment; a tactical use of criminal law to define and thus buttress the authority of VAD processes and this new form of death itself. I expand on this tactical use of criminal law here by reflecting on criminal law's deployment to define and give authority to VAD itself, as well as the VAD processes defined in the Act.

As to the definition of a voluntary assisted death 'itself', criminal law's deployment to establish this new form of death is best seen in a historical light. The form of death now described as a voluntary assisted death has historically constituted a serious criminal offence, namely, some form of homicide offence either directly or by way of accessorial liability. With the advent of the Act, one might expect or have hoped for an evacuation of the criminal law from the scene of a voluntary assisted death. And, in one sense, this has been achieved; the criminal law has been 'peeled back' from application to the scene of a voluntary assisted death. However, this withdrawal is a withdrawal from a tightly defined space, and it is the criminal law that is used to mark out and construct what a voluntary assisted death in fact 'is'; as that which takes place within the boundaries established by the (redescribed and much expanded) criminal law. In this sense, criminal law has been evacuated from the tightly defined space of 'voluntary assisted death', but it is this very evacuation that achieves the definition of a voluntary assisted death, in and through the movement of withdrawal and establishment of (even firmer) criminal legal boundaries around such deaths. In this sense, criminal law provides both the 'topographical features' and 'borders', which together produce voluntary

---

58 One reading of this might be that the Act is entirely an instrument of the criminal law and these 'administrative processes' are therefore a set of criminal offence elements, albeit rendered in an unusual level of detail.

assisted deaths. Its re-inscription in the domain of death – with expanded reach and a larger number of offences – defines what a voluntary assisted death in fact 'is'.[59]

In addition to the use of the criminal law's jurisdiction to produce voluntary assisted death 'itself', the criminal law is also mobilised in the VAD regime in order to establish the various processes used to govern and administer VAD. The governance of VAD relies on a mixture of procedures and pronouncements on various question of 'status' and the working through of detailed processes in order to navigate access to a voluntary assisted death. Like voluntary assisted death 'itself', these processes and statuses are fundamentally a product of the criminal law. In a manner similar to that of the criminal law's production of the new form of (voluntary assisted) death that the Act ushers in, the criminal law's sanctioning regime defines the specific processes and statuses used by VAD to gain access to such a death. It does so through the same practice of shaping the boundaries of those processes that lead to the newly decriminalised terrain of voluntary assisted death. Guarded on all sides by the criminal law and its offences, these processes are the only ones that may facilitate access to a voluntary assisted death, and their very nature and pathway are defined by the tactical arrangement of criminal law's jurisdiction by the Act.

To illustrate with a practical example: Why might it matter at all that whether or not a 'co-ordinating medical practitioner' will make an application for a self-administration permit 'in the prescribed form'?;[60] or that a person will return the voluntary assisted dying substance to a pharmacist at the dispensing pharmacy?;[61] or will inform the person to whom the voluntary assisted dying substance is being dispensed that they are 'under no obligation to self-administer' the substance?[62] It is because the Act provides that a registered health practitioner or other person will be criminally sanctioned (in both senses of the term) based on their acting in accordance with the processes as established by the Act. The 'stick' of the criminal law is that which provides an imprimatur and power to the otherwise 'free floating' processes described in the Act. It gives them shape and effect. Without the criminal law's buttressing of the boundaries

---

59 This could, of course, be achieved by an alternate legal ordering – through administrative or civil processes perhaps. However, in this instance, it is criminal law that performs this work.
60 *Voluntary Assisted Dying Act* (n 2) s 55.
61 Ibid.
62 Ibid s 58.

of these processes, these processes would struggle, or be unable, to establish their authority. This is no mere 'stick', designed to ensure that a process is followed. Rather, the criminal law here shapes and establishes a very *particular* process, the violation of which will halt access to VAD and cause the sanctioning regime to punish – up to and including with life imprisonment – those who fail to follow the process in its fine detail.

The net increase in serious criminal offences and the widening of the jurisdiction of criminal law in this field of practice makes it clear that the Act is deeply invested in the use of the criminal law. The form of use of the criminal sanction as that which produces both voluntary assisted dying 'itself' and the complex of VAD processes and status questions only adds to the claim that the Act is itself deeply and fundamentally reliant upon the criminal sanction in order to produce and operate VAD, in Victoria at least. The 'legal mechanics' of these processes remain reliant upon the criminal sanctioning regime established by the Act, and the Act's operation, enforcement and authority emanates from its criminal sanction regime. The legal rationale for these various 'processes', including those that involve administrative decision-making or which might enliven rights to administrative review, remain traceable directly to the question of whether or not acts performed by persons will or will not enliven criminal sanction.[63] I am not claiming that the act is *only* or purely an act of criminal law. It is not. It establishes and relies upon, for example, decisions and activities of the executive at times – however, these remain enclosed within the broader criminal sanction regime, where the successful completion or compliance with administrative processes establishes the proof of a criminal offence.

The distribution of (voluntary assisted) death through the criminal sanction

In this final section, I want to argue that criminal law, in the guise of the Act, distributes death according to the biopolitical model of Foucault. To do so I will attempt to elaborate how the criminal legal/juridical sanction is the mechanism by which the criminal law performs a distribution of death, and thus its biopolitical role.

---

63   In other words, these 'processes' may be thought of, simply, as (some of) the elements of offences rendered in unusually detailed form. Given both the historical and now expanded criminalisation of particular forms of death, these processes that the Act describes are best understood – from a position of law – as detailed elaborations of when criminal sanction will or will not apply.

According to the literature and debate surrounding VAD and similar regimes, these regimes offend against important principles of human dignity and care or, alternatively, provide a salutary system that is responsive to community demand for more adequate control over their end of life. Arguments in the former camp have tended to focus on the difficulties and dangers of VAD implementation and the significant risks to individuals, the meaning of healthcare and resourcing for end-of-life care. Those arguments in the latter camp have seen the ongoing criminal sanctioning of forms of VAD-like activity as an embarrassment to an 'enlightened' liberal politics and an affront to patient/human autonomy, while generating accusations of a lack of mercy in the face of human suffering.[64]

What I want to propose here is a different perspective on VAD.[65] One that is perhaps at a higher generality than these competing perspectives. This view is that VAD can be fruitfully understood as a biopolitical apparatus that differentially distributes death within a population by use of the criminal sanction. What this particular distribution should look like is a secondary question. Rather, what I want to do here is to show that a differential distribution is being put into effect by use of the criminal law. To do so, I will return briefly to Foucault and describe how his understanding of the biopolitics that is centred on the governance of life can come to kill.

For Foucault, biopower and biopolitics are focused upon the production and administration of life up to the limit of biopolitical authority, the limit of life: death. VAD regimes introduce a tension to theorisation of biopolitical governance. This is a tension between the death-orientation of VAD and the life-preserving orientation of the biopolitical state. Appearing as a form of conflict within the theorisation of biopolitics, an individual's wish 'to die' being facilitated by the state seems to conflict with the state's role according to biopolitical theory as that which has

---

64 I would add a third approach, that has not been advanced in the literature as yet – safety. Given the consistent inability of the health system to offer services that are safe, even simple services uncontrolled by strict regulation, I wonder if the health system will be able to offer VAD services in a 'safe' manner. If past performance is anything to go by, then VAD will be subject to workarounds and other quality and safety failures. Although, if VAD proves successful – in the sense of safe – then this might also be an argument for a re-regulation of other health system functions along the lines of VAD including criminal sanctioning for system stakeholders and practitioners.

65 Although I don't wish to say that this view is superior to the existing debate regarding the nature and impacts of VAD.

a role to 'protect' and 'foster' life.[66] As Jennifer Hardes puts it, if we accept Foucault's claims that biopolitical governance aims to *cultivate* the life of a population, then cases where individuals actively desire death disrupt such a life-advancing biopolitical logic and should be opposed by the biopolitical state.[67]

Foucault asserts that a biopolitical regime of power 'allows' individuals within populations to die (that are 'let die') rather than having death inflicted upon them in the manner of sovereign power of old. However, with the construction and identification of a particular division or 'biosocial collectivity',[68] as Rabinow and Rose term it, a 'break'[69] opens up in the populace that allows the operation of biopower to make or let die in a particular way,[70] addressed to a particular subpopulation. 'Race' was one such biosocial collectivity that Foucault reflected on. Racial groups, the racial 'hierarchy' and all of the attendant quasi-biological framing of the discourse of 'race' as a biosocial collectivity all function to create a break within the broader populace, a break that creates new opportunities for the differential application of biopower as between these newly formulated groupings that *appear* to be biologically based. Regardless of the particular subpopulation, this division into various subpopulations along allegedly biological lines is

> a way of fragmenting the field of the biological that power controls … It is a way of separating out the groups that exist within a population … a way of establishing a biological type *caesura* within a population that appears to be a biological domain.[71]

---

66   See Hanafin on this question: Patrick Hanafin, 'Rights of Passage: Law and the Biopolitics of Dying' in Rosi Braidotti, Claire Colebrook and Patrick Hanafin (eds), *Deleuze and Law: Forensic Futures* (Palgrave Macmillan, 2009) 47; but see Hardes who engages with Derrida to read this conundrum in a criminal legal context: Jennifer J Hardes, 'Fear, Sovereignty, and the Right to Die' (2013) 3(1) *Societies* 66.

67   Hardes (n 66).

68   Rabinow and Rose (n 16) 197, 207.

69   Ibid 201 (such divisions allow power to 'subdivide a population into subspecies, to designate these in terms of in terms of a biological substrate, and initiate and sustain an array of dynamic relations in which the exclusion, incarceration or death of those who are inferior can be seen as something that will make life in general healthier and purer'). See and compare Golder's discussion of the same material: Golder (n 6) 101–3.

70   See the discussion of the differences between 'making' and 'letting' die, Rabinow and Rose (n 16), see for example 203, 211.

71   Foucault, *Society Must Be Defended* (n 27) 255. See also Golder's presentation of this line of thought at: Golder (n 6) 102.

In short, it is a separation of those that are worthy of life and those that are not, of 'what must live, and what must die'.[72]

In the VAD regime, the criminal law – and those who cooperate with it – bring about a differential distribution of death through the criminal sanction, enacting either a form of lethal violence or merciful death, by way of the creation and use of the emergent biosocial collectivity of 'the dying'. Using this new biosocial category as its principle of division (the 'biological type *caesura*' of VAD), the state is able to classify and sort those who may and those who may not die by way of VAD, and in so doing identifying those that are worthy of life and those that are not, of 'what must live, and what must die'.[73]

The construction of this new group within the population is achieved primarily by the criminal sanction applying differentially to both persons who seek death and those who – as agents of the state and biomedicine – may grant it.[74] The biopolitical effect of this criminal sanctioning regime results in particular persons – 'the dying' – being exposed differentially to death. This new biopolitical category 'enlivens possibilities for regulation', allowing 'for greater calculated exposure to violence and death'.[75] Thus, by allowing some and disallowing others, the VAD criminal sanction results in *differential* access to a voluntary assisted death and thus a differential distribution of death within the population as a whole. In the manner described above, the criminal legal apparatus is used to enact the state's biopolitical function of protecting and cultivating life until that life is no longer a life worth living and passes beyond the limit of biopower's domain.

The VAD regime does more than simply 'allow' or 'disallow' access to a voluntary assisted death, in the manner of an administrative process. Rather, it provides a differential exposure to such deaths by the tactical withdrawal (allowing) and application (disallowing) of the existing and now greatly expanded criminal offence regime. Using its newly constructed socio-biological collectivity of 'the dying' as the vector upon which the criminal law is either withdrawn or applied, two moves are made. On the

---

72 Foucault, *Society Must Be Defended* (n 27) 255.
73 Ibid.
74 As the work of Courtney Hempton and Catherine Mills shows, Hempton and Mills, 'Constitution of "the Dying"' (n 7).
75 Linda Steele, 'Disabling Forensic Mental Health Detention: The Carcerality of the Disabled Body' (2017) 19(3) *Punishment & Society* 327, 331.

one hand the criminal legal sanction of VAD 'carves out' and exempts those whose lives are no longer worth living/protecting/cultivating from the biopolitical protection of the state through its criminal prohibition and sanction against killing. At the same time, the criminal sanction of VAD sorts persons, admitting some persons and not others to access VAD, authorising particular persons to kill with protection from criminal liability by the state for their instituting death.

In fashioning this tactical 'allowing' and 'disallowing' of the criminal law, the state sanctions either lethal violence or dignified death – depending on the perspective adopted – against 'the dying' by its structuring of the field by strategic (re)description of liability. While doing so, it also reinforces the status of this group as 'life not worth living' through its strengthening of the criminal law at the boundaries of this socio-biological collectivity – introducing new criminal laws for making and letting die those who do not belong to that subcategory of the population to be governed.

Conclusion

This chapter is a first attempt at testing whether the criminal law is simply a supplement to other more 'biopolitical' technologies of power or whether criminal law itself can function as a fundamental component of the biopolitical apparatus. I have argued above that the criminal law – through the mechanism of the sanction that can both allow and disallow – operates to construct and make functional the biopolitics of VAD. In so doing, I have used Ben Golder's refocusing of biopolitics to highlight its work as a mechanism for the differential distribution of death, in which death/VAD is distributed along the division between 'the dying' and others. Those who belong to this socio-biological collectivity of 'the dying' are killed by the state's withdrawal and application of criminal law. If VAD achieves this differential distribution of death, abandoning particular collectivities to a greater exposure to death, then this is achieved through the medium of the criminal law sanction.

How (criminal) law itself advances biopolitics is a question that few have tackled, preferring to ignore 'black letter' law or to give it a treatment in such broad brush strokes that the legal materials are 'lost' or misinterpreted in the process. This is to say that bringing VAD, criminal law and biopolitical analysis together advances theory and method in the analytics of biopower.

This analysis advance practice in two ways. First, all of the analysis and critique – both in support, questioning or critical of VAD – is really a wrestling with what shape we wish our biopolitics to be. Worries about the differential effects of VAD on marginalised communities or vulnerable persons, or claims of its salutary aspects for individual autonomy, are competing claims about a distribution of death and thus about the shape of our biopolitics. Understanding how the Act itself activates and achieves its biopolitical ends through the criminal law – whatever they may in fact be and whatever we may think of them – is to describe and explain how the act and VAD really 'works' biopolitically. Second, an attentiveness to formal legal materials and their operation creates the opportunity for analysis to contribute to reform. If, as Foucault boldly wrote, 'knowledge is not for knowing, knowledge is for cutting',[76] closer attention to formal law and its effects is necessary. Without such a detailed attention we close off much of the potential for a Foucauldian analysis of law to have any purchase on law and legal practices informed by it.

Bibliography

A Articles/books/reports

Braidotti, R, 'Biomacht und nekro-Politik. Überlegungen zu einer Ethik der Nachhaltigkeit [Bio-Power and Necro-Politics. Reflections on an Ethic of Sustainability]' (2007) 13(2) *Springerin: Hefte fur Gegenwartskunst* 18

Braidotti, Rosi, 'The Politics of "Life Itself" and New Ways of Dying' in Diana Coole and Samantha Frost (eds), *New Materialisms: Ontology, Agency, and Politics* (Duke University Press, 2010) doi.org/10.1215/9780822392996-009

Carter, David J, 'HIV Transmission, Public Health Detention and the Recalcitrant Subject of Discipline: *Kuoth, Lam v R* and the Co-Constitution of Public Health and Criminal Law' (2016) 25(2) *Griffith Law Review* 172 doi.org/10.1080/10383441.2016.1238563

Carter, David J, 'Transmission of HIV and the Criminal Law: Examining the Impact of Pre-Exposure Prophylaxis and Treatment-as-Prevention' (2020) 43(3) *Melbourne University Law Review* 937

---

76 Michel Foucault, 'Nietzsche, Genealogy and History' in Paul Rabinow (ed), *The Foucault Reader* (Pantheon Books, 1984) 88.

Carter, David J, 'The Use of Coercive Public Health and Human Biosecurity Law in Australia: An Empirical Analysis' (2020) 43 *University of New South Wales Law Journal* 117

Faunce, Thomas, 'Justins v The Queen: Assisted Suicide, Juries and the Discretion to Prosecute' (2011) 18 *Journal of Law and Medicine* 706

Foucault, Michel, *The History of Sexuality. Volume 1: The Will to Knowledge*, tr Robert Hurley (Penguin, 1998)

Foucault, Michel, 'Nietzsche, Genealogy and History' in Paul Rabinow (ed), *The Foucault Reader* (Pantheon Books, 1984) 76

Foucault, Michel, *'Society Must Be Defended': Lectures at the Collège de France, 1975–1976* (Picador, Reprint ed, 2003)

Golder, Ben, 'The Distribution of Death: Notes towards a Bio-Political Theory of Criminal Law' in Matthew Stone, Illan rua Wall and Costas Douzinas (eds), *New Critical Legal Thinking: Law and the Political* (Taylor & Francis, 2012) 91

Golder, Ben and Peter Fitzpatrick, *Foucault's Law* (Routledge-Cavendish, 2009)

Hanafin, Patrick, 'Rights of Passage: Law and the Biopolitics of Dying' in Rosi Braidotti, Claire Colebrook and Patrick Hanafin (eds), *Deleuze and Law: Forensic Futures* (Palgrave Macmillan, 2009) 47 doi.org/10.1057/9780230244771_4

Hardes, Jennifer J, 'Fear, Sovereignty, and the Right to Die' (2013) 3(1) *Societies* 66 doi.org/10.3390/soc3010066

Hempton, Courtney and Catherine Mills, 'Constitution of "the Already Dying": The Emergence of Voluntary Assisted Dying in Victoria' (2021) 18(2) *Journal of Bioethical Inquiry* 265 doi.org/10.1007/s11673-021-10107-1

Hempton, Courtney and Catherine Mills, 'Constitution of "the Dying": Voluntary Assisted Dying Law Reform in the Australian State of Victoria' (Conference Paper, Australasian Association of Bioethics and Health Law, 2 July 2018)

Kubiak, Anna E, 'Assisted Dying in the Context of Biopower' (2015) 21(1) *Anthropological Notebooks* 23

Kubiak, Anna E, 'The Discourse of Biopower against Disturbances of the Boundary between Life and Death' (2011) 15(Special) *Annales Universitatis Apulensis Series Historica* 481

McDorman, Todd F, 'Controlling Death: Bio-Power and the Right-to-Die Controversy' (2005) 2(3) *Communication and Critical/Cultural Studies* 257 doi.org/10.1080/14791420500198571

Neilson, Brett, 'Anti-Ageing Cultures, Biopolitics and Globalisation' (2006) 12(2) *Cultural Studies Review* 149 doi.org/10.5130/csr.v12i2.2341

Özpolat, Gürhan, 'Between Foucault and Agamben: An Overview of the Problem of Euthanasia in the context of Biopolitics' (2017) 7(2) *Beytulhikme An International Journal of Philosophy* 15 doi.org/10.18491/beytulhikme.373466

Rabinow, Paul and Nikolas Rose, 'Biopower Today' (2006) 1(2) *BioSocieties* 195 doi.org/10.1017/S1745855206040014

Steele, Linda, 'Disabling Forensic Mental Health Detention: The Carcerality of the Disabled Body' (2017) 19(3) *Punishment & Society* 327 doi.org/10.1177/1462474516680204

Veitch, Kenneth, 'Medical Law and the Power of Life and Death' (2006) 2(2) *International Journal of Law in Context* 137

B Legislation

Voluntary Assisted Dying Act 2017 (Vic)

Voluntary Assisted Dying Act 2019 (WA)

C Other

Silva, Kristian, 'Voluntary Euthanasia Patients Caught in Red-Tape Bottleneck', *ABC News* (online, 18 July 2019) <https://www.abc.net.au/news/2019-07-18/voluntary-euthanasia-patients-caught-in-red-tape-bottleneck/11320626>

Victoria, *Parliamentary Debates*, Legislative Council, 21 September 2017, 2949 (Jill Hennessy, Minister for Health)

List of Contributors

Dr David J Carter

Dr David Carter is a National Health and Medical Research Council Early Career Fellow and Senior Lecturer in the Faculty of Law at University of Technology Sydney (UTS). His expertise is in the legal, regulatory and governance challenges involved in the delivery of safe, effective and sustainable healthcare services. At present, he teaches and writes on the regulatory practice of health law, public health law and criminal law, applying theoretical and empirical methods in aid of advancing legal and regulatory strategies for reducing the burden of healthcare-related harm and death.

Dr Penny Crofts

Dr Penny Crofts is a Professor at the Faculty of Law, UTS. Penny specialises in criminal law and legal constructions of culpability. Her research is cross-disciplinary, drawing upon a range of historical, philosophical, empirical and literary materials to enrich her analysis of the law. Penny is currently undertaking a large project entitled 'Rethinking institutional culpability: Criminal law, horror and philosophy', funded by an Australian Research Council grant.

Dr Daniel J Fleming

Dr Daniel Fleming is head of ethics for St Vincent's Health Australia. Fleming is Adjunct Professor in the Faculty of Medicine at the University of Notre Dame, Australia, and an Associate Member of the Law | Health | Justice Research Centre at UTS. Fleming holds a PhD in moral philosophy and theology, and is widely published in the areas of moral philosophy, theological ethics, moral education and healthcare ethics.

Courtney Hempton

Courtney Hempton is a bioethicist and interdisciplinary researcher. She has disciplinary training in psychology and bioethics, and research interests in health law, policy, and practice, particularly the regulation of dying and death, ageing, and mental health. Courtney is currently a PhD Candidate with the Monash Bioethics Centre at Monash University. Her doctoral research is on the biopolitics of 'voluntary assisted dying', with focus on the emergence of law, policies, and practices in the Australian state of Victoria.

Dr Jessica Ison

Dr Jessica Ison is a Post-Doctoral Research Fellow at the Judith Lumley Centre, La Trobe University. Her research examines responses to and the prevention of drug and alcohol-facilitated sexual violence. Her PhD focused on the regulation and criminalisation of sex and sexuality particularly concerning queers and animals. Jess is the coordinator of the La Trobe Violence Against Women Network.

Dr Elise Mansfield

Dr Elise Mansfield is a Postdoctoral Research Associate, in the Health Behaviour Research Collaborative at the School of Medicine and Public Health, College of Health, Medicine and Wellbeing, University of Newcastle, NSW. Her research interests include quality of care, wellbeing, and medico-legal issues for older adults and individuals with chronic disease and their caregivers.

Dr Nola M Ries

Dr Nola Ries is a Professor with the Faculty of Law, UTS. She is a cross-disciplinary researcher with expertise in health law and policy. Her work focuses on law, ageing and health, legal aspects of health system reform, and the governance of health research. Nola is a recipient of research grants from funders such as the Australian Research Council, the National Health and Medical Research Council and the Australian Association of Gerontology.

Dr Hamish Robertson

Dr Hamish Robertson is a Senior Lecturer in the Centre for Health Services Management at UTS. A geographer with experience in health, ageing, disability and multicultural issues, his PhD research was on the geography of Alzheimer's disease. His research focuses on spatial science applications in the health, ageing and disability sectors including spatial visualisation as a tool for collaborative research and analysis. He also writes in the areas of big data, health informatics, 'race', diversity and cultural heritage issues.

Dr Marc Trabsky

Dr Marc Trabsky is a Senior Lecturer at La Trobe Law School and an Australian Research Council DECRA Fellow from 2022–2025 (DE220100064). His first monograph, *Law and the Dead: Technology, Relations and Institutions* (Routledge, 2019), was awarded the Law and Society Association of Australia and New Zealand Book Prize for 2019. His forthcoming monograph, *Death: New Trajectories in Law*, will be published by Routledge in 2022.

Professor Joanne Travaglia

Professor Joanne Travaglia is the Director of the Centre for Health Services Management, in the School of Public Health UTS. Her particular interests are the implementation of policy and theory in practice, knowledge creation and management in the public sector, social and organisational origins of errors and adverse events, clinical governance and its enactment, interprofessional and interdisciplinary collaboration and learning, mixed method research, disaster theory and the management of workplace diversity.

Dr Nigel Zimmermann

Dr Nigel Zimmermann is a Senior Fellow with the PM Glynn Institute at Australian Catholic University and an Adjunct Senior Lecturer with the Institute for Ethics & Society at the University of Notre Dame Australia. Based in Melbourne, Nigel holds a PhD from the University of Edinburgh, as well as Master's degrees in theology (Brisbane College of Theology) and bioethics and medical law (St Mary's University Twickenham). He was a Wingate Scholar in the UK and is the editor of *Streams of Light: Easter Messages from Australian Bishops During Lockdown 2020* and co-editor (with Sandra Lynch) of *Faith and Reason: Vistas and Horizons* (both in 2021). Nigel is published in ethics and theology, with a focus on Emmanuel Levinas and Karol Wojtyla.

www.ingramcontent.com/pod-product-compliance
Lightning Source LLC
Chambersburg PA
CBHW042320210326
41599CB00048B/7172